VARIATION, TRANSFORMATION AND MEANING

T0358676

VERHANDELINGEN
VAN HET KONINKLIJK INSTITUUT
VOOR TAAL-, LAND- EN VOLKENKUNDE

144

VARIATION, TRANSFORMATION AND MEANING

STUDIES ON INDONESIAN LITERATURES IN HONOUR OF A. TEEUW

Edited by

J.J. RAS and S.O. ROBSON

1991
KITLV Press
Leiden

Published by:

KITLV Press
Koninklijk Instituut voor Taal-, Land- en Volkenkunde
(Royal Institute of Linguistics and Anthropology)
P.O. Box 9515
2300 RA Leiden
The Netherlands

CIP-GEGEVENS KONINKLIJKE BIBIOTHEEK, DEN HAAG

Variation

Variation, transformation and meaning : studies on Indonesian literatures in honour of
A. Teeuw / ed. by J.J. Ras and S.O. Robson. – Leiden : KITLV Press. –
(Verhandelingen van het Koninklijk Instituut voor Taal-, Land- en Volkenkunde : 144)
Met index.
ISBN 90-6718-027-0
Trefw.: Indonesische letterkunde.

ISBN 90 6718 027 0

Printed in the Netherlands

Contents

J.J. RAS

Introduction

This volume contains the papers presented at the symposium held in honour of Professor A. Teeuw on the occasion of his retirement as a member of the Leiden University staff in September 1986.

Since these papers were written specially for this occasion by friends and pupils, this book may be considered as a counterpart of the collection of essays in honour of Teeuw entitled *A Man of Indonesian Letters*. If the latter reflects the wide variety of topics on which friends around him in the Leiden academic context were working at the time of his retirement, the symposium reflects the impact of Professor Teeuw's presence in the international world of Indonesian letters as the leading scholar in the field during a period of over forty years.

Teeuw entered this world as a Javanist. He translated the Old Javanese text *Bhomakāwya* for his Ph.D. thesis and the *kakawin* genre has remained dear to him throughout his academic career. We find a reflection of this aspect in P.J. Worsley's contribution to the symposium, which deals with Mpu Tantular's kakawin *Arjunawijaya*.

In spite of his dealings with Old Javanese literature, Teeuw is internationally more widely known as a student of modern Indonesian literature. His debut in this field was the little book entitled *Voltooid Voorspel* (Jakarta 1950), which deals with modern Indonesian literature between the two World Wars. It was this book which set the tone for much of Teeuw's later work and interests.

The symposium was not merely a tribute to Teeuw. It reflects the impact which the European 'man of Indonesian letters' has had on the study of Indonesian literatures, in the Western world as well as in Indonesia itself. *Voltooid Voorspel* (Finished Overture) shows us Teeuw as an idealistic and assertive young scholar offering his judgements on modern Indonesian writers and their work. It is not a coincidence that Teeuw begins his book with a discussion of the person and work of Takdir Alisjahbana. As the most talented, idealistic – and also assertive – participant in modern Indonesian culture and leading Indonesian artist and scholar of the time, Takdir was the natural 'native' counterpart for the young European lecturer in the training college for teachers of Indonesian in the Batavia/Jakarta of the late forties.

Teeuw recognized the fact that this modern Indonesian literature confronts us with two problems. On the one hand it was the product of a vanguard of young creative artists, for whom literature was a channel to reach a public in their struggle for cultural modernization and a new national identity. On the other hand it was – and still is – a topic for academic research and teaching by scholars who tend to turn their backs on authors and their message to the readers. In the third place there was the problem of the medium in which this literature was written, the *Bahasa Indonesia*.

Since this Indonesian language was the continuation of the old lingua franca known as Malay, Teeuw had, somehow, to come to terms with it. And so his first approach to the 'Finished Overture' of modern Indonesian literature was through a discussion of the history of the Malay language and the problems faced by the modern writers who used it as a medium for artistic expression.

By including the post-war generation (Angkatan 1945) in his coverage Teeuw made the 'Finished Overture' grow into *Pokok dan Tokoh dalam Kesusasteraan Indonesia Baru* (Themes and personalities in modern Indonesian literature, Jakarta 1952).

Teeuw was, as a matter of fact, the first European witness standing full-time at the cradle of 'Modern Indonesian Literature' and constantly 'reading' the baby's pulse. At the same time, as a lecturer at the Jakarta teacher-training college, he was given the task of forming for himself and for his students an idea of what was going on in this field of literature, both linguistically and from an artistic point of view. He did so – as most of us would have done – by stocktaking, absorbing and trying to put into words the effect of this reading on himself, aesthetically and intellectually. In 1952 his observation post was shifted from Jakarta to Utrecht and still later from Utrecht to Leiden. Was this Utrecht intermezzo in which he taught linguistics an aberration? Only he himself can give the answer. *Pokok dan Tokoh* went through a number of reprints and provided the conception for a new book: *Modern Indonesian Literature* (The Hague 1967). When this book was reprinted and expanded by the addition of a second volume in 1979, a final stage seemed to have been reached: a scholarly inventory in historical perspective of 'themes and personalities' in modern Indonesian literature, as complete as was feasible, was here offered to the international student of literature. Since there was no comparable introduction to modern Indonesian literature available, it soon became the authoritative handbook on the subject in the various universities where Indonesian literature is studied and taught nowadays.

Writing on 'Critics and criticism' Teeuw remarks:

'Literary criticism in the stricter sense of the word is indeed a rather underdeveloped area in Indonesian literature. Before the war Pujangga Baru represented the first attempt at literary criticism, and in the post-war period it was first of all H.B. Jassin who led the way in this kind of activity. The latter acquired great authority, both because of the quantity and solidity of his work and by the leading role he played as the editor or co-editor of literary magazines, or of literary pages or sections of general magazines, so much so that he came to be referred to as the Pope of Indonesian literary criticism, an epithet coined by the Protestant author Gajus Siagian which has subsequently been often used by way of either censure or praise.' (Teeuw 1979, II: 69-70.)

It is indeed true that H.B. Jassin owes this dominant and distinguished position to his zeal, devotion and industry as a documenter, conservator and stimulator of literature. With his critical work he dominated the field of Indonesian literature and did meritorious work in promoting the work of young writers.

Developing a broad theoretical framework for the study of literature and literary theory on an academic level, something he found lacking up to that moment, was the task Teeuw obviously set for himself while completing the work on volume II of *Modern Indonesian Literature* during a year of sabbatical leave spent on the Gadjah Mada campus in Yogyakarta during the academic year 1977-78. A systematic study of the field of literary theory was called for. It was made possible and was stimulated by teaching commitments in Indonesia and The Netherlands from 1977 onwards. As appears from the linguistic medium used, it was Teeuw's face-to-face meeting with his Indonesian students which was to furnish the principal stimulus for writing his introduction to the theory of literature entitled *Sastra dan Ilmu Sastra* (Jakarta 1984). It is this latest major publication which completes the picture of the 'man of Indonesian letters' to whom the symposium on Indonesian literatures was offered as a tribute to his scholarship. Teeuw himself presented his book with the following words:

'What is offered here is indeed a theory of literature, complete and comprehensive in the sense that it is based on the semiotic model of literature which accounts for all factors and aspects essential to the understanding of the phenomenon of literature as a specific medium for communication in any society. In this sense it may be said that this book is not only a text-book of literary theory specially written for the scholarly world and students of literature in Indonesia, but at the same time offers a new and original contribution to literary studies and the theory of literature in general.' (Teeuw 1984:6.)

Teeuw's approach to literary studies – as said above – is based on the semiotic model of the literary work as a sign. In accordance with this he acknowledges quite early in his book (1984:6-7, 42-53) that the study of literature needs linguistics as a basis. In view of this indebtedness of modern literary theory to linguistic theory, so frankly professed, and considering the fact that reading and interpretation are the central topics in today's international literary discussions, it is only natural that Leiden's most prominent linguist and Teeuw's long-time colleague and friend, Professor E.M. Uhlenbeck, should open the symposium on Variation and Transformation with a paper on interpretational problems of the speech act and written language. Together with Teeuw's closing address it furnishes an appropriate theoretical frame enclosing the totality of the presentations. In view of their importance for the central themes of the symposium, detailed synopses of both Uhlenbeck's opening address and Teeuw's closing address are given here.

Uhlenbeck: the speech act and the written text

Since Derrida published his *De la grammatologie* in 1967, the truths of traditional philology, the principles of New Criticism and those of various structural approaches have been challenged. No more interest for the author and his literary work! The reader writes the text! Only the *reader's* act of interpretation is all-important! These and other extreme views are advocated in exuberant arguments filled with exaggerations, paradoxes, and aphorisms. Instead of surveying the various viewpoints found in modern literary studies, it seems preferable to examine the relationship between language and linguistics as against that between literature and the study of literature.

Considering the verbal nature of literature, one might expect literary theorists to examine to what extent insight gained in language may contribute to a general theory of literature. This is indeed what happened. Prestigious terminology has been borrowed, but in an often superficial way. Linguistic theories have been imitated and the result adopted as a model, notwithstanding the fact that there is an obvious lack of similarity between a language and the literature which makes use of it. Also critical attitudes can be observed, for instance when Derrida rejects the Saussurean evaluation of writing as an epiphenomenon in relation to language. Other theorists of literature show an obvious lack of appreciation as to the use that could be derived for their studies from linguistics.

Since literature uses language as its medium, Uhlenbeck wishes to look into those characteristics of language and language use which seem to be relevant for the study of literature, namely speech, semantics and written language.

Important for interpretational purposes is that the speech act does not function all by itself but in conjunction with knowledge derived from extra-linguistic sources shared by speaker and hearer. As members of the same society they have a common knowledge of their cultural environment (1). They also have a shared knowledge of the situation in which the speech act takes place (2), and they have a certain amount of knowledge, large or small, about each other (3). As a consequence, a spoken sentence does not necessarily provide all the information needed for its correct interpretation.

As for the semantic information provided by the sentence and the words it contains, Uhlenbeck observes that a sentence consists of a sequence of words enclosed by an intonational frame. But words are not fixed entities. Their meanings may vary by metaphorical use and polysemy. Furthermore, words may have different types of meaning, depending on the class to which they belong, while the speaker may also form new words on the basis of existing ones by using certain productive morphological processes. Thus, by free combinability of semantically very flexible words the speaker has the possibility of creating a multitude of new ad hoc units. In spoken language the hearer, in his or her act of interpretation, has to cope with this whole diversity of information. An extra dimension is added to this by the intonational component of the sentence, which conveys information about the emotional state of the speaker, about topic-comment organization, modality, and sentence segmentation.

In written language writer and reader are often separated by space and time. The greater part of the para- and extra-linguistic sources of information are not available. On the other hand the reader may reflect on the text, and may go back and forth through it. The act of interpretation may be repeated and its result altered. The writer may make use of this and employ a greater spectrum of writing techniques. Thus the distance between writer and reader opens up new possibilities with regard to interpretation. This is of importance for the use of language as an instrument for literary use.

Written language leaves ample room for creative use on the part of the writer and for interpretation on the part of the reader. In addition all products of language use possess a limited amount of indeterminacy. An important goal of literary research is to determine the area of this indeterminacy in each work and to find out to what extent and by which strategies it is made to serve literary purposes. This means that, while the text has to remain a central point of focus for the study of literature, the links with the author and the prospective readers may never be disregarded. The study of the author's meaning and the interpretational possibilities of the reader are not mutually exclusive but complementary. Traditional philological studies which by means of textual criticism try to come as close as possible to literary works of the past also set themselves a legitimate goal, provided each manuscript is examined within its own cultural and literary context. Approaches which concentrate on one single factor will yield only limited results with partial validity. The ultimate question remains: what is it that transforms ordinary linguistic utterances into literature?

Teeuw: it doesn't say what it says

Very much the same developments in literary theory and their consequences are in focus in the paper presented by Professor Teeuw, which was at the same time the closing address of the symposium and the speaker's farewell lecture to the Leiden *civitas academica*. But whereas Uhlenbeck begins his opening address with a critical note, laying bare some obvious weaknesses in the theories of the deconstructivists, Teeuw takes a rather ambivalent stand and demonstrates this right from the start by his motto: 'it does not say what it says – or does it?'

Teeuw directs his attention to the manuscript culture and he wishes to deal in the first place with the role of the editor. The manuscripts in which a text is handed down tend to become more and more different from each other, owing to repeated copying. A text which is handed down by copying suffers changes in the course of this process, either because of errors or because of wilful deviation from the original by the copyist. It has been the task of the philologist to restore the text to its original form.

As a scholarly discipline, philology developed in Indonesian studies when the need arose for 'authoritative versions' of texts for the printing presses. One of the methods employed was the stemmatic method, which provided a technique for weighing divergent readings against one another on the basis of the genealogical relation between the manuscripts of a text.

The stemmatic method was never systematically applied in Indonesian philology. Sometimes it proved impossible to set up a stemma, or the condition of the manuscripts did not allow application of this method. Some editors simply chose another method of editing their texts for unspecified reasons. The classical method of philology fell into discredit, just as had happened in Middle Dutch philology. Reasons for this were that texts are so often anonymous (1), that the manuscript tradition is often preceded by an oral tradition (2), that the choices between a correct and a corrupt reading often seem arbitrary (3), that copyists themselves have already done a job of creative language-conscious rewriting (4), that the idea of a near-perfect original text is often a fiction (5), or that recovery of the original text may be a loss because in modern literary studies there is more interest in readers and users of texts than in authors (6). Textual criticism nowadays seems caught in an inner contradiction. It is impossible for a textual critic to establish a norm for correct or corrupt readings on the one hand, while on the other hand the critic advocates the idea of the uniqueness and unpredictability of that text. One cannot at the same time be reader as a literary critic and as a textual critic.

The period of New Criticism, in which the text was considered essential and close reading was the slogan of the day, passed. The reader was discovered as the one who re-creates the dead artefact of the mere text through his creative act of reading. In the eyes of Derrida and Barthes, reading is not reconstruction of the true and original meaning of the text, but deconstruction of what it seems to say and a replacement of the wordings of the text by another construct of words. The text as an original, independent signifying whole is no longer considered to exist. What one reads does not depend on the words of the text, but on the whole literary context surrounding each specific reader. Therefore it is senseless to search for the original text and its proper meaning. In this way of thinking, choices by the textual critic between variant readings become uninteresting and irrelevant.

The Australian Vickers took this to its logical conclusion in his treatment of the Balinese *kidung Malat*. The text is of such little importance to him that – alas – future researchers interested in the *Malat* will have to start all over again from the manuscripts. In this total disregard for the text Vickers may feel backed up by Barthes and Derrida, who argue that it is even fundamentally impossible to explain or expound texts or linguistic utterances of any kind. Words always have their meanings in terms of opposition to other words, and this makes it impossible to give a true representation of that meaning. Every linguistic utterance is unique and basically can never be explained by any other linguistic utterance. Textual criticism is futile, editing dubious, analysing ambivalent and interpreting fundamentally impossible.

In spite of this seeming deadlock, Teeuw sees a possibility for textual critics and literary critics to proceed together on the road of Indonesian literary studies. In the first place there is the fact that language has a referential function and that linguistic signs are means to deal with things. Secondly, we simply cannot work without edited and published texts. The nature of the available manuscript material and the situation of its transmission are decisive for the method to be used in each individual case. Furthermore, it is important to look at the nature of the texts themselves and to distinguish between texts according to their origin, way of transmission, and function. Also the aim of the edition has to be kept in mind.

Most important of all is that textual criticism and literary criticism cannot do without each other. One cannot practise textual criticism without literary analysis and one cannot study literature without the capacity to apply textual criticism to the material.

Conclusion

Summarizing, we can say that in the light of recent developments in international literary theory Uhlenbeck discussed the following issues: 1. interpretation in spoken as well as in written language: the question of meaning; 2. the link between the writer and the reader of a text; 3. the question of what it is that transforms a linguistic utterance into literature. On the other hand Teeuw, as a student of literature, highlighted in his closing address: 1. reading as a creative activity: the meaning of the text for the individual reader or copyist in the manuscript culture; 2. textual criticism and the implications of the literary criticism of the deconstructivists; 3. variation in textual traditions and, in connection with this, the role of the editor.

The confrontations of Uhlenbeck and Teeuw with modern trends in literary theory clearly demonstrate that we are facing three fundamental problems. The first one is that of interpretation of the literary text, the second that of our dealings with the manuscript tradition, while the third one is that of the attitude of students of Southeast Asian literature vis-à-vis modern developments in literary theory. The three problems are interrelated, but the first one can only be solved with the help of linguistic theory, the second is mainly a question of common sense, while the third one is a mixed issue in which personal prefer- ence, practical needs of the profession, and the position of the individual scholar in the literary culture all play their parts. It is this last question to which the participants in the symposium have given their answers. The variety of answers and the different angles from which the problem appeared to be viewed make it necessary to reproduce the complete texts of the papers presented in the symposium. If anywhere, then here Derrida's dictum 'the reader writes the text' might be accepted as valid. In the intertextual *bricolage* of symposium papers every reader is bound to 'weave his own tissue of quotations'. Before turning our attention to the full texts of the papers, how- ever, we shall try to give a bird's-eye view of how the various guest speakers as members of an international body of researchers each handled the issues at stake on the factual basis of his or her specific line of research.

Survey of the symposium papers in the perspective of the central questions

'What does the reader do with his text?' was the question preoccupying Derrida, Barthes and many other modern theorists of literature. This very question is also posed by Professor Sulastin Sutrisno. However, she does not pose it in an abstract way, as may be expected from a general theorist and philosopher, but in her quality of 'possessor' of a specific type of literature. As heir to a tradition, she gives it a place in her own 'intertextual cadre' and silently translates the word 'reader' into 'audience'. Thus, speaking about the concrete case of Classical Malay literature, her answer is clear. She states that it developed as a local literature, primarily featuring regional culture. Specific to the Malay social and cultural context is that moral teaching forms the central focus of literary life. The texts express values in Malay society and are predominantly exemplary in character. They reflect life as a social reality and document Malay cultural life.

Malay society was an open society. It could absorb foreigners, provided these were prepared to speak like Malays (*bahasa*), to behave like Malays (*adat*) and to embrace Islam (*agama*). In view of the didactic and moralistic nature of Malay literature, Islamic texts occupy a major place. Then come custom and history, heroic texts strengthening the morale and texts for pure entertainment. The aesthetic concept is that of beauty emanating from the greatness of God. Since most of the texts were anonymous, the copyists were free to change their texts. A new version was a new creation, in view of the didactic and moralistic nature of literature easily accepted as better than the original. There were also other accepted forms of reception. The text could be studied from various points of view: as providing a picture of the past or an image of women, for the sake of its language, and so on. Transformation into other forms of literature also occurred, for instance prose into poetry, or borrowing from older work for entirely new creations.

The question now is: what can the Malay and Indonesian heirs do with the bulk of their literary heritage? How do the readers and listeners of the heritage receive the cultural heritage of their ancestors? The answer is that to its heirs Classical Malay literature is a philosophy of life. In every literary expression one of the basic elements of literary activity that enriched the spirit is made explicit. Modern reception in Indonesia is mostly limited to those who deal with the classical heritage professionally, but this does not mean that literary works are a dead thing. They are kept alive in a variety of perspectives.

Modern reception of traditional literature and, in connection with this, 'the recognizing of present significance in past meanings' form the topic discussed by Professor Achadiati Ikram.[1] She wants to know what the position of traditional literature in modern society is. What role can it play in the preservation or remodelling of cultural values? Two answers are possible here,

---

[1]   This paper was read at the symposium, but has not been published in this volume, as it has already been published elsewhere.

namely: 1. old cultural values should be preserved; 2. old values form an obstacle to modernization and we can do without them. To decide this, a search for present significance in past meanings is called for.

Knowledge of traditional literature is disappearing in Indonesia. This is understandable because present-day society has no facilities for acquiring it. The written literature of the past was meant to be listened to, to be 'enjoyed together', but modern society has no use for this type of entertainment. Preservation of an old form can be observed in *macapatan* in Jakarta: texts are recited in evening sessions, sometimes by a skilled artist. But it is an empty performance: the real meaning of the words is not discussed. A third answer to the above question might be compartmentalization. This might offer a solution to the conflict between Indonesian as the national language and the regional language reserved for the intimate sphere of family life and adat (custom).

In studies of older texts by Indonesians there is a tendency to search for an inner meaning. Perhaps this is connected with a desire to demonstrate the benefits of traditional texts. In this approach appreciation of *wulang* (teaching) as the greatest merit of literature can be recognized. The *Hikayat Sri Rama* provides us with the picture of the ideal king. In the *Aśramawāsaparwa* the old king Dhṛtarāshṭra instructs Yudhishṭhira how to obtain success and happiness in life as a human being and as a king. But what is the inner and deeper meaning, which is more important but understood only by those who take the trouble to look beneath the surface? Animal stories convey teachings in a humorous, informal, and indirect manner. The narrative is the surface, while the communication of ideas and concepts forms the inner meaning. Modern indigenous scholars are very intent on finding values applicable in modern life in the older texts, and indeed most teachings preached represent universally recognized virtues still having their intrinsic value.

Laughter and the challenge of authority in a Malay folk story are discussed by Professor H.M.J. Maier in an attempt at text interpretation following an analysis of the Malay narrative tradition. Following Frye, Maier makes a preliminary division of narratives into myths, dealing with power relations, religious concepts, laws or history of the community, vindicating social cohesion and cultural identity; and tales, primarily meant for amusement. The Malays themselves, Maier observes, distinguished between *hikayat* and *cerita*, representing the same opposition. The opposition myth vs. tale, *hikayat* vs. *cerita* may be extended so as to comprise normative vs. amusing, written vs. oral, stylized vs. dialectal, and perhaps even court culture vs. folk culture, although we should not forget that there has been interaction between the court and the peasantry. The written tradition was preserved in the form of manuscripts; oral performances were given by professional storytellers and have been recorded only in recent times.

Malay narrativity has always been dominated by written and printed texts. The folk romances of the oral tradition have received little attention from scholars, except where they were written down as in the case of certain *penglipur lara* tales. Yet it is here that we find laughter, for example in the stories of Pak Pandir.

Following Frye once more, we may recognize a 'tale' as a 'romance' by the concept of adventure; the hero goes through one adventure after another without developing or aging, until he has completed the major adventure which keeps the narrative as a whole together: the quest. There are three stages: the perilous journey, the crucial struggle, and the exaltation of the hero, who is in every respect an example to the public. Romances are found in the written as well as in the oral tradition. In principle they may be distinguished from each other by certain standard oppositions. These concern: 1. the hero's origin (exalted/humble); 2. the language (stylized/colloquial); 3. the world presented (magic/realistic).

This attempt at analysing the Malay narrative tradition is tested with a text interpretation of the story of the Bearded Civet Cat (*Musang Berjanggut*), a text which, though presented in written form, belongs in every respect to the category of romances in the oral group of the tales, a story which calls into question all conventions and traditions.

Variation and poetic diction in Minangkabau oral literature are treated by Dr Nigel Phillips in his description of two non-standard forms of *kaba*. Oral storytelling filling a whole night or several nights is still popular in Minangkabau, especially on the occasion of weddings and other celebrations. This form of literature confronts us with a number of problems which have so far been left undiscussed. In the first place there is the occasional character of this form of literature and its social function. A storytelling session implies the coming together of a number of people for a celebration and their listening collectively to a story selected for the occasion. We are concerned here with a form of traditional literature which is still very much alive: new stories on modern topics are created in inherited forms.

Dendang pauah and *Rebab pesisir selatan* are two hitherto undescribed forms of Minangkabau storytelling. A special characteristic of dendang pauah is that it is not composed in rhythmic prose interspersed with *pantun* like standard kaba, but entirely in the form of pantun sung by the performer and separated from each other by pauses of a few seconds filled with flute-playing. A question arising here is: on what account should we consider dendang pauah as poetry, whereas we call standard kaba 'prose'? Is it the form, pantun? Or the fact that it is sung? Has it something to do with the music that accompanies it, or is it the formulaic character of its diction? Can we maintain that standard kaba is prose, or should it be styled poetry as well? And on what grounds? Then there is the problem of interpretation. The problem of meaning in pantun can be quite complicated, as we all know. The 'author' producing the 'communication' sits face to face with his audience. Who is 'writing' the text? What about the characteristics of oral literature as against those of written literature established for Malay? Is that not a question which should be brought up?

As soon as we bring the rebab pesisir selatan into the discussion, the problem becomes still more complex. This form of storytelling is formally very like ordinary kaba, excepting three features: 1. the use of long sequences of pantun describing travel, in which the first part mentions the places passed through, while the second half or *isi* describes the sad feelings of the traveller; 2. the singer's imitation of the voices of characters in the story; 3. the relative lack of parallelisms and other forms of redundancy. The stories in recorded examples of rebab pasisir selatan are not traditional, but composed by the singer while performing before his audience. Cassette copies are sold and can therefore be edited and transcribed by anybody interested in the texts. It is obvious that the kaba tradition with its variants is highly relevant for the problems of meaning, interpretation, variation and transformation discussed by previous speakers.

The writer, his texts and the reading public in late 19th century Batavia is discussed by Dr H. Chambert-Loir in his paper dealing with a book-lender's family and their activities as copyists and authors of Classical Malay texts. He presents a fascinating case of transition from traditional Malay literature to more modern forms. The writers were Muhammad Bakir and Ahmad Beramka, sons of Guru Cit Sapirin bin Usman al-Fadli. They copied texts, romantic as well as religious, prose as well as poetry, which they hired out to their customers. From postscripts in the form of *syair* added by Muhammad Bakir in some of his books we get a glimpse of the relations between writer and reader. Sometimes the writer breaks in on the narration and supplies personal comment on a scene. The books contain only popular literature meant for entertainment, no texts dealing with history, theology or law. We find Sri Rama, Panji Semirang, Kèn Tambuhan and a number of wayang stories, some of which may have been composed by Muh. Bakir himself, all written in Classical Malay, but sometimes mixed with modern words and idioms, probably the *bahasa Melayu tinggi* of that period (± 1880). Bakir's brother Beramka worked some 20 years later. From him *syair* have been preserved describing historical events. The author obtained his material for these from current events described in literary works by other authors, sometimes printed, prose as well as poetry, or reported in local newspapers. The language Beramka uses is Malay as spoken in the big cities before the standardization by Balai Poestaka. It also contains Chinese Malay elements. In the period of about 20 years between Bakir and Beramka we observe a transition from Classical Malay to rather modern Malay, from traditional topics to modern topics. We witness continuity and coexistence of the classical/traditional heritage and modern forms and topics. Beramka's literature focuses on facts, not on persons; it describes acts, not actors. This literature is informative and entertaining. It provides an example, though usually not a positive one. Through the evolution from one brother to the other we also perceive the interaction with the public, whose taste is changing. Since the books were rented out there was direct contact between the author and his readers.

Contacts between the orally transmitted narrative tradition of Sundanese folklore and modern written forms of literature were studied by Dr Yus Rusyana. He observes that folklore did not die when the competing modern genre of the novel was introduced in West Java. Orally transmitted narrative material has been written down and published in magazines, newspapers, local histories, almanacs and diaries. But it has also been used by writers and integrated into novels. There we witness the merging of two totally different forms of literature: the folklore tradition, which is oral, old and imaginary, and the novel, which is written, new and realistic. Exploitation of narrative materials borrowed from the oral tradition means that they suffer trans-formation by the writer's creativity and adaptation to the conventions of the novel. We are confronted here with problems of interpretation of oral texts, transformation, and blending. Borrowed folkloristic elements may be of different kinds, such as: complete narratives, prophesies, metaphoric descrip-tions, popular sayings about omens or old forms of poetry. Narratives may provide the basis or major part of a plot; then the whole sequence of events in the novel is based on the oral tradition. Another possibility is that a minor part of a novel is based on folklore, in the form of a story told on a certain occasion or an explanation given by one of the characters.

A particular aspect of the contact between folklore and novel writing is the coming together of two different sets of conventions. Folklore stories are anonymous, while novels have an author. Characters in folklore may remain vague and stereotyped, while in the novel attention is paid to particular individuals and to the complexity of human interrelations. The world in folklore has a different type of reality: place and time are perceived in different ways. The perception of real and unreal and the relation of cause and effect are different from our daily experience. The novel, on the other hand, pretends to give an authentic report of human experience. Human characters are placed against the background of a particularized place. Time is important in connection with the structure of the plot and the development of the characters. It is obvious that this all has important consequences for questions of meaning and interpretation. Narration takes place on different levels, and as a consequence the relation between author and reader is not the same throughout the text.

The person of the author in relation to the hero of his text is brought into focus by Dr C.W. Watson in his paper on Hamka's autobiography. Autobiography as pretended self-portrayal of the writer is a literary genre with certain specific characteristics of its own. Yet it also shares certain fictive conventions with other modes of self-expression, such as lyrical poetry and the novel. One of the reactions against the New Criticism was a tendency among some critics to turn once more to biographical information as an integral element of critical interpretation, and this is what stimulated the critical study of autobiography.

If we accept that the fiction of a novel is firmly rooted in the personal experience of the writer, we also have to acknowledge that autobiography follows a method of composition which is essentially fictive. Autobiography then may be defined as the writing of essentially true narrative in which the writer has participated.

A notable absence in Hamka's work is the mention of domestic life, reference to family and intimate friends. The explanation is that for Indonesian autobiographers their public identity has become their self-identity. There is a reluctance to display emotion or give an account of highly personal experience. This also applies to religious experience. Being a Muslim in Indonesia means participating in the religious rituals of Islam and abiding by specific Islamic prohibitions. The reward for undertaking the minimal requirements is acceptance into the local social community. The penalty for rejecting Islam is social alienation. This explains the absence of a spiritual dimension in Indonesian autobiographies. As a consequence of this interplay of social conventions in autobiographical writing, one has to conclude that there can never be true autobiography, only biography, since through the experience of self-reflection the writer is always a different person from the one being described. This observation has consequences for questions of meaning and interpretation. A variety of critical approaches to literature can be brought to bear to make an Indonesian text yield up its meanings: reception theory, biographical information, linguistic analysis, narratology and *explication du texte*. These are not mutually exclusive. The point of convergence is close attention to the text, the sine qua non of all responsible literary criticism.

Transformation and meaning in the 14th century Arjunawijaya *kakawin* form the object of Professor P.J. Worsley's enquiries.

Kakawin was an artistic production in pre-Islamic Java which both in form and content was the exact equivalent of the Indian *mahākāvya*. It was a highly prestigious type of epic court poetry, created in written form by the author, but intended to be sung in an artistic way and listened to by the audience. Themes were mostly borrowed from the great Sanskrit epics *Mahābhārata* and *Rāmā-yaṇa*.

Mpu Monaguṇa, himself a kakawin writer, called this genre *māyākāra* (creating illusion). This means that we may expect to be confronted with things like surface meaning and inner meaning. The surface meaning is conveyed by the plain words of the narrative. In search of the inner meaning of the *Arjunawijaya* kakawin we are helped by the author, who calls his work a *palambang*, which may be translated as 'allegory'. This would imply that the kakawin is meant to convey its message in a metaphorical way.

The narrative contents of the *Arjunawijaya* kakawin are taken from the *Uttarakaṇḍa,* the Old Javanese prose version of the 7th part of the Sanskrit *Rāmāyaṇa*. Here we are told how Rāma, after the defeat of Rāwaṇa, is visited by a number of sages. One of these, Pulastya, tells Rāma the history of Rāwaṇa prior to his enmity with Rāma. This history also forms the contents of the kakawin, but in a very special way, for the kakawin is not just a simple transformation of the prose narrative into verse. The plot of the story has undergone a number of significant changes. It is here that we should begin our search for the inner meaning of the kakawin, asking ourselves what is essential for the recognition of the theme and what modifications may have been necessary in order to turn the story into a meaningful allegory. To do this we have to separate the general tendency of the story in its new form from the secondary messages contained in its various parts. The main theme is that of the world-destroying demon king who attacks the virtuous king, who together with his queen protects the world and ensures the well-being of the priests and the common people. The demon king is defeated but not killed. He submits to the virtuous king and will meet his death at a much later stage when he comes into open conflict with Wiṣṇu's *awatāra* Rāma. Careful reading of the kakawin lays bare narrational strategies which situate meanings in such a way that the message of the author comes through.

Variation and transformation in the context of literature teaching is what occupies Dr E.U. Kratz. Moving on from what has been achieved by Professor Teeuw, he looks forward to problems that are still in need of discussion. Modern literary theory and its impact on Indonesian studies are not the most significant aspect here, but rather the fact that, because of the passage of time, observers of Indonesian literature are no longer pure eyewitnesses but have to look back as well. The developments of the 1930's have gained a historical dimension. However, for lack of documentation and published studies, newcomers are unable to answer several of the questions raised by a historical approach. How do we define contemporary Indonesian literature? Where does it begin and what does it consist of? Where does the demarcation line lie between 'dead' and 'living' literature? Where do we draw the borderlines between national, regional and provincial literature? How do we differentiate between good and bad quality, between serious and trivial, if we admit that terms such as *sastra majalah, sastra pop, bacaan liar,* and so on have misleading connotations? What is the position of 19th century Malay writing and that of the dime novels of the early 20th century? What are the origins of modern Indonesian literature, seeing that it cannot be viewed as a continuation of traditional Malay writing? Is it an imitation of Dutch literature of the 1880's, as is often maintained, or is it part of a universal process of modernization involving other aspects of life and society as well? How do we distinguish features, trends, movements and periods if we no longer wish to use the rather biological concept of generations? In a new analysis attention might be focused on changes in the use of language and style.

Much of Indonesian literary criticism has been written by persons who are involved in creative writing themselves and who are consequently also involved in the ongoing historical process. Can we accept their conclusions at face value, or should we make their criticism an object of study on its own? The example of *Perdebatan Sastra Kontekstual,* a 500-page comprehensive anthology of programmatic articles and polemics on the concept of contextual literature published in 1984, would seem to furnish an argument in favour of the latter.

With this paper, touching on the problems with which we began our introduction, the circle is complete and the reader is invited to examine the verbatim texts of the papers dedicated to 'the man of Indonesian letters'.

E.M. UHLENBECK

Linguistics, interpretation, and the study of literature

I

To the interested observer, especially if he happens to be a sober-minded linguist, literary studies to-day offer a fascinating spectacle. The truths of traditional, classical philology, the principles of the New Criticism as well as those of various structural approaches, are being challenged and often downright rejected in the post-structuralist writings which from 1967 onward, the year of De· la's *De la grammatologie*, began to emanate from Paris and from centres such as Yale and Cornell. New emphases have replaced the old ones. The author, formerly a main focus of literary interest, was demoted to a more modest status, and now in French publications called the scriptor, to indicate his degradation. The literary work itself, by many students of literature past and present considered to be the central object of literary research, was reduced to not much more than an occasion for triggering the all-important interpretative activity of the largely sovereign reader, whose new position of eminence is reflected succinctly by Derrida's well-known dictum that the reader writes the text, and even more dramatically by Barthes, who has stated that the birth of the reader must be at the cost of the death of the author.

With the advent of post-structuralism,[1] a term which suggests much more uniformity and unity than actually existed, the study of literature in the Western world seems more than ever to be in a state of turmoil and ferment. One gets the impression that anything goes, that arguments can be constructed in favour of every point of view, no matter how extreme or unusual. It is not surprising that there is widespread uncertainty about whether literary studies will ever become a discipline able to master the staggering complexity and diversity of its subject matter. Others even question the desirability of such a development.

A second striking characteristic of present-day literary studies cannot escape

---

[1] For surveys, see Suleiman 1980, Young 1981, Culler 1983. Highly relevant is also Smith 1978, especially part III.

one's attention: its extravagance or, to use a German term which seems particularly fitting: its *Ueberschwenglichkeit* of expression. There is especially in French essays a remarkable penchant for exuberance and exaggeration, for paradoxes and aphorisms, sometimes coupled with a certain disregard for logical consistence. Although a number of these extreme views rest on very shaky foundations, running counter to well-established facts, they may – as we shall see later – upon closer inspection, at least in some cases, be appreciated as justifiable, if immoderate, reactions to one-sided conclusions in the past too easily accepted as gospel truths.

It cannot be the purpose of my contribution, which is supposed to function as an introduction to this Symposium, to try to achieve the impossible and to present some sort of survey of the vast range of conflicting viewpoints which nowadays find expression in modern literary studies. Apart from the fact that I completely lack the expertise for such an enterprise, it seems that for a student of general linguistics there is a more useful task to fulfil: to examine the relationship between language and linguistics on the one hand, and literature and the study of literature on the other. I intend to do this from two different points of view.

First I will look into the ways linguistics and linguistic theories have been treated and made use of in recent literary studies. I hope that this will lead to a more balanced evaluation, especially of some post-structuralist tenets. Secondly I will try to answer the more general theoretical question: to what extent insight gained in language may contribute to a general theory of literature. I have reason to believe that literary theorists have still insufficiently exploited the indisputable fact that literature, as Barthes has put it, *est de nature verbale*.

Before embarking on this program a few words to explain the title I have chosen. That linguistics and the study of literature are part of it will have become clear from what I have said so far. The position of the term 'interpretation' between them is to symbolize the fact that it is this concept which is a crucial one, indispensable both in linguistic and literary theory.

I trust that this short introduction will be sufficient as an indication of what will follow.

II

Literary studies reveal at least four different attitudes toward linguistics. The first one is perhaps the most conspicuous and certainly the most superficial one. It consists of the uninhibited borrowing of current linguistic terminology, probably caused by the prestige linguistics has acquired within the humanities as a truly scientific discipline. It is not too difficult to trace the linguistic origin of the terms which are most in favour. The use of terms such as 'system', 'sign', 'langue/parole', 'syntagmatic/paradigmatic', immediately betrays the influence of De Saussure's *Cours*, and terms like 'code' and 'message', 'metonymy' and 'metaphor', 'similarity' and 'contiguity', point to the French translation of a few studies by Roman Jakobson, while 'deep structure' and 'surface structure', 'competence' and 'performance', 'intuitive knowledge' and the like indicate some Chomskyan contagion. Several of these terms are used in French literary writings for concepts and in ways which are quite foreign to their original linguistic habitat. Mounin complained some years ago that with certain literary authors everything all of a sudden has become *signe* (Mounin 1968:10). The same is certainly true of terms like 'metaphor' and 'meaning'. This confusing practice, no doubt an aspect of the extravagance just mentioned, is one of the reasons why some of these literary writings suffer from a vagueness and a lack of clarity difficult to accept in scientific discourse.

A much more direct influence is exerted by linguistics when one of its theories is explicitly adopted as a model, and even considered an absolute condition for ever arriving at a viable literary theory. A clear case has been Culler, who in 1975 in two publications, namely in his contribution to the volume of studies edited by Fowler and in his *Structuralist Poetics*, introduced a certain set of notions, quite analogous to those found in generative grammar. Chomsky's concept of linguistic competence is paralleled by literary competence, and the intuitions a native speaker of a language is assumed to possess, by the intuitions of the reader of literature. Accordingly Culler declares in his *Structuralist Poetics* that 'since literature itself is a system of signs and in this respect like a language, one postulates a poetics which would study literature as linguistics studies language, taking its cue from linguistics wherever that seemed possible' (Culler 1975:96). There are two serious weaknesses in this reasoning. First of all it does not take into account the doubt that has, within linguistics, been thrown on the validity of Chomsky's conception of language as a closed, tightly organized, abstract system of interlocking rules. A second, even more serious weakness is the lack of similarity between a language and the literature which makes use of that language. Even if it were correct to characterize language as a system of signs, one still would have to show that the systematic nature posited for the whole of a literature is comparable to that found in language.

The intuitions of a native speaker, supposed to reflect his innate language basis, are not at all on a par with the intuitions which readers possibly have, and the same is true for competence as used in linguistics in contrast with

performance, and what Culler calls literary competence. Moreover, the whole
idea of an analogy between the study of language and the study of literature
implies a far too simple view of the relations between the two. It implies the
existence of two parallel disciplines with different but basically comparable
objects of study. The relationship between language and literature is, however,
much more complicated, just because language is used in literature. Literature
cannot be understood without knowledge of language, while linguistic
knowledge is at the same time fundamentally insufficient for understanding
literature. It is therefore not surprising that the theory of narrative structure
developed by Culler in the publications just mentioned owes little to the
Chomskyan framework in which this theory is placed. To quote Barbara Smith:
'Culler's concluding observations and proposals may be understood and defined
quite independently of their origins in the Chomskyan model and could have
been formulated without that model' (Smith 1978:184).

This lack of integration is not accidental. There is a structural incompatibil-
ity which will be readily understood if one takes into account the development
of generative grammar since 1970. In harmony with its psychological orientation, generative grammar remains focused on core grammar, supposed to
represent the universal, innate basis of the human faculty of language. This
leads to a severe reduction of its empirical domain, as not only the rich variety
of phenomena of actual language use, but also large areas of syntax, of old the
central interest of generative grammar, are no longer a subject of study.
Secondly, generative grammar is engaged – as Verhagen has recently shown –
in an attempt to reduce the relations between form and meaning to relations
between aspects of form only. For the study of literature, however, the
semantic aspect of language is all-important.

This import of concepts from generative grammar has at least the virtue that
it implies a positive appreciation of linguistics. There are, however, also quite
different, much more critical if not antagonistic attitudes towards linguistics. I
am referring to studies by literary philosophers like Derrida and Barthes.[2]
They tried to expose certain theoretical weaknesses, first of all in De Saussure's
Cours, advancing new points of view in areas of vital importance for the study
of literature. One of the most important issues is the relationship between
language and writing. In the *Cours* writing occupied a subordinate place in
relation to spoken language, which was viewed as the sole object of linguistic
study. Moreover, the role of writing was only seen as representational. It
served to represent and to make visible the sound form of the word. It is

---

[2]   The influence of Chomsky on Barthes seems to have been rather superficial (see Barthes
1966:57), certainly in comparison with Jakobson's influence.

against these views that Derrida directed his arrows in *De la grammatologie*. In this monograph of more than 400 densely printed pages devoted, as the title indicates, to a new science of writing, Derrida made an attempt – a truly revolutionary one – to reject the Saussurean evaluation of writing as an epiphenomenon in relation to language, and to accord to writing a much more central position, with his concept of *archi-écriture* coming close to presenting a radically different historical perspective on the relation between language and writing. It is impossible in this discussion to present a critical assessment of this unusual book, which not only discusses writing, but also De Saussure's conception of language, as Derrida suspected an intimate link between De Saussure's evaluation of writing and his conception of language. One thing is certain: a linguist cannot have a high opinion of Derrida's work. Throughout his book one finds statements which no linguist would be ready to accept. In some cases they are exactly the converse of what are considered in linguistics to be established facts. For instance, the opinion that language is but a moment, or an aspect of writing, and that the concept of writing transcends and includes the concept of language. As Mounin has rightly observed in his *Clefs pour la langue française*, pronouncements such as these do not take into account three simple facts: (1) that every child everywhere learns to speak before it learns – in quite a different way – to write, (2) that everywhere, in all civilizations, writing is a recent phenomenon which developed hundreds of thousands of years after language, and (3) that even at present there are still languages which are never written and which are fully equivalent to languages which are written (Mounin 1975:128). These facts permit a fundamental conclusion. If it is true, and there is ample evidence in favour of it, that all languages are individual elaborations of one and the same model, then one cannot but conclude that the study of language must be based primarily on spoken language.[3] However, this does not at all imply that written language should be viewed as a phenomenon of ancillary and secondary importance. On the contrary. It constitutes, as Vachek emphasized nearly half a century ago, a topic which deserves to be studied in its own right. The development of written language into a form of language use that is semi-independent of the oral mode offers new possibilities which the oral use of language does not permit at all, or only to some extent. As we will see later, it is exactly these new possibilities which are of special relevance for the study of written literature. This is the important grain of

---

[3]   This is overlooked by Mooij in his account of the attitude of De Saussure and others towards writing. The genetic argument as formulated by him did not play a role. Even to-day linguists sometimes experience difficulties in distinguishing between oral and written language (Mooij 1981).

truth buried beneath the linguistically ill-founded conception of Derrida.

Closely related to this new appreciation of writing and written language is the new status of the reader, to which I already alluded in my introduction. Here again post-structuralism has hit upon an important truth which again was presented, however, in a mass of *Ueberschwenglichkeit*, hard to digest. This second truth is the discovery that a literary work of art is not a closed, unequivocal, finished product, created at a certain moment by its author, but an entity which not only needs interpretation by a reader in order to come to life, but also leaves room for several interpretations, neither necessarily identical with the interpretation intended by the author, nor necessarily foreseen or even foreseeable by him. This is what Barthes in his *S/Z* and in his *Critique et vérité* has called *le pluriel* or *la pluralité* of a text (1966:50; 1970:11-2).

One might say at this point that a fourth attitude towards linguistics makes itself felt, namely an attitude of indifference and underestimation of the assistance the study of language could render to the student of literature. One would have expected that the realization of the necessity and the plurality of interpretation would have led literary theorists to study linguistic semantics or to start an inquiry into the interpretational process that listeners have to perform every day, but this is not what happened. Not even when texts are analysed. Barthes's rich commentary to Balzac's 'Sarrasine' in *S/Z* testifies to his general sensitivity to semantic differences and implications, but is marred by vagueness and lack of precision caused by the absence of distinctions available from linguistics and indispensable for a really illuminating analysis. Barthes even explicitly states that the object of semantics is not to be found in the analysis of words (1970:99). To take a close look at language and the way language functions in actual speech is a move apparently not considered, or considered not effective.[4] The same can be observed in Culler's *Prolegomena to a Theory of Reading*. Culler is aware that interpretation is not a random process, but a process governed by certain operations or strategies, but even he does not arrive at the conclusion that one has to go back to language and the semantic potentialities of its basic units. Many of us have seen Zadkine's statue, which so dramatically symbolizes what the city of Rotterdam lost during the war. Literary studies devoted to the reader and the reading process sometimes remind me of that statue, as what I consider the heart of the matter is missing: the analysis of the role which word-meaning plays in actual language use.

The same lack of expectation of what linguistics might do for the study of

---

[4]   Compare, however, Barthes's view: 'Un long chemin reste sans doute à parcourir avant que nous puissions disposer d'une linguistique du discours, c'est-à-dire d'une véritable science de la litérature, conforme à la nature verbale de son objet' (Barthes 1966:63).

literary texts may be observed in relation to other linguistic trends. Linguistics nowadays covers much more than generative grammar. Since 1970 a great variety of approaches have developed not only in the United State, but also in Germany and other European countries. The burgeoning fields of text-grammar and discourse analysis constitute one of the most remarkable reactions to generative grammar. Potentially these two fields, which are gradually coalescing, are of importance to the study of literature, and this for two reasons. Like literature, their focus is on language use, on performance and on pragmatics – to use the current catchwords – and secondly they are interested in texts, which are viewed as communicative events. It is true that these fields are still in the very first stage of their development. The four volumes of the recently completed *Handbook of Discourse Analysis*, edited by Van Dijk, make this abundantly clear. Moreover, many seem to be averse to theory, or consider the development of general theories as highly premature. As De Beaugrande, one of the contributors to the *Handbook*, has stated: theory, research, and practice should be considered provisional. Nevertheless one would expect a rapprochement between discourse analysis and literary studies, but as Sinclair notes in his article 'On the integration of linguistic description', which also appeared in the *Handbook*: 'literary critics have remained largely aloof, maintaining that there is a difference in kind between descriptive and evaluative study' (Sinclair 1985:17).

And with this brief discussion I would like to conclude this part of my discourse. The harvest has not been impressive. Superficial borrowing of prestigious terminology, imitation of theories which do not hold much promise, largely misguided attacks on Saussurean linguistics, lack of appreciation as to what linguistics could do for literary studies. It is high time I moved to the more constructive part of my article, devoted to the contribution that a linguistic approach which accords semantics a central place may make to literary theory.

III

Since literature uses language as its medium, it seems reasonable to look into those characteristics of language and language use which one may expect to be relevant for the study of literature. This will be done in three sections; the first discusses speech, the oral form of language use, the second discusses semantics, and the third written language.

The first fact to observe is that speech does not fulfil its various functions all by itself, but in conjunction with cognitive information derived from sources outside language. Within this cognitive information, within this extralinguistic knowledge, three components are to be distinguished.

The first derives from the fact that speaking and hearing are done by members of a society who – whatever their position – have a certain variable amount of practical, factual knowledge of their environment, of the culture in which they live and in which they participate. Next to this knowledge related to everyday existence, there is a second source of knowledge which is more directly bound with the speech event. Speaking and hearing do not take place *in vacuo*, but always at a given moment in a certain situation, a cover term for (1) the situation which prompts the speaker to speak, (2) the situation in which the speech event is embedded, and (3) the situation in which the hearer interprets what is said to him. Finally there is a third component: the knowledge which speaker and hearer have about each other, a knowledge which may comprise a great deal, but which may also be minimal.

This brief analysis enables us to establish an important truth. In every speech event the hearer has to perform a complex, still insufficiently understood task of inference, of interpretation. This task consists of integrating cognitive information from different sources: from the semantic information supplied by what is spoken, and from the three kinds of extralinguistic knowledge just mentioned. This process of interpretation, if successful, leads to comprehension of the utterance by the hearer (Uhlenbeck 1978).

These sources of outside information are not a luxury: they play an essential role in the functioning of speech. This becomes clear if one realizes to what extent spoken sentences are underspecified and underdetermined. If I say: *I brought along something to read*, no specification is given as to the person who is supposed to read what the speaker has brought along: is it the speaker himself or the addressee? And if somebody says: *John walked*, is he then referring to a single event or to a habitual activity of John? And what about the sentence *I went to Mary's garden* Did the speaker go to a garden owned by Mary, or merely to a garden where she liked to sit, or perhaps to a garden in which she had never been, but about which she had often spoken? As Declerck has shown, the sentence *In his speeches, the doctor refers to those patients* permits – in the absence of any situational or contextual clues – no less than sixteen different interpretations (Declerck 1986:165).

Both for linguists and for students of literature it is important to understand that it is a fallacy to assume that a sentence all by itself furnishes all the information needed for its interpretation. Or, to put it differently, it would be a serious mistake to confuse the final result of the interpretational process with the semantic information derivable from the sentence. This conclusion brings us in a natural way to the second section: the examination of the semantic information provided by the sentence and the words it contains.

Sentences are characterized by the presence of two components: a shorter or longer sequence of words enclosed by an intonational frame, consisting of a configuration of differences in pitch and duration, sometimes articulated by pauses and by other means into smaller segments. Sentences function in close conjunction with paralinguistic factors of various kinds, partly visible, partly audible; partly related to the voice of the speaker, partly to the sentence spoken.

Words are in two respects independent of the sentence, the framework in which they occur in actual speech. From the point of view of speech production, the word comes before the sentence. Speakers use words in making up sentences. They do not select sentences from a fixed repertoire. Secondly, words retain their identity when occurring in different sentences. In *I feel strong, This is strong tea, He has a strong mind,* the same word *strong* is used three times. Words have a certain permanency. They remain available to the native speaker, while sentences are ad hoc entities, constructed in accordance with the syntactic rules of the language. Finally, words are ordered linearly within the sentence; this is a design feature of speech which should not be confused with the potential a word has for combining with other words into groups according to language-specific rules. Words then are entities which have a sound-form, a meaning, and a potential of combining, usually called its valence. Of these three aspects, meaning and valence are of central importance in the context of this contribution.

The term 'meaning', so often used for quite disparate phenomena, and insufficiently distinguished from what the word *meaning* means in English, will be used here only for the semantic aspect of words. It will be defined as knowledge bound up with a word-form and used in speech. Furthermore a distinction will be made between meaning as a cognitive potential that a word has, and the meaning a word has in individual instances of language use.

Not all words have the same kind of meaning. At least five different types have to be distinguished. First of all the appellatives, a type which comprises the traditional classes of nouns, verbs, and adjectives. They are relatively independent of situation and context, and contain a certain descriptive knowledge about things, processes, and qualities thought to be present in the world outside us. A second type is formed by the deictic words, to which the pronouns belong. They do not describe like the appellatives, but point to entities in relation to the speech event or its participants. The other three types are the proper names, which only identify, technical-relational words, to which conjunctions and prepositions belong, and finally the interjections, exclamations, adhortatives, and other similar words.

This inventory shows that the speakers of a language have at their disposal a set of different semantic tools which they may use in various ways and in various combinations, in accordance with their specific semantic potential and the rules existing for their combination. However, this characterization of words as semantic tools should not lead to the conclusion that word-meanings are some sort of fixed entities, just like other tools we use in everyday life. Actually they are forms of integrated knowledge, and their most remarkable properties are their flexibility and their openness.

In order to get a closer view of these properties, we shall return to the word *strong*. Earlier we observed that in the three sentences *I feel strong*, *This is strong tea*, and *He has a strong mind*, there can be no doubt that one and the same word *strong* is used. There is, however, a second observation to be made. The meaning of *strong* is not exactly the same in the three sentences. In the first *strong* may be paraphrased as 'having physical power', in the second as 'concentrated', in the third as 'intellectually powerful', and if we also take into account sentences such as *This fruit has a strong odour*, *He presented strong arguments*, and *His love is not very strong*, *strong* again has in each case a somewhat different meaning, drawn out – so to speak – by the different nouns with which it is combined in one group. But, in all these cases the identity of *strong* is not affected. Our certainty that one and the same word has been used is not shaken.

From the observation of instances such as these, one cannot but conclude that within the meaning of an appellative word certain differences, certain distinctions may exist which are integrated into one unit. They shade into each other, forming a continuous range like colours in a spectrum. Traditionally this phenomenon is called polysemy, an unfortunate term as it suggests plurality of meanings, while what we actually have are closely related differences within one meaning. Polysemy has important consequences, as it allows subtle differences between the distinctions within a word applied by a speaker and those applied by the hearer in his interpretation of the same word. This lack of congruity is the more likely to occur as there is no good reason for assuming that semantic knowledge of words is the same for all native speakers of a language: a word may have for some a much more richly articulated meaning than for others. Moreover, polysemy allows different interpretational attitudes. One may try to recover the distinctions in meaning applied by the speaker or the writer, but one may also impose one's own interpretation by actualizing other distinctions in meaning.

Moreover, two of the three creative uses of word meaning are based on polysemy. The first is metaphorical use, for instance when I say to one of my young granddaughters: *Come out of your house*, when she is hiding under my writing-desk in Voorhout. I then use the distinction of 'living quarters' or 'shelter' within the word meaning of *house* with the exclusion of all other distinctions, applying the word *house* to something which is not normally called a house. This metaphorical use, here illustrated by a simple example, is a cover term for several possibilities of creative use, as Levin has shown by his analysis of the simple *The stone died* (Levin 1977:48).

A second possibility for creative handling of word meaning, also based on polysemy, is much less well-known. I am referring to the fact that distinctions within word meaning may serve as a point of departure for the speaker or writer for elaboration in various directions. In my contribution to the second Festschrift for Roman Jakobson of 1967, I showed this in relation to the word *nation*, by tracing its semantic development through a text of 35 lines, printed as an advertisement in the *San Francisco Examiner*. The title of this patriotic piece, written in a kind of Walt Whitman style, was *I am the nation*, suggesting that it was the American nation which addressed the reader. This offered new opportunities for using the word *nation*.

To appreciate the third form of creative use, we have to take into consideration what is generally called the thing-meant or the referent. In the case of an appellative word such as *dog*, the meaning consists of the knowledge native speakers of English have about a certain category of animals, a knowledge which includes the fact that they may talk about this category or its individual members by means of the sound form /dog/. However, with other words, such as *man*, the situation is more complicated, because with *man* one may refer not only – as with *dog* – to one class of things, but at least to four different ones: to adult males, to husbands, to male servants, and finally to mankind. And with words such as *house* and *tree* there are even more different categories of things.

Here again, one has to observe that the number of different categories of things to which a word may refer is not fixed.[5] The possibility of further extension to new categories remains open. Recently I came across such a case in Dutch while reading a catalogue of a nursery in which a 'little knee', in Dutch *knietje*, was advertised, which – as an illustration showed – appeared to be a yellow pad, which may come in handy for putting one's knees on, when gardening or repairing a flat tire. At about the same time I found that in recent anthropological studies by Brown and Witkowski, and Casagrande and Hale, the

---

[5]   Reichling has introduced the term 'distributive use' (Reichling 1969:45).

same sort of extension has been reported for various languages.

Before concluding my brief account of word meaning, I have to add a few words about a phenomenon of a marginal character which – although not absent from speech – is known to play an important role at least in some cases of literary language use. It may happen that for a speaker or a writer positive or negative associations have become attached to certain words, because of past personal experiences. Such words have for their user, and for him only, acquired what is usually called associative knowledge. Its presence in actual speech cannot be discovered by the hearer or the reader during the process of interpretation, as this associative meaning does not constitute transient knowledge. It is only by a systematic search that preference for certain words or sets of semantically more or less related words may be discovered, which may furnish important interpretive clues.

As we have seen, a speaker can do many things with the meaning of individual words. He has also at his disposal two quite different processes by which he may increase the number of words.

The first is furnished by morphology and consists of the expansion of the lexicon on the base of productive categories. This expansion may be called natural, because neither the speaker nor the hearer has any awareness that the words formed by such processes are new or not.

Next to this regular potential for making new words, there exists a second, quite different way, which one can hardly call a process, because of its incidental character. While morphological expansion rests on processes of word formation gradually mastered by the native speaker, this second kind of expansion rests on language reflection and is dependent on a certain measure of inventivity. A recent example is the combination *caught white-handed*, formed on the basis of the familiar *caught red-handed*, and considered to be more fitting, as it was said of cocaine smugglers.

Productivity is not a property of morphology alone. It also plays a role in syntax. The valence of words is organized not on an individual, but on a categorial basis. The English words which belong to the morphological category of adjectives are combinable with the words of the category of nouns, for instance within the frame of the group article + adjective + noun. Two facts have to be emphasized. There is no freedom as far as the structure of the group is concerned. The order of its constituents is fixed: the article takes first place, it has to be followed by the adjective and the noun in that order. There is, however, complete freedom for combining any single adjective with any single noun. From the point of view of semantics anything goes. *The love of two desk lamps*, the title of a recent article in *Time*, is as permissible as the more usual *the love of two people*, as both groups respect the same syntactic frame.

Free combinability within fixed syntactic patterns is a universal property of language. There are two reasons why language cannot do without it. First of all combining words into groups offers the speaker the possibility of creating a multitude of new ad hoc units, so that his lexical repertoire is, as it were, temporarily expanded without, however, burdening his memory. Except for being an efficient device for lexical expansion, the combining of words into groups sets in motion a process of semantic interaction between the meanings of the words combined in the construction, thereby counterbalancing the flexibility of word meaning. Word meanings determine each other, but – and this is of the highest importance for literary language – this determination remains incomplete. For full determination an appeal has to be made to the extralinguistic sources which we discussed earlier.

This completes my rapid survey of the forms of knowledge related to the word component of the sentence with which the hearer has to cope in his interpretational task. However, this is not all: there is a further dimension. This semantic knowledge functions in conjunction with a great diversity of information, originating from the intonational component of the sentence. The nature of this information is different from the largely semantic-cognitive knowledge deriving from the word component. It may comprise personal and social information about the speaker and his emotional state, thematic information, that is information relative to the so-called topic/comment organization, and also information about the modality of the sentence, for instance whether a statement is made or a question is asked, and last but not least there is the mechanism of sentence segmentation, which provides the speaker with subtle means for bringing about slight but significant differences in the presentation of the information, allowing him the foregrounding of one segment at the expense of others.

And now the third section: written language. It is obvious that there is no face-to-face interaction possible in the written use of language (Iser 1980). There are no paralinguistic sources of information either, while the twenty-odd punctuation marks are only a poor substitute for the intonational means functioning in oral use.

A second difference lies in the extralinguistic information. Because of the purpose of writing, this will tend to be less than in oral use. Only when writer and reader are contemporaries belonging to the same cultural community will the first of the three components we distinguished within extralinguistic knowledge be present and it remains possible that writer and reader have some knowledge about each other. But as far as situational knowledge is concerned, things are radically different, as normally there will be no situation shared by writer and reader.[6] If a writer considers it necessary to present situational information, the only method open to him is to present it in the text itself. This can be done in widely different ways. Information about the setting of a story may precede the telling of the story itself, but may also be built up gradually. Compare for instance a Javanese *lakon* with its elaborate descriptive beginning, with Butor's *La modification*, in which the reader is plunged into the story without any previous introduction whatsoever. One might say that in this respect the writer is able to control a factor which is largely beyond the influence of the speaker. A writer may deliberately refrain from presenting any situational information if that suits his purpose, and if he wants to present it, he may choose from a variety of strategies. Moreover, he is able to furnish relevant situational information more precisely and explicitly, just because of the linguistic means he employs.

There are, however, other aspects of written language which open up quite new dimensions. These have to do with its visibility, with the interpretational process, and with the position of writer and reader. Written language allows greater complexity of syntactic structures, because text and context remain present and accessible for the reader, while in spoken language the hearer is dependent on memory for textual retrieval.

The interpretational process is much more sophisticated in written language than in oral use. First of all there is in written use reiterability of interpretation, which is largely absent in oral language use. From the point of view of the reader, repeated interpretation may lead to a better understanding, or at least to an understanding different from the result of an earlier interpretation.

Secondly, there is ample opportunity for the reader for an unhurried reflection on the content of the text and on his own initial interpretation of it. This may lead – as Stutterheim pointed out many years ago – to a more richly articulated reading experience, as knowledge acquired by reflection may be integrated in a renewed interpretation (Stutterheim 1953:Chapter 3).

Thirdly, the written use of language makes it possible to overcome the limitation put on interpretation by the linearity principle, operative in oral language use, as a written text allows the reader to go back and forth through it, no longer restricted to one single interpretational direction. Moreover, the fact that in the written use of language the context remains available for

---

6   Compare Barthes (1966:54): 'l'oeuvre n'est entourée, désignée, protégée, dirigée par aucune situation, aucune vie pratique n'est là pour nous dire le sens qu'il faut lui donner'. For the function of the situation in linguistics and in poetry, see Mounin 1969:255-85.

repeated inspection, may allow more precise interpretation than the context in oral language use, which is hard to retain in memory, and consequently is soon lost sight of.

The writer who is aware of the special possibilities of interpretation open to the reader may deliberately make use of the fact that the reader may repeat his interpretational efforts and may study the text carefully. This implies that a broader spectrum of writing techniques is at his disposal in comparison with the speaker, who knows that normally only one interpretational chance is given to the hearer.

As to the relations between writer and reader, it is clear that they are only partly parallel with the relations between speaker and hearer. Written language makes possible temporal and spatial distance between addresser and addressee, thereby overcoming two limitations characteristic of oral use. A writer and a reader may not even know each other and may even be totally unaware of each other's existence. This distance and this indeterminacy of the reader may be exploited by the writer. He can – to mention only one possibility – address himself explicitly in the text to a reader of his choice, at the same time aiming at a quite different readership. One might say that written language use allows a certain multiplication of the reader, not in the trivial sense of a plurality of readers, but of different kinds or categories of readers. The writer can even go so far as to give the impression that what he writes is not meant for any reader, in spite of the fact that writing, like speaking, remains an intentional act directed towards others.

This brief comparison between written and oral language use reinforces the importance of the distinction between oral and written literature, and establishes the need for a detailed comparative study of the mechanisms involved in their production and in their interpretation. Such a comparison would be illuminating for both. It should include hybrid forms of language use, for instance written texts meant to be recited, such as the Old Javanese Rāmāyaṇa *kakawin*, which can be shown to employ devices which may be absent in texts written in order to be read.

IV

And now it is time to conclude. Our inquiry into language as an instrument for literary use showed in the first place that language is not some sort of Nessus garment from which we, like Hercules, cannot free ourselves. Such an extreme version of the Sapir-Whorf hypothesis rests on insufficient appreciation of the essentially open character of language. Far from being a rigid system, it is a complicated and subtle composite of freedom and constraint, of on the one hand obligatory features to which speaker and hearer, writer and reader alike have to adhere, and on the other hand areas where there is ample room for choice, for inventivity, for creative use and interpretation.

Secondly, it appears that for all products of language use the conclusion holds that they possess a limited degree of indeterminacy,[7] caused by the very nature of language, and by its use in close conjunction with outside sources of information. Recognition of this indeterminacy makes us realize an important goal of literary research: to determine the areas of this indeterminacy in each work, and to find out to what extent and by what sort of strategies this indeterminacy, this elbow room,[8] is made to serve literary purposes.

Thirdly, our cursory examination of language may be seen as an attempt to set in motion a *systematic* inquiry into the literary devices permitted by the semantic tools at the disposal of literary language use. Studies such as Levin's recent work on the semantics of metaphor and Balk's commentary on a poem of Vasalis are examples of what I have in mind.

Fourthly, I believe that the attention given to language at least permits us to understand the very relative validity of slogans such as: the text and nothing but the text. I agree with Kummer that the text has to remain a central focus for the study of literature – and actual practice is in accordance with this view – but it should never become the sole focus. The links which a work of art made of language has with its author and with its prospective readers, and its links with the outside world, preclude acceptance of such a one-sided standpoint.

Fifthly and finally, the analysis of language as literary instrument may contribute to our understanding of the value of competing approaches. It seems to me that they are complementary rather than mutually exclusive, being concerned with different aspects of literary works. The study of polysemy and in general of word meaning, for instance, shows that attempts to study what is called author's meaning may be combined and accommodated within studies focusing on the reader and his interpretational possibilities. Those who study the cultural background of the life of a poet, expecting that knowledge acquired from such sources may contribute to our understanding and appreciation of his oeuvre, are no doubt engaged in a legitimate enterprise. However, even if such studies have solved the vexed problem of determining what is relevant, a problem inherent in such studies, one has to realize that only limited results can be expected from such an approach which concentrates on one single factor. The same may be said of those traditional philological studies which by means

[7]   For a different view, see Hirsch 1967:44 sq.

[8]   Compare Iser's concept of 'blanks' (Iser 1980:109 sq.).

of textual criticism of the usual kind try to come as close as possible to literary works of the past. Such studies set themselves also a legitimate goal, provided that each manuscript used is examined within its own cultural and literary context, and traditional concepts such as scribal error and omission are revised and refined. An equally useful complement to such traditional concerns are the more recent attempts to follow the historical development of the interpretations a literary work has received during the time of its existence. Again, all such approaches have their limits, as they are concerned only with some aspect of a literary work.

The most pressing task for literary theory at the moment seems therefore to expose the partial validity of current approaches, and to reconcile them by assigning each of them its proper place within one coherent theoretical conception. Such a conception has to provide an answer to Jakobson's and Mounin's fundamental query about what it is that transforms ordinary linguistic utterances into literature (Jakobson 1960:350; Mounin 1969:11). This haunting question, which is similar to the one asked by Taco Roorda more than a century ago (Roorda 1863), will, however, be answered only by a theory of literature erected on the basis of an intimate knowledge of speech and language.

Bibliography

Balk-Smit Duyzentkunst, F.
1979   'Grammaticalness & poetry or how to live slowly', *Dutch Crossing* 9:114-24.
Barthes, R.
1966   *Critique et vérité*. Paris: Seuil.
1970   *S/Z*. Paris: Seuil.
Beaugrande, R. de
1985   'Text linguistics in discourse studies', in: T.A. van Dijk (ed.), *Handbook of discourse analysis*, vol. 1, Disciplines of discourse, pp. 41-70. London: Academic Press.
Brown, C.H. and S.R. Witkowski
1983   'Polysemy, lexical change and cultural importance', *Man* N.S. 18:72-89.
Casagrande, J.B. and K.L. Hale
1967   'Semantic relationships in Papago folk-definitions', in: D.H. Hymes and W.E. Bittle (eds), *Studies in Southwestern Ethnolinguistics*, pp. 165-93. The Hague/Paris: Mouton.

Culler, J.
1975a   *Structuralist poetics; Structuralism, linguistics and the study of literature.* Ithaca, N.Y.: Cornell University Press.
1975b   'Defining narrative units', in: R. Fowler (ed.), *Style and structure in literature; Essays in the New Stylistics,* pp. 123-42. Oxford: Blackwell.
1980   'Prolegomena to a theory of reading', in: S.R. Suleiman and I. Crosman (eds), *The reader in the text; Essays on audience and interpretation,* pp. 46-66. Princeton: Princeton University Press.
1983   *On deconstruction; Theory and criticism after structuralism.* London/Henley: Routledge and Kegan Paul.
Declerck, J.
1986   'The manifold interpretations of generic sentences', *Lingua* 68:149-88.
Derrida, J.
1967   *De la grammatologie.* Paris: Minuit.
Dijk, T.A. van (ed.)
1985   *Handbook of discourse analysis.* London: Academic Press. 4 vols.
Hirsch Jr., E.D.
1967   *Validity in interpretation.* New Haven/London: Yale University Press.
Iser, W.
1980   'Interaction between text and reader', in: S.R. Suleiman and I. Crosman (eds), *The reader in the text; Essays on audience and interpretation,* pp. 106-19. Princeton: Princeton University Press.
Jakobson, R.
1960   'Closing statement: Linguistics and poetics', in: Th.A. Sebeok (ed.), *Style in language,* pp. 350-77. Cambridge, Mass.: MIT Press.
Kummer, E.
1985   *Literatuur en ideologie: Proust en Ter Braak.* Amsterdam: Huis aan de Drie Grachten.
Levin, S.R.
1977   *The semantics of metaphor.* Baltimore/London: Hopkins.
Mooij, J.J.A.
1981   *Idee en verbeelding.* Assen: Van Gorcum.

Mounin, G.

1968   *Clefs pour la linguistique.* Paris: Seghers.

1969   *La communication poétique, précédé de Avez-vous lu Char?* Paris: Gallimard.

1975   *Clefs pour la langue française.* Paris: Seghers.

Reichling, A.

1969   *Verzamelde studies over hedendaagse problemen der taalwetenschap.* Vijfde druk. Zwolle: Tjeenk Willink. [Eerste druk 1961.]

Roorda, T.

1863   *Over dichtmaat, versmaat en versbouw, inzonderheid in de Hollandsche, Duitsche, Fransche, Grieksche en Romeinsche, Arabische en Oud-Indische poëzie.* 's-Gravenhage: Nijhoff.

Saussure, F. de

1916   *Cours de linguistique générale.* Lausanne/Paris: Payot.

Sinclair, J.McH.

1985   'On the integration of linguistic description', in: T.A. van Dijk (ed.), *Handbook of discourse analysis*, vol. 2, pp. 13-28.

Smith, B.H.

1978   *On the margins of discourse. The relation of literature to language.* Chicago/London: University of Chicago Press.

Stutterheim, C.F.P.

1953   *Problemen der literatuurwetenschap.* Antwerpen/Amsterdam: Standaard.

Suleiman, S.

1980   'Introduction; Varieties of audience-oriented criticism', in: S.R. Suleiman and I. Crosman (eds), *The reader in the text; Essays on audience and interpretation*, pp. 3-45. Princeton: Princeton University Press.

Uhlenbeck, E.M.

1967   'Language in action', in: *To honor Roman Jakobson*, pp. 2060-6. [Janua Linguarum Series Maior 33.] The Hague/Paris: Mouton.

1978   'On the distinction between linguistics and pragmatics', in: D. Gerber and H.W. Sinaiko (eds), *Language interpretation and communication*, pp. 185-98. New York/London: Plenum Press.

Vachek, J.

1939   'Zum Problem der geschriebenen Sprache', *Travaux du Cercle Linguistique de Prague* 8:94-104.

Verhagen, A.
1983   'Strukturele ambivalentie in de generatieve taalkunde;' *Forum
             der Letteren* 24:179-98.
Young, R.
1981   *Untying the text; A post-structuralist reader.* Boston/London/
             Henley: Routledge and Kegan Paul.

SULASTIN SUTRISNO

Classical Malay literature and its heirs

Introduction

Classical Malay literature – ending about the middle of the 19th century, Abdullah's period – like any other local literature in 'Nusantara' during its glorious era flourished, was nourished, developed, and deeply felt by the young as well as the old Malay people. Contemplations, thoughts and feelings which were examined and tested and carried on as a whole from generation to generation orally and in writing were regarded as guides of exemplary as well as disgraceful deeds which should be abided by. Violations of these guidelines would bring shame to the violator and his family.

The Malay people actively carried on a literary tradition so that good as well as bad value criteria in social life were very deeply rooted in the minds of the people. When Malay literature was still in the form of oral tradition, it was transmitted from generation to generation by word of mouth. Part of the oral literature was composed to attain a certain purpose. People were engaged in exchanging *pantun* in rice-planting rituals in the hope that harvests would be abundant; in wedding ceremonies in the hope that the bride and bridegroom would lead a peaceful and happy life; in birth rites in the hope that the baby would grow well and healthy, and to protect it against evil things. The ceremonies held for magical purposes were normally led by a man with magic powers who was well versed in choosing words possessing magical powers. Oral literature was also utilized by professional storytellers to entertain, such as the fables and other humorous stories. Oral tales, however, were not the only form of literature, as there emerged a form of written literature. Along with the written tradition found in inscriptions of the 15th century in Malaysia – most of which were written in Arabic (Teeuw 1961:9-12) – we could observe the growth of written Malay literature in Malaka, that is the emergence of the written literature of the palace around AD 1500 known as *hikayat*. The Arabic word hikayat means story, thus the use of this word in Malay literature is indicative of the fact that elements of Islam have been incorporated into the tradition of Malay written literature; this fact is further supported by the use of

Arabic script in the Trengganu Inscription (1303). In Malay society with the coming of Islam it was agreed that the Malay identity should be based on three factors: speaking Malay, carrying on Malay custom, and embracing Islam (Wan Ghalib 1985:1). Classical Malay literary works were based on these three factors.

Malay literary works used the medium of Malay, which since the 16th century had spread widely throughout 'Nusantara' as the lingua franca. Linguistic contacts with other nations resulted in cultural contacts, so that Malay as well as Malay culture picked up foreign elements from the language and literature of other regions, and vice versa. In Malay literature for example Nuruddin Arraniri and Abdullah Munsyi, who were not brought up in a Malay cultural society and had no Malay ancestors, wrote their masterpieces in Malay (Khaidir Anwar 1985:16). Moreover, Abdullah was quite interested in Malay and Malay culture. He succeeded in inspiring the Malay people to take an interest in their own language; he then published *Sejarah Melayu* and translated the *Hikayat Pancatantra* from Tamil into Malay (1835) under the title *Hikayat Galilah dan Daminah* (Datoek Besar and Roolvink 1953:13).

It is therefore not surprising that in the linguistic and cultural contacts with foreign nations there are a number of borrowed words from Sanskrit, Arabic, Portuguese, Chinese, Dutch, Persian, and Tamil (Teeuw 1961:38-41). Translations of the Bible and the Kuran into Malay, the writing of various Malay dictionaries and the thorough study of Malay (Teeuw 1961) will show the important role of Malay in expressing all the aspects of life of the Malay people.

Besides, in the use of Malay will also be observed the relation between language and culture, such as prohibition or language taboo, for instance a prohibition on mentioning the name of something which is feared when a person is walking or travelling at a certain time or place so as not to meet with danger; for example, a snake should be referred to as a root. The relation between language and culture is also reflected in the expression 'Bahasa menunjukkan bangsa', meaning that a person using good language is a good person, and a person using bad language shows that he is not of noble birth (Pamuntjak, Iskandar and Modjoindo 1951).

Custom is unwritten law and is the source of law, and this law of the people was then perfected with Islamic law (Wan Ghalib 1985:3). This law has come down to the people through various expressions showing clearly the basis of Malay law reinforced by the 'Sunnah Nabi' and the Holy Kuran. This Principle cannot be altered, as can be observed in the statement: 'Adat berwaris kepada Nabi, Adat berkalifah kepada Adam, Adat tersirat dalam sunnah, Adat dikungkung Kitabullah' (Custom is inherited from the Prophet, Custom has Adam as its Caliph, Custom is contained in the Tradition, Custom is fettered by Scripture') (Wan Ghalib 1985:5-6).

Besides there is still a custom which arranges the good and ideal character of man on the basis of the conception of Malay custom, for instance a good king is described in *Adat Raja-Raja Melayu* (Panuti Sudjiman 1979:196) as follows:

'[...] adalah raja itu telah dijadikan Allah subhānahu wa taala akan gembala segala manusia, yang di dalam daerah takluk perpegangan raja itu, supaya jangan menjadi pergaduhan dan rusak segala manusia itu yang di bawah takhta kerajaan; [...] kalakian maka adalah raja itu telah dikaruniai Allah taala dilebihkan daulatnya, yakni tuahnya [...]. Maka tatkala itu segala manusia pun kasih sayang dan takut akan dia [...] mereka itu pun menurutlah sekarang perkataannya dan memuji-muji atas segala kelakuannya [...] masyhurlah wartanya pada segala negeri asing-asing. Maka menjadi besarlah kerajaan raja itu.'

'[...] Now that king has been appointed by Almighty God as a shepherd of all the people who are in the lands subject to him, lest there be any conflict or injury to all those who are beneath his royal sceptre [...]; such a king has been granted by God an increase of authority, that is, his holy power [...]. Then all the people love him and fear him [...], they now comply with his commands and praise all his doings [...], his fame spreads to every foreign country. That king's rule becomes great.'

Some praiseworthy characteristics are also explained:

'arif yaitu amat pandai barang sesuatu perbuatan dan pekerjaan dan peraturan dan perkataan, budi bicaranya serta mengetahui kesudahannya.
budiman artiya, berakal; barang sesuatu perbuatannya dengan sempurna, tiada memberi cedera kesudahannya.
bangsawan artinya, orang yang berbangsa turun-temurun tiada bercampur [...].
setiawan artinya, barang yang telah dijanjikan selamanya diteguhkan.
dermawan yaitu yang sangat murah, hatinya; barang siapa meminta tiada ditahannya adanya' (Panuti Sudjiman1979:228).

'"Wise", that is very clever in all his acts, works, rulings, sayings and deliberations, as well as considering their effect.
"Intelligent" means resourceful; whatever he undertakes is accomplished, it does not bring about any harm.
"Noble" means that a man is of aristocratic descent, unsullied.
"True" means that whatever is promised is always fulfilled.
"Bountiful" refers to great generosity of spirit; no matter who asks, he is not refused.'

Seven characteristics of a righteous king have also been preserved, for instance in the *Hikayat Sri Rama*; cleverness, justice, love, outer attractive characteristics, courage for the sake of self-esteem, martial ability, and asceticism (Achadiati Ikram 1980:10). What has been written in those manuscripts about kings is a guide for heads of state stipulating their rights and duties to rule the country and people safely in reaching a peaceful, just and prosperous society.

As already mentioned, the Malay people very much uphold the observance of spiritual life, so moral teaching is the central focus of literary life. With the coming of Islam, spiritual and mental life are materialized in Islamic religious life. Aceh has produced masterpieces by prominent figures in heterodox mysticism such as Hamzah Fansuri and Syamsuddin, whereas Nuruddin Arraniri and Abdul Rauf represent orthodox mysticism.

Besides, Malay literature with this strong Islamic colour generally deals with the spread of Islam and Islamic teaching as the centre of narration; therefore it is logical that the stories deal with the life of the Prophet Muhammad, his apostles, the other prophets, Islamic missionaries, and Islamic heroes. Finally there are stories based on Islamic sources and fictitious stories inspired by Islam (Winstedt 1969; Liaw Yock Fang 1982). These groups of stories are quite well known in 'Nusantara' and several of these stories have been translated into regional languages. Culture, tradition and pre-Islamic concepts are as far as possible altered, adjusted to Islamic norms and religious duties, for example 'yang empunya cerita' in oral tradition changes into 'sahibu'l hikayat', the *Hikayat Sri Rama* from India has been Islamized so as not to contradict good Islamic teachings. The influence and spirit of Islam on Malay literary works is tremendous and deeply rooted in the minds of the Malay people, so that Malay literature functions as a means of Islamic propaganda and religious conviction in Islam (Hamdan Hassan 1980:89). All other social functions of Malay literature develop from these main functions.

Classical Malay literature: a cultural heritage

Literature reflects life as a social reality, so literature usually is very closely connected with certain social customs; therefore in a traditional society, for example, it is quite difficult to distinguish between poetry and religious cermonies, magic, or games (Wellek and Warren 1970:91). Literature as one of the branches of art is a manifestation and reflection of life and is a record of various aspects of culture. Art is never separate from society and is an integral part of culture as well as an expression of cultural creativity itself (Umar Kayam 1981-82:52).

Thus the Malay literary treasure is a document of the cultural life of the Malay people. It is impossible to understand Malay literary works without understanding the social-cultural background which creates those works. On the other hand, through Malay literary works we can obtain a picture of the cultural life of the Malay people. The study of Malay culture naturally involves a thorough study of Malay literature, because the poet's world or the world of words is built upon a foundation of elements in the real world, an illumination of an aspect of the world as it really is (Daiches 1956:37) in the cultural context, which applies in society.

It has been mentioned above how the Malay identity in the form of language, custom, and religion as a cultural aspect is upheld by the Malay people. There is still quite a lot of ancestral heritage in the form of teachings and guidance expressed in sayings, expressions, proverbs, *pantun, seloka*, and so on. The *Gurindam Dua Belas* written by Raja Ali Haji is very well known because of having valuable teachings. Religious advice taught though sayings and other figurative language has become part of culture throughout Indonesia (Wan Ghalib 1985:15) because it really has a universal value for the society in 'Nusantara'.

Patterns of good manners involving behaviour, using decent language, decent dress, one's attitude in facing various social strata, humility, mutual aid, concord, and the like are preserved in various forms of figurative language and are still alive nowadays, although not quite so much employed as they used to be in former days. In fact, a simple proverb might have an essence requiring a long explanation. Actually, these concise expressions convey a deep and profound meaning.

Except in the form of various short expressions mentioned before, all other Malay literary genres conveyed orally as well as in writing in the form of poetry and prose are sources of information on Classical Malay culture, among others the paternalistic Malay culture, the Malay personality which is shrouded in customs, tradition, and conventional religion, so that Malay can hardly come out of the metaphysical era (Thabrani Rab 1985:8-10).

Another aspect of inner life is manifested in comfort, jokes, education, the spirit of heroism, historical awareness, guide to law, respectively expressed in *cerita pelipur lara* (Winstedt: folk romance), farcical tales, animal fables, heroic tales, Malay histories, and digests of law. These literary activities are in accordance with an Islamic view: that taking up art (including literature) is a form of devotion, an activity to guide civilization and culture in this world in line with the guidance of God (Shahnon Ahmad 1981:90).

Ancient Malay society has left an inheritance of quite rich spiritual value. Besides the inheritance still presented in its original place, Classical Malay manuscripts are scattered far beyond the boundaries of their places of origin, which is a sign of positive response from non-Malay societies with their respective literary and cultural backgrounds.

Classical Malay literature and its Indonesian heirs

Since the introduction of Islam, Malay literature has played the role of spreading the tradition of writing in Malay in the Malay world and preserving existing literature or literature that had just been introduced into Malay literature by bringing forth Islamic values (Shafie Abu Bakar 1980:49).

It is thus understandable that Malay literature, like Javanese literature, is an ancient tradition, having the largest repertory of texts after the repertory of Javanese literature (Ismail Hussein 1984:8). The question now is: What can the Malay or Indonesians, as the direct heirs, do with the bulk of this literary heritage? How do the readers and listeners of the heritage receive (Jauss 1970) the cultural heritage of their ancestors?

In the *Sejarah Melayu* (SM) (Situmorang and Teeuw 1952) it is reported that the king requested the treasurer to arrange the writing of the hikayat to preserve the knowledge of events, regulations, and customs of all Malay kings for the sake of posterity, that their descendants may learn, remember, and benefit from them (p. 2). The request contains two objectives: first, that the descendants who are explicitly addressed in the text receive and preserve the heritage; secondly, that the descendants may benefit from them. The term descendants, as it is used here, means the readers and listeners of the hikayat, because, although the hikayat was handed down in a written form, it was not meant to be read alone by individuals; rather, one person read while others listened, as is mentioned in the *Hikayat Andaken Penurat* (Robson 1969:21): '[...] inilah hikayat cerita Jawa [...] dipatut oleh dalang yang arif lagi bijaksana [...] barang siapa "membaca" dia atau "menengarkan" dia [...]'.

It is also mentioned in the *Sejarah Melayu* that on the evening before the attack on Malaka by the Portuguese, all of the commanders requested that the war hikayat, the *Hikayat Muhammad Hanafiyyah* (HMH), be read in order that they might benefit from it (pp. 297-8), that is, become as courageous as Muhammad Hanafiyyah. The king selected the *Hikayat Amir Hamzah* because he thought the courage of the hero, Amir Hamzah, was enough, but at the insistence of one of the *pertuanan* (nobles), Tun Isap, the HMH was also released. HMH was read the whole night to those who were awaiting the day for the attack. The literary work thus was given meaning by its readers (Segers 1980:9).

The content of SM is, on the one hand, a message from the ancestors about the texts that they bequeathed; and on the other hand, it is a reception of the message by the heirs by reading the hikayat so as to restore one of its functions, that is, to obtain the advantage of boosting the fighting spirit.

Apart from the utility function, Malay literary works also fulfil the enjoyment function (Wellek and Warren 1970:30), i.e. to entertain as mentioned in the *Hikayat Panji Kuda Semirang* (Lukman Ali and Hutagalung 1973): '[...] inilah cerita orang dahulu kala, hikayat namanya, [...] akan penghibur hati yang masygul [...]' (p. 1); likewise the *Hikayat Percintaan Kasih Kemudaan* (Ahmad Kotot 1975) says that: '[...] hikayat ini dikarangkan hendak memberi kesukaan kepada anak muda [...] moga tertarik hatinya membaca hikayat atau syair sambil terpungut akan maksud yang berfaedah' (p. xv).

In the *Hikayat Hang Tuah* (Shellabear 1908-09) the king is said to have asked Hang Jebat to read some hikayat. The king enjoyed the reading by Hang Jebat so much that he fell asleep on Hang Jebat's lap (III:67). This is proof that the reading of the hikayat provided enjoyment for the king.

The fact that the tales were old but continuously handed down through the generations is proven by the quotation above, which reads 'the account of ancestors'. The quotation from the *Hikayat Malim Deman* (1976) verifies the age of the tales, which extends over centuries. In other words, the tales were received and preserved because their contents met the reader's expectation: 'Inilah warita orang dahulu kala, entahkan beberapa zaman lamanya cerita dibawa air yang hilir, angin yang lalu dan burung yang terbang' (p. iii).

The function of Indonesian literature can only be revealed by the literary works themselves, and likewise, the aesthetic concepts that underlie Classical Malay literature can only be traced in the Malay texts. The main aspect of the aesthetic concepts in Malay literature with Islamic influence is closely related to the beauty that emanates from the greatness of God the Creator. According to Braginsky (1975), there are three aspects in the Malay concept of beauty. The first aspect is the ontological aspect of beauty, which is expressed in God's affluence as shown in the following quotation: 'Sakali peristiwa Allah subhanahu wata'ala menunjukkan kekayaannya kepada hambanya [...]' (*Hikayat Si Miskin* 1965:1). The poet or author feels that he is not capable of creating; therefore, he asks for God's protection or assistance, 'Dengan nama Allah Tuhan semesta – Saya mengarangkan satu cerita' (Ahmad Grozali 1978:15). 'Dengan nama Allah aku memulai kitab ini, [...] kami minta tolong atas segala pekerjaan dunia dan akhirat' (Rosmera 1965:244).

Due to the affluence, greatness, or power of God the Creator, the absolute beauty (*al-Jamal, Yang Maha Elok*) of the Lord is impressed on the beauty of the phenomenal world (*husn, indah*) in works of art. The meaning of the word *elok* above refers to *indah*, which is something invisible, and which has a good quality (Poerwadarminta 1976), while *indah* refers to what is grasped from the outside, which is impressive as a work of art including literary works, as exemplified in the following: 'Ini hikayat terlalu "indah" ceritanya daripada cerita yang lain' (Jumsari Jusuf 1982:15).

The second aspect is the aspect of immanence in beauty, which impresses and which is expressed in the description of a situation that involves variety, harmony, and order.

> 'Surat itu dibubuhkan pada ceper emas yang bertatahkan ratna mutu manikam. Setelah sudah dinaikkan orang ke atas gajah maka terkembanglah payung ubur-ubur enam belas kekuningan daripada intan dikarang [...] tunggul panji-panji pun berkibaranlah pelbagai warnanya. Maka raja Budak pun semayam di atas singgasana yang bertatahkan ratna mutu manikam berumbai-rumbaikan emas sepuluh mutu bertatahkan intan lazuardi adatnya baginda itu [...].' (Jumsari Jusuf 1982:99-100.)

> 'The letter was laid on a golden salver studded with precious stones. After it had been raised onto the elephant's back sixteen golden parasols with fringes of diamonds were unfurled [...], flags and variegated pennants fluttered. Raja Budak was seated upon a throne inlaid with jewels, hung with fringes of 24-carat gold and set with diamonds and lapis lazuli in royal style [...].'

The third aspect is the psychological aspect, which involves the impact on the reader, who may be struck with awe or ecstasy by the variety; the excessive beauty is comforting and relieving, as shown in tales for entertainment such as the *Hikayat Raja Muda* (1964:1), as related by Pawang Ana, the storyteller:

> 'Alkissah, maka adalah sebuah negeri bernama Benua Tua, maka rajanya bernama Sultan Degar Alam, cukup dengan menteri, hulubalang, sida-sida bentara, terlalu banyak rakyat tenteranya, [...]. Pada suatu hari baginda keluar ke peseban agung, bersemayam di atas takhta singgasana yang keemasan yang bertatahkan ratna mutu manikam berumbai-rumbaikan mutiara dikarang, cukup dengan alat orang berjawatkan perkakas kerajaan empat puluh hulubalang di kanan, empat puluh di kiri, yang sedia menyandang pedang yang keemasan, sekaliannya itu hulubalang pahlawan yang pilihan: semuanya sudah turun-temurun tahan dipanah, tahan digergaji dan tahan dibakar, tahan direndam dan tahan dipahat dan tahan pula dimasukkan ke dalam mulut meriam menjadi peluru, ditembak tiada binasa, bulu roma sehelai pun tiada gugur.'

> 'It is told that once there was a land named Benua Tua. Its king was called Sultan Degar Alam, and he was well endowed with ministers, chiefs, heralds and a great many followers [...]. On a certain day His Majesty proceeded to the great audience hall and sat in state upon a golden throne inlaid with precious stones and adorned with fringes of pearl, complete with attendants bearing the regalia, forty chiefs on the right and forty on the left, standing ready with a golden sword over the shoulder. All those chiefs were chosen heroes, each one from a line that could resist arrows, could be sawn or burnt, could be submerged in water or chiselled, could be put in the mouth of a cannon as cannon-ball and fired without being killed or a single hair of his body harmed.'

The ecstacy which overpowers the reader as he experiences the beauty of artistic creation in Malay literature is similar to being carried away in experiencing beauty in Old Javanese literature as claimed by Zoetmulder. The art of writing poetry in ancient Java was given the name *kalangön*, that is 'beauty'; for it was the creation and enjoyment of the products of literary art which conveyed the ecstasy (*langö*) of losing oneself in the experience of beauty (Zoetmulder 1974:v). The enjoyment, utility, and aesthetic elements in Classical Malay literature constitute the basic elements of the reception of those Malay literary works.

A form of reception that was widely practised is the copying of manuscripts by hand, because many people wanted to keep them as part of their personal collection due to the fear that the original manuscripts might be lost, deteriorate, or be destroyed in a fire. It might also be the case that people kept the manuscripts in order to gain some magical power due to a belief in the sacredness of those manuscripts. Manuscripts that were considered important were copied for political, religious, educational, and other reasons. With the exception of religious texts, in the process of copying the manuscripts, the copyists were free to add, delete, or change the manuscripts according to their liking, so as to conform with the situation and condition of the period. Thus it is very likely that a given copy of the original manuscript is not a complete or perfect copy. Sometimes the differences were so great that different versions appeared. Actually, the copying of manuscripts is a kind of reception both in form and essence, thus reception and creation combined.

Another kind of reception takes the form of studying a literary work from various aspects, like the *Hikayat Hang Tuah*, for example, which has been scrutinized in no less than 15 writings by modern Malay writers, among others as a work of fiction, a historical work, its technique of presentation, the image of women depicted in it, its traditional values, the main events in it, its language, and a comparison with other literary works (Sulastin Sutrisno 1983:32-3).

In Classical Malay literary miscellanies, excerpts from this hikayat are always found as an example of a traditional tale. The reception also took other forms, such as drama performance, over the radio and on television under the title *Hang Jebat Mendurhaka* (Treason of Hang Jebat), or a film like *Hang Tuah*. The name of the main character was used as the name of the first Indonesian man-of-war, of streets, and of *keris* at the Palace of Perak (Sulastin Sutrisno 1983:32-4). As another example of reception, Amir Hamzah wrote a poem in rhymed couplets entitled 'Hang Tuah' which is 39 stanzas long and taken from the *Hikayat Hang Tuah*. The re-creation by Amir Hamzah differs from the original story in an essential way, that is, concerning the end of the main character. In the *Hikayat Hang Tuah* Hang Tuah does not die, but becomes a saint, while in the modern poem by Amir Hamzah, Hang Tuah is depicted as an ordinary human being who dies in the end. A reception in the form of a complete translation of the work into German was done by Hans Overbeck, who entitled it *Hikayat Hang Tuah; Die Geschichte von Hang Tuah*, and he praised it as 'das schönste Buch der malayischen Literatur' (1922). Similarly, the *Sejarah Melayu* was reinvestigated by Umar Junus in *Sejarah Melayu; Menemukan diri kembali* (1984). He views SM as a literary work, or more appropriately as a work of fiction that is always alive in the interpretation of its readers and writers. Umar Junus applied a modern approach to this classical work of literature, by making use of the receptive-aesthetic theory, intertextuality, and semiotics.

Umar Junus is of the opinion that *Sejarah Melayu* as a literary work should be viewed in the light of modern theories that are usually applied only to modern literary works; that classical works of literature may also be analysed using modern theories and approaches to literature; that an appropriate approach will broaden the perspective of investigating classical literature and eliminate the dividing line between modern (beginning about 1920) and Classical Malay literature due to the fact that modern works of literature deliberately seek strength in traditional literature in the plot, style, or technique of presentation (Umar Junus 1984:163-4).

A reception of *Sejarah Melayu* was also done by Muhammad Haji Salleh, who recomposed it in *Sajak-sajak Sejarah Melayu* (1981). Each tale was transformed from prose to poetry; the old and the new were composed into a new creation that can be enjoyed by modern readers. The author enriched his poetic perspective by digging into the roots and tradition that could increase the value of this classical work of literature beyond the time of its creation.

In Malay literature we can also find works translated from Javanese as stated at the beginning of the texts of the stories of Panji and wayang, such as in the *Hikayat Darma Wangsa* and the *Hikayat Pandawa* 'dipindahkan dari bahasa Jawa kepada bahasa Melayu' (Van Ronkel 1909). These stories were later accepted as indigenous and became very popular, like other works from other regions, such as the *Hikayat Raja-Raja Pasai* from Pasai and mystical poetry by Hamzah Fansuri.

Re-examinations of classical literary works are continually being made, such as the *Hikayat Abdullah* by Goenawan Mohamad, who claims that Hikayat Abdullah is not merely a work of literature or just a series of legends. Its author is considered the first reporter of actual events, and also as the first writer to introduce realism into Malay writing. He also claims that Abdullah was the first sign of a new era who blended foreign influence and his strict, non-Western tradition, and Abdullah is considered as an exponent of the 20th century when he praised Lord Minto for treating the convicts in a humane way and when he criticized the despotic practices of the sultans. 'What is praised in Hikayat Abdullah are things that we are also likely to praise', writes Goenawan Mohamad (1986:22).

Concerning modern creation using classical literary tradition or convention, Rachmat Djoko Pradopo (1981) mentioned some examples. Below are some examples cited to illustrate the reception of classical literary works by modern society: Sanusi Pané wrote *Sandyakalaning Majapahit*, a play which was an adaptation of a Javanese tale *Damarwulan*. Rustam Effendi wrote *Bebasari*, a dramatic verse which made use of material taken from *Ramayana*. Chairil Anwar wrote a poem entitled 'Cerita buat Dien Tamaela' based on the belief of the people of Maluku. Asrul Sani wrote a poem in the style of incantation of magic spells entitled 'Mantera'. Rendra wrote ballads by using traditional materials and belief in the supernatural in a collection entitled *Ballada orang-orang tercinta*. Soebagio Sastrowardojo dug out materials from traditional tales and composed 'Candi Prambanan' and 'Nawang Wulan'. Sutardji Calzoum Bachri reintroduced the style of spells in poetry. In the area of short stories, Danarto wrote 'Nostalgia', which has as its background the story from 'wayang Bharatayuddha'. There are novels that have the Javanese wayang tradition as their background, such as *Arjuna mencari cinta* by Yudhistira Ardi Noegraha. The novel *Burung-burung manyar* by Y.B. Mangunwijaya is another example of the use of the Javanese tradition and wayang as background. *Pengakuan Pariyem* by Linus Suryadi A.G. makes use of the Javanese tradition of myth and legend as its background (Rachmat Djoko Pradopo 1981:32-41). Wisran Hadi made use of classical Minangkabau tradition adapted from Malin Kundang, Malin Deman, and also from Sangkuriang in his modern play *Puti bungsu* (Umar Junus 1981:112-3).

There are a host of other forms of reception in every kind of literary genre, but the brief illustrations, citations and limited examples above testify that the message of the ancestors to preserve the spiritual heritage has, to a certain extent, been fulfilled as it is contained in the texts themselves. The reception is continued by the younger generation by applying their respective orientation of authorship and approach. Considering the vast repertoire of Malay literature, the number of recipients of the literary heritage is very small, as it is limited to those who are actively involved in literature as part of their duty, or hobby, and those who are interested in literature.

Conclusion

To its heirs, Classical Malay literature is a philosophy of life. In every literary
expression, both oral and written, long and short, one of the basic elements of
literary activity that enriches the spirit is made explicit. Literary works are not
a dead thing, because they are kept alive in a variety of perspectives as shown in
the aforementioned examples and also in the following survey. *Warisan puisi
Melayu* (Mohd. Taib Osman 1979) brings forth various kinds of *pantun, syair,
gurindam, seloka,* and *ikatan puisi bebas.* In his survey, Mohd. Taib Osman
found that although traditional poetry was restricted by some fixed formulas, in
all new creation some deviation could be found which could be considered a
manifestation of creativity. In Malay traditional communities, poetry, especially
pantun was widely exploited, particularly in celebrations where reciprocal
recitals were popular, while *syair* were employed as a vehicle for ideas
concerning philosophy, religious knowledge, or advice. Poetry was considered
a form of communication (Mohd. Taib Osman 1979:v-viii), so it persisted in
everyday interaction.

In *Warisan prosa klasik* (Mohd. Taib Osman and Abu Hassan Sham 1980) we
can find folklore, historical literature, epic literature, and other stories. We can
find in them depictions of universal human experience which are not limited to
a certain period or culture, such as love, family ties and togetherness, anger,
revenge, treason, good and bad luck, joy, and moral or ethical teaching that
exceed the limits of the background of a community or a period. The awareness
and reception of literary conventions handed down from the past have enriched
the experience of the present generation (Mohd. Taib Osman and Abu Hassan
Sham 1980:vi).

From all of the examples we can draw the conclusion that intimacy with
ancient literature has opened up a new horizon for the development of both
language and modern literature. In order to produce literature of high quality,
a writer has to be able to dig out and utilize the forms of literary beauty that
were achieved in literary works of the past (Achadiati Ikram 1976:4-5). In that
way ancient or traditional literature can be perceived as a contribution to the
development of modern literature.

To investigate classical literature, an approach that makes use of modern
theories that are appropriate to the object of research can be applied. A text
edition will be more attractive if along with an analysis of the function of the
text for its creators the meaning and benefit to the recipients are also appended.
An ancient text has its own status and distinction as a work of literature within
the cultural pattern of ancient Malay, so the text should be interpreted in

accordance with the socio-cultural context of the community that produced it. To cite an example, some modern readers may admire Hang Jebat as their hero, but according to the text itself, that is to say, in the period and community that the text was produced, it was Hang Tuah who was the hero.

Research on Classical Malay literature must be encouraged and continued. The number of contributions made by foreign researchers and experts as heirs in general must be continued and counterbalanced by intensive research, both quantitatively and qualitatively, by the heirs of Malay literature themselves. There is no need to allot duties. Every interested researcher, regardless of his or her origin, is equally appreciated for making an effort to bring to light the cultural values contained in the object being researched. It is hoped that such research will reveal the special characteristics of the classical literary works and at the same time reveal their international value as works of literature. Thus, it is only appropriate that the traditional tales should find their place within the study of literature in general and be valued as a legitimate part of world literature. Their contribution to the development of modern literature is also a contribution to the development of modern culture in the context of a modern world.

Bibliography

Ahmad, Shahnon
1980   'Sastra Melayu dan Islam (Bahasan kepada kertaskerja saudara Shafei Abu Bakar)', in: *Kesusasteraan Melayu dan Islam*, pp. 72-86. Kuala Lumpur: Sarjana Enterprise.
Ali, Lukman and M.S. Hutagalung
1973   *Hikayat Panji Kuda Semirang*. Jakarta: Departemen Pendidikan dan Kebudayaan, Direktorat Jendral Kebudayaan.
Anwar, Khaidir
1985   Sumbangan bahasa Melayu (Riau) terhadap perkembangan bahasa Indonesia; Paper Pertemuan Ilmiah Kebudayaan Melayu, Proyek Inventarisasi dan Dokumentasi Kebudayaan Daerah di Tanjung Pinang.
Bakar, Shafie Abu
1980   'Sastra Melayu dan Islam', in: *Kesusasteraan Melayu dan Islam*, pp. 42-71. Kuala Lumpur: Sarjana Enterprise.

Braginsky, V.I.
1979   The concept of 'the Beautiful' (Indah), in: *Malay Classical literature and its Muslim roots; Paper Persidangan Antarabangsa Pengajian Melayu*. Kuala Lumpur: University Malaysia.

Daiches, David
1956   *Critical approaches to literature*. London/New York/Toronto: Longmans, Green.

Datoek Besar, R.A. and R. Roolvink
1953   *Hikajat Abdullah*. Djakarta/Amsterdam: Djambatan.

Ghalib, Wan
1985   *Adat istiadat dalam pergaulan orang Melayu di Riau; Paper Pertemuan ilmiah kebudayaan Melayu*. Proyek inventarisasi dan dokumentasi kebudayaan daerah di Tanjung Pinang.

Grozali, Ahmad
1978   *Syair Si Pahit Lidah*. Jakarta: Departemen Pendidikan dan Kebudayaan, Proyek Penerbitan Buku Bacaan dan Sastra Indonesia dan Daerah.

Hassan Hamdan
1980   'Sastera Melayu dan Islam', in: *Kesusasteraan Melayu dan Islam*, pp. 144-76. Kuala Lumpur: Sarjana Enterprise.

Hikayat Malim Deman
1963   *Hikayat Malim Deman*. Kuala Lumpur: Fajar Bakti.

Hikayat Raja Muda
1964   *Hikayat Raja Muda*. Kuala Lumpur: Oxford University Press.

Hikayat Si Miskin
1965   *Hikayat Si Miskin*. Kuala Lumpur: Oxford University Press.

Hussein, Ismail
1974   *The study of traditional Malay literature with a selected bibliography*. Kuala Lumpur: Dewan Bahasa dan Pustaka, Kementerian Pelajaran Malaysia.

1984   *Antara dunia Melayu dengan dunia Indonesia*. Kuala Lumpur: Bintang Kuala Lumpur.

Ikram, Achadiati
1976   'Sastra lama sebagai penunjang pengembangan sastra modern', *Bahasa dan Sastra* 1-6:2-13.

1980   *Hikayat Sri Rama; Suntingan naskah disertai telaah amanat dan struktur*. Jakarta: Penerbit Universitas Indonesia.

Jauss, Hans Robert
1970   Literaturgeschichte als Provokation. Frankfurt am Main: Suhr

kamp. [Partly translated: 'Literary history as a challenge to literary theory', in: Ralph Cohen (ed.), *New directions in literary history*, 1974:11-41.]

Junus, Umar
1981   *Mitos dan komunikasi.* Jakarta: Sinar Harapan.
1984   *Sejarah Melayu; Menemukan diri kembali.* Petaling Jaya: Fajar Bakti.

Jusuf, Jumsari
1982   *Hikayat Raja Budak.* Jakarta: Departemen Pendidikan dan Kebudayaan, Proyek Penerbitan Buku Bacaan Sastra Indonesia dan Daerah.

Kayam, Umar
1981-82   'Kreativitas dalam seni dan masyarakat suatu dimensi dalam proses pembentukan nilai budaya dalam masyarakat', *Analisis Kebudayaan* 2-2:52-7.

Kotot, Ahmad
1975   *Hikayat percintaan kasih kemudaan.* Kuala Lumpur: Dewan Bahasa dan Pustaka Kementerian Pelajaran Malaysia.

Liaw Yock Fang
1975   *Sejarah kesusastraan Melayu Klassik.* Singapura: Pustaka Nasional.

Mohamad Goenawan
1986   'Hikayat Abdullah', *Tempo* 16-23(2 Agustus):22.

Osman, Mohd. Taib
1979   *Warisan puisi Melayu.* Kuala Lumpur: Dewan bahasa dan Pustaka Kementerian Pelajaran Malaysia.

Osman, Mohd. Taib dan Abu Hassan Sham
1980   *Warisan prosa klasik.* Kuala Lumpur: Dewan Bahasa dan Pustaka Kementerian Pelajaran Malaysia.

Overbeck, H.
1922   *Hikajat Hang Tuah; Die Geschichte von Hang Tuah.* München: Müller.

Pamuntjak, K.St., Iskandar, and A.Dt. Modjoindo
1951   *Peribahasa.* Tjetakan Ke-6. Djakarta: Balai Pustaka.

Poerwadarminta, W.J.S.
1976   *Kamus umum bahasa Indonesia.* Jakarta: Balai Pustaka.

Pradopo, Rachmat Djoko
1981   'Bangkitnya konvensi dan tradisi Nusantara dalam kesusastraan Indonesia modern', *Bahasa dan Sastra* 7-4:32-42.

Rab, Thabrani
1985   *Pribadi Melayu; Paper Pertemuan Ilmiah Kebudayaan Melayu.*
            Proyek Inventarisasi dan Dokumentasi Kebudayaan Daerah di
            Tanjung Pinang.

Robson, S.O.
1969   *Hikajat Andaken Penurat.* The Hague: Nijhoff. [KITLV, Biblio-
            theca Indonesica 2.]

Rosmera
1965   *Hikayat Malik Saiful-Lizan.* Singapura: Malaysia Publications.

Salleh, Muhammad Haji
1981   *Sajak-Sajak Sejarah Melayu.* Kuala Lumpur: Dewan Bahasa dan
            Pustaka Kementerian Pelajaran Malaysia.

Segers, Rien T.
1980   *Het lezen van literatuur.* Baarn: Ambo.

Shellabear, W.G.
1908-09   *Hikayat Hang Tuah.* Singapura: Methodist Publishing House. 4
            vols.

Situmorang, T.D. and A. Teeuw
1952   *Sedjarah Melaju menurut terbitan Abdullah (bin Abdulkadier
            Munsji).* Djakarta: Djambatan.

Sudjiman, Panuti Hadimurti Mohammed
1979   *Adat Raja-Raja Melayu; A critical edition together with a com-
            mentary on court ceremonials.* [Ph.D. thesis, Australian National
            University, Canberra.]

Sutrisno, Sulastin
1983   *Hikayat Hang Tuah; Analisa struktur dan fungsi.* Yogyakarta:
            Gadjah Mada University Press.

Teeuw, A.
1961   *A critical survey of studies on Malay and Bahasa Indonesia.*
            's-Gravenhage: Nijhoff. [KITLV, Bibliographical Series 5.]

Wellek, René and Austin Warren
1970   *Theory of literature.* Harcourt: Peregrine Books, Brace and
            World.

Winstedt, R.O.
1969   *A history of Classical Malay literature.* Third edition. Kuala
            Lumpur: Oxford University Press. [First edition 1939.]

Zoetmulder, P.J.
1974   *Kalangwan; A survey of Old Javanese literature.* The Hague:
            Nijhoff. [KITLV, Translation Series 16.]

H.M.J. MAIER

The laughter of Kemala al-Arifin
The tale of the bearded civet cat

> 'Laughter liberates not only from external censorship
> but first of all from the great interior censor; it
> liberates from the fear that developed in man during
> thousands of years: fear of the sacred, of prohibitions,
> of the past, of power' (Bakhtin 1984:94).

In Malay narratives that have been preserved in manuscripts dating from before 1900, laughter is a rare phenomenon. Reading through the teachings of wise men, the adventures of states, the exploits of Sri Rama, the Pandawa, Inu Kertapati or Indraputra, we hardly ever come across a scene that gives rise to unrestrained laughter – neither from the hero nor from us. A prince may laugh on meeting an old friend, a ruler may laugh on hearing witty repartee, yet heroes are so much involved in fighting out their conflicts and fulfilling their missions, heroines are so much engrossed in efforts to evade and protect their heroes, villains are so occupied by their invidious and violent schemes, that none of them seems to realize that laughter is a creative force that could overcome their awe of the sacred and death as well as their fear of the world and life. An occasional smile is all, but then, there is usually something ambiguous, something restrained about a smile: it hides uneasiness as much as it suggests amusement, and this holds for the smiles of the heroes as much as for those of the public. In short, it seems as though Malay scribes did not give much value to offering fun, and the culture they supported with their narratives was a grim one.

Narratives are a crucial feature of any human community. Some of them are more important for its members than others: in explaining and describing power relations, religious concepts, laws or the history of their community, they vindicate a certain social cohesion and cultural identity – they are myths. The other narratives, though not necessarily without some moral value, are primarily meant for amusement, for pleasure – they are tales. These terms are Frye's, who adds that such a distinction between sacred and secular narratives does not run parallel to differences in narrative schemes. Most members of both groups can be categorized formally as what Frye calls 'romances', the distinction between myths and tales being primarily a matter of function, of authority (Frye 1982:6).

Frye's distinction seems very well suited to bringing some sort of order to a narrative tradition which, until the end of the nineteenth century, provided the Malay-speaking communities on the Malay peninsula and the east coast of Sumatra with a distinct cultural identity. There, too, was a corpus of narratives that tended to stick together, 'a large interconnected body of narrative that covers all the religious and historical revelation that its society is concerned with, or concerned about', preserving the themes, sentences, and images that the Malays needed to make sense of the world and of themselves. Circling around this 'mythology' were tales, constantly dispersing, wandering within Malay-speaking communities and beyond, picking up and dropping elements of other narratives on the way, absorbing elements of myths, and being incorporated into myths.

This picture of Malay narrativity as moving between the poles of myth and tale is not just a scholarly construct. The Malays themselves made the distinction, too, between *hikayat* and *cerita* (*ceritera*). The distinction can be extended further: it is a distinction between writing and speaking, and still further than that: between a uniform stylized language and a variety of dialectal, colloquial forms.

Some time before the end of the nineteenth century, the body of myths was definitely domesticated in writing. Contained in a heavily stilted language, laced with repetitions, steeped in commonplaces, stock phrases and typescenes, the hikayat called up a world that was inaccessible to narrators as well as to their public. Presenting themselves as stories from the days of yore in a never-never land, they were ascribed authority, truth, and validity because of their continuous references to Tradition, that transcendental origin of the rules and regulations of Malay thought and action.

Meanwhile, cerita continued to travel around with the people who preserved them in their voice, in dialectal and colloquial forms, more or less stylized in a way that made them different from everyday discourse but close enough so that their audiences appreciated the references to real-life situations – the coughing, hesitations, nonsense phrases, and intonations which the narrator's voice allowed itself could only add to the amusing appreciation of its closeness to its public's everyday world.

Is not this another beautiful set of oppositions: myth vs. tale, normative vs. amusing, written vs. oral, stylized vs. dialectal, past vs. present, traditions vs.

realism? It is tempting to summarize these oppositions in the opposition of court culture vs. folk culture, but the construction of such a strict dichotomy would imply a disregard for the complex interaction between the court and the peasantry, and hence an underestimation of the dynamics of Malay culture. There are questions involved that seem to be more urgent: should writing, in Malay culture, be regarded as a supplement to speaking or, conversely, should speaking be considered as a complement to writing, or, for that matter, as a substitution? Myths cannot exist without tales, writing can only exist because there is speaking, but what is the nature of such oppositions and where should the force that created this difference be located?

Data about oral performances prior to the end of the nineteenth century are scarce. In Malay narratives there are only some scattered remarks – about a prince reciting a manuscript, a ruler listening to a recitation – that could be read as indications of how the voice was used. The accounts of Malayists on the performances they watched are too casual and inconsistent to construct a clear picture of how a Malay teller of tales operated. Oral culture has left few traces indeed.

More data about the preparation and use of manuscripts are available: the preserved manuscripts themselves provide us with some indications. The fact, however, that so many manuscripts have been lost or are inaccessible makes every effort to go beyond some general statements a very hazardous endeavour.

Overall, we can be certain that we will never acquire a full view on Malay narrativity as a whole: for every manuscript we have, a number of manuscripts are lost, for every oral performance that has been recorded, a great number of performances have evaporated without leaving a trace.

Starting out with summarizing what has been accepted as authoritative within Malay studies may be the most efficient way to set up some sort of construction of literary life in the Malay-speaking areas – if only to serve as the basis for a subversion. With a smile, maybe, or with a laugh. The authoritative view of Malay narrativity, the result of a century of mainly Dutch and British scholarship, gives a clear priority to writing over speaking, to manuscripts over oral performances. The most obvious explanations for this preference are so self-evident that they hardly need to be repeated. Writing is the cultural form our predecessors were more sympathetic with because of their education and their close familiarity with the Scripture. Contacts with the natives were primarily contacts with people who identified with court life rather than with village life and, therefore, offered a vision of the Malay world that focused on forms of court culture in which writing was given a prominent place. The disinterest Western scholarship showed for popular art forms appears like a mere supplement to their interest in written texts, strengthened by the anxiety of a certain class consciousness and feelings of racial superiority.

There is yet another explanation for this preference for manuscripts. For social and practical reasons, it has not always been easy for scholars and administrators to get more than a careful glimpse of village life. Oral traditions have been relatively inaccessible to Westerners, and, of course, it is hard for (wo)men of letters to write and speak about something they have never seen. In these days of post-colonialism, too, access to these forms of orality requires a great amount of persistence and sometimes even courage. It is so much more comfortable to lean back in an easy chair in a study and dream away over pencil and paper.

Malaysian scholars who have entered the mainstream of Malay studies do have access to these oral forms, and so does Amin Sweeney, who has done more than anyone else to bring oral traditions to the attention of Malayists. Their reports create a feeling of *memento mori*: professional storytellers, whose predecessors must have been wandering in considerable numbers through the Malay lands at the turn of this century, are becoming rare these days; they are being replaced by new channels of culture, like television, cinema, comics, music, and newspapers, which in their turn, are having a strong impact on amateur storytelling.

Of course, since the turn of the century Malayists have undertaken efforts to record oral performances. Next to manuscripts and books, tapes and films have created another kind of signifier that awaits interpretation. More than that, these recordings are the best informants available for the reconstruction of the oral component of Malay narrativity in days of yore. It should, however, be realized that such a reconstruction is as much a construction – using twentieth-century recordings to show how Malay tellers of tales performed up to the nineteenth century is a shaky enterprise and, if it is accepted as relevant at all, it can certainly not claim to be more than tentative and hypothetical.

Each medium has its own possibilities and limitations. The crucial question that the transformation of a spoken text into a written one gives rise to – tapes and films will not be discussed here because of the as yet restricted access to them – has never been satisfactorily answered: what is the most appropriate way to transfer the voice into writing and print? If one tries to repeat the voice of the narrator as carefully as possible, a great deal of sound is lost: the melody of the narrative, the singing, the chant that form integral parts of the performance, but also the sounds in which the narrating voice is embedded: the sizzling lamb, the matchbox used as a rhythm-stick, the crying baby, the whispering people, the slamming door, the rain on the roof, the clink of the fresh glass of coffee placed in front of the narrator – none of these can be accurately put on paper. Conversely, it would be equally impossible to make an accurate reconstruction of the performance of a storyteller from the letters of the page. And if we do indeed tear the voice away from its context and restrict ourselves bookishly to an attempt to repeat only the sounds of the narrator as carefully as possible in writing, the result is an unreadable text, full of disturbing interjections, repetitions, dots, loose phrases. Well preserved in the libraries, now and then perfunctorily quoted, but never carefully read or analysed. Reading makes different demands from listening.

Fortunately, most of the tales that have been transferred from voice to script so far have been consciously adapted to current conventions of reading; they are unreliable representations of their sources, and in their assimilation to new tastes and new requirements they follow the best of Malay scribal traditions. Naturally, there are all sorts of variations in these transferences. In most cases, the original presentation of the narrative has been 'translated' into what is considered standard Malay, presented in one of the standard spellings; some of these have tried to preserve a local, or rather colloquial, flavour by preserving dialectal elements, others have tried to preserve something of the different registers that were used, still others have added explanatory footnotes and an introduction.

The British, not unaware of the problems that are involved in transforming a tale from one medium into the other, had a clear preference for one possibility: they had the tales transformed into the 'literary' Malay of the hikayat tradition. Some tales were published in the most powerful scholarly journal of the day in order to give British readers a more complete idea of what 'Malay literature' was. Others were printed as books that were used as reading material in the vernacular schools. Leaving aside the question of why the British tried to degrade the narratives about Raja Muda, Malim Dewa, and Anggun Ce' Tunggal into children's tales, it is important to note that these tales, in this printed form, did not enjoy much popularity among the Malays. Apparently the stilted style drew these tales too emphatically into Malay mythology, giving them too much authority, too much normative power – and, as a result, they lost much of the realistic flavour and amusing recognition they must have had for their original audiences.

Curiously enough, it was these very cerita which, once fixed in writing, became relatively popular among the Europeans (Wilkinson 1907:17). More than the hikayat and the *kitab*, they offered European readers some realistic glimpses of the daily life of the Malays, from wedding ceremonies to educational methods, from observations of animal behaviour to fishing techniques.

'Accepting the popular theory that simple speech was prosaic, he [the storyteller] substituted imagery for gorgeous words. He shunned references to the habits of birds like the phoenix and the harpy, and confined himself to the more familar ways of sparrows, doves, quails and hawks. Where the learned man talked of "sun-gods" and the "curtain of dawn", the lettered rhapsodist spoke of "the hour at which the robin's note is heard". [...] Whatever may be its faults in other respects, the imagery of these village singers has one great merit: it is intensely real.' (Wilkinson 1907:7-9.)

Secondly, they had, for Western scholars, the originality and sensitivity of genuine literature. As Winstedt (1969:31-20) himself formulated it in his inimitable prose: they 'are the cream of Malay fiction, because in them the local colour takes the place of the tedious conventional descriptions in the many slavish copies from Indian models'.

Realism and literariness – an uneasy combination within the framework of modern literary theory, and this uneasiness is not worked out by Winstedt himself: only three pages of his book on Malay texts are devoted to the description of these 'genuine' Malay tales, whereas the rest of it is used to describe precisely those 'tedious' and 'conventional' hikayat. Disproportionate, yet understandable: for most of us, Malay narrativity is still dominated by written and printed texts – the use of the careless and self-contradictory term 'oral literature' should be a sufficient indication that the tales that are presented by the voice are approached against the background of writing.

Criticizing others is a way to create space for oneself; it is a rhetorical device which some Indonesianists are unable to appreciate, even though their field of study covers communities in which rhetoric is so all-pervasively present. Criticism certainly does not exclude admiration and respect; the British did have an admirable knowledge of the Malay world, and their seemingly commonsense observations could not only be interpreted as characteristic of a now reprehensible frame of mind, but can also be used as a starting point for a study of tales that is more in accordance with current scholarly discourses and interests.

'Romances' is the term British Malayists used for tales; the Malay communities reminded the members of a greatly industrialized nation of the Middle Ages in Europe, and narratives like the Tale of Raja Muda and the Tale of Anggun Ce' Tunggal reminded them of the romances and chansons of mediaeval literature: the stories about heroes wandering through a world full of wonders and mysteries reflected a certain frame of mind, primitive or not very civilized.

'Folk romances' is the term Wilkinson used for orally performed tales; for him, they formed a part of the great corpus of romances that included most of the hikayat as well. In his terminology, the myth of Iskander as well as the tale of Malim Dewa, the myth of Rama as well as the tale of Awang Sulung Merah Muda are romances, because they all are variations on a single masterplot: the hero is a prince in a prosperous and famous land; his birth and youth are attended by all sorts of favourable omens; at age fifteen he sets out to find his partner, overcomes a number of fierce enemies with his supernatural weapons, finds his loved one, and acquires another three wives on the way; eventually he returns safely with his loved ones, and is appointed ruler in his land of origin (Wilkinson 1907:21-2).

As for the oral variation of romance, Wilkinson deserves another quotation:

'The rhapsodist – the *penglipur lara* or "soother of cares" as he is prettily called – chants his story or poem or romance to a circle of appreciative listeners who do not trouble to enquire whether the plot of the poet is original but who revel in the pleasure afforded them by the sweet voice of the singer, by the courtly grace of his diction, and by the references that he continually makes to the "tender grace of the day that is dead", the ideal age, the golden past that can never come back to the Malay except in the dreamy imaginations evoked by melody and song.' (Wilkinson 1907:59.)

These notions of romance – constructed on a tripartite scheme (youth, adventures, happy return) and having a nostalgic effect on its public – lead us back to Frye, whose precious descriptions of romance offer ample possibilities to develop a rewarding understanding of Malay narrativity within a more scholarly framework (Frye 1957:186-205 and 1982). What makes us recognize a narrative as a romance is the concept of adventure: the hero goes through one adventure after the other, without developing, without aging, until he has completed the major adventure which keeps the narrative as a whole together: the quest. Romances can be divided into three stages: the stage of the perilous journey, the crucial struggle, and thirdly, the exaltation of the hero. The struggle is the crucial part, and the enemy is in every respect the reverse of the hero, whose values and concepts the public is supposed to take as an example. As for the emotions that are called up by romance: 'the childlike quality of romance is marked by its extraordinary persistent nostalgia, its search for some kind of imaginative golden age in time or space'.

Romance seems to take the central place in every narrative system (Frye 1982:28-31). Malay narrativity is no exception to this rule; in terms of both Wilkinson's impressionistic sketch and Frye's scholarly analysis, a great number of both cerita and hikayat can indeed be categorized as romance, although next to their similarities, there are many formal differences between, say, the *Hikayat Amir Hamzah* and the *Cerita Raja Muda*, the *Hikayat Pandawa Lima* and the *Cerita Musang Berjanggut*. Scholarship is always trying to

establish order, if only to substitute it, subsequently, for another harmonious
unity. If we try to detect a hierarchy within Malay narrativity, three formal
features could be used as yardsticks for determining the hikayat model and the
cerita model: the origin of the hero – divine in the hikayat, human in the cerita;
the language – highly stylized and uniform in the hikayat, conversational in the
cerita; and the world presented – a magic world in the past in the hikayat, a
realistic world in the present in the cerita.

High on the scale of such a hierarchy are the narratives about Amir Hamzah,
Iskander, Rama, and Panji, which in a very stilted language present the magic
and glory of days of yore in faraway countries; they were the most normative
and authoritative hikayat in that the Malays tended to use them as models of
behaviour and thinking. The narratives about the village idiot Pak Pandir,
which in colloquial and casual language present the world of the Malay village,
are the best example of the lowest form of cerita, more often than not deviating
from the narrative scheme of romance, and hence declining altogether and
becoming just anecdotes. Realistic tales, and very amusing indeed.

Penglipur lara narratives are somewhere in between these two extremes of
Malay narrativity. They had an ambiguous potential. They could be made so
stilted that they were gradually incorporated into the corpus of myths, the
hikayat style being substituted for distorted everyday language, turning the
entertaining adventures of a hero into a story about the human search for God,
the Truth. The *Hikayat Parang Puting* seems to be a late example of this, and it
is tempting to consider the *Hikayat Inderaputra* as an early example of the same
phenomenon. On the other hand, penglipur lara could also be so low on the
scale that they became primarily amusing tales if not anecdotes, presented in
strongly dialectal language, situated in the world of everyday life and laughter
(Frye 1957:136-40).

The following discussion centres on the *Cerita Musang Berjanggut* (Tale of
the Bearded Civet Cat), a cerita that seems a solid starting point for the study of
Malay narrativity as a whole. With a laugh.

Every text interpretation should be preceded by a second thought on the way
the text is presented, and the Tale of the Bearded Civet Cat is an interesting case
indeed. R.O. Winstedt, with the assistance of A.J. Sturrock, published the tale as
'Musang Berjanggut' in the Journal of the Straits Branch of the Royal Asiatic
Society in 1909; the usual addition of either hikayat or cerita is lacking –
apparently the editors did not know what to do with it. Data about its
provenance and origin are scarcely given. The version that was published – 52
pages in print – was written down by Winstedt's trusted informant, Raja Yahya
bin Raja Muhammad Ali of Perak, from the mouth of a storyteller not

mentioned by name. As in the case of the publication of the tales about Anggun Ce' Tunggal and Raja Muda, it can be safely assumed that Raja Yahya transformed the *Musang Berjanggut* as much as possible into a conventional hikayat, interlarded with 'rhythmical prose'.

Winstedt called it the 'most rollicking farce' of Malay literature. This is a highly questionable qualification if we take the Pak Pandir stories into consideration, but in itself it may serve as a clear indication that the Tale of the Bearded Civet Cat must have caused a lot of laughter among its Malay audiences. A lot of fun, no doubt.

Laughter, and with it realism. The Tale of the Bearded Civet Cat (henceforth MB) is a rustic story; its heroes are a couple of commoners who outwit the court, show its weakness in a series of slapstick scenes but in the end are made part of that same court. Behind the laughter we see an ambiguous attitude toward the state of affairs in a Malay community: the tale reveals the hypocrisy of a court but also the willingness of commoners, human, all too human, to give in to its glamour and power.

The following sentence could be seen as the kernel of the MB: 'maka kedua laki isteri pun tertawa sehingga muntahkan angin oleh teramat sangat sukacita melihatkan termasa raja2 dan orang besar2 jadi suatu permainan yang teramat indah sekali' [Both man and wife laughed till they broke wind, they so enjoyed watching the wonderful spectacle of kings and high officials being held to ridicule].

It is one of the last scenes of a tale in which, as will be shown, the dominating values of the Malay community as well as the powerful narrative scheme of romance are radically challenged; the physical manner in which the laughter about authority is described here makes it the narrative's most vital manifestation of this challenge.

From the beginning, all conventions and traditions are called into question. The hero, Kemala al-Arifin (KA), son of a trader, is adopted by the Sultan of the state of Shahar Desa, who has remained infertile with his four wives. Not a land of plenty, this Shahar Desa, no justice, no wealth, no influx of foreigners, as in other romances. A sterile country, indeed, and when Kemala al-Arifin is fifteen years old and his foster-father orders him to marry the daughter of someone at his court, the lad is very resolute in his rejection: 'When something is sold, it is far away. When something is hung, it is high. When something is burnt, it is destroyed. When something is soaked, it is wet' – for KA it is a simple fact that this country does not have women (*perempuan*), only females (*betina*). The court is flabbergasted and insulted by this insolence, and with a smile the ruler can only send his foster-son away, ordering him to return within a year with such a 'woman'. KA takes leave of his foster-father, who gives him money for his journey, and then says good-bye to his real parents; he prepares provisions – putting a mixture of uncooked rice, spices, peanuts, small fish, and grated coconut in a bag – and sets out on his quest for a 'woman'.

It is a strange quest indeed: no combats with ogres and giants, no confrontations with wicked villains and bloodthirsty animals, no acquisition of talismans and charms – just a peaceful battle in wit and intelligence, using food and words. KA is received by simple people, but every time he asks the daughter of the house to prepare a meal from his provisions, she serves him the family's food instead – the strange mixture in his bag seems impossible to cook. Eventually, after many a month, he meets a farmer, Paman, who has a beautiful daughter, Dang Seri Arif Laksana (DSAL), who spends her days sewing in her parents' house rather than working in the fields. She succeeds in separating the various foods in his bag and cooks them the way KA wants. 'Only now have I reached my aim; the waves called passion are singing.' When DSAL also turns out to have the wit to provide her father with an explanation for the enigmatic behaviour of KA at the time he was shown to their house, the hero gives thanks to Allah. He feels happy 'as if a mountain of jewels has fallen on him' and asks Paman for his daughter: 'If you, please, want to do good for me and have mercy on me, a wanderer, a humble and poor foreigner, then I would ask you if I could serve you in replacing that leaking roof, that broken floor, in collecting wood, and in pounding your resin'.

His request is accepted by the farmer, who blushes as if 'the moon and the sun have fallen on him': 'If you do not mind having a crossbeam for your pillow, a floor for your sleeping-mat, and smoke for your mosquito net'. Elaborate marriage ceremonies are performed in accordance with village traditions, attended by the bride's relatives and paid by the bridegroom, with a lot of merriment, singing, and laughter – 'everybody, young and old, men and women, small and big, poured and spattered water over each other, running and chasing around. Some picked up mud and cowdung and earth and tried to besmear the others, running around. Everybody was shouting and laughing, and those who were playing music were soaking wet, assaulted by the others. It was a lot of fun.'

When all ceremonies are finished, husband and wife test each other's wit once more, this time in a series of rhymed riddles. And KA loved his wife like 'Adam did Hawa, like Rajunia did Sergandi, like Yusuf did Zuleikha, they were inseparable'.

Then the couple return to Shahar Desa, where the Sultan is anxiously waiting for his foster-son's return, but, as it turns out, not to praise him. In a very

unroyal manner, His Majesty falls in love with DSAL at first sight. 'He stood
agape in astonishment, unaware of himself – it seemed as if His Majesty would
faint and he had the feeling that he was looking at a nymph from Heaven; he
was speechless so that the arrow of Sergandi pierced right through his heart.
His Majesty was drowned in the deepest sea, called the Sea of Passion, blown
away by the wind, called the Wind of Passion, because at that time DSAL
looked like a beam of the beautiful Light shining brightly in the palace.'
Not only the Sultan is suddenly possessed by Lust; his closest associates, the
raja muda, the *bendahara*, the *menteri*, the *temenggung*, and the *kadi* are
equally struck by a desire to tempt the newly-wed woman. The Sultan thinks
out a ruse in order to lure KA away from his house and his spouse: His Majesty
feigns having a serious disease and asks his foster-son to find him a bearded
civet cat, the heart of which is the only possible medicine for his own aching
heart. Whereupon the dignitaries of the court start scheming, just like the ruler
himself.

Thus, once again KA sets out on a quest, and this one is even stranger than
the first: he stays at home and leaves the trials to his wife. DSAL devises a ruse:
she tells KA to pretend to set out on his search and then to hide on top of the
house, while she takes care of those lustful dignitaries. So it happens. The very
night after his pretended departure, KA witnesses from his hiding place how
the most prominent leaders of the state, drunken with passion, one after the
other come to his house with very secular intentions and are properly received
by his wife. None of them, however, is given the time to satisfy his lust: the
kadi has to hide in a chest on the arrival of the temenggung, who hides on a
shelf on the arrival of the menteri, who hides on another shelf on the arrival of
the bendahara, who hides in the kitchen on the arrival of the raja muda, who
pretends to be a lamppost on the arrival of the Sultan himself. For His Majesty,
DSAL has something very special in store: she wants to ride him, like a horse,
seven times around the room, a request which the Sultan, overwhelmed with
passion, readily complies with. While they are running around, the menteri
feels a sudden thirst, finds a coconut, and lacking another tool, smashes it open
on the head of the temenggung. A wild shriek, and all the courtiers throw
themselves panic-stricken out of the house and return home – except for the
kadi, who is caught in the chest.

Once again KA is impressed by the intelligence of his wife, and on her
advice he brings the chest to the court, claiming that he has caught the bearded
civet cat His Majesty had asked him for. One after the other, the Sultan
included, the dignitaries throw a glance into the chest; they recognize the kadi,
but as soon as the kadi threatens to reveal their adventure of the night before,

they feel compelled to say that this indeed must be the bearded civet cat. His Majesty is satisfied, and on his order the chest is brought back to KA's house, where the couple have 'farting laughter' about the 'wonderful spectacle at court'. The kadi is released and makes friends with KA, who promises him that he will keep secret the humiliation of the state's religious leader. Eventually, the Sultan summons the couple to the palace and justifies his nocturnal adventure to his foster-son and his wife by explaining that he wanted to find out what a real 'woman' is like. KA is promised a monthly allowance, both he and his wife are given new names and are appointed in the most important positions of the court; moreover, each of the compromised courtiers gives them a considerable sum of money – to 'mend their house'. And ever since, there has been justice and peace in the state of Shahar Desa.

In all, KA and his wife have reasons enough for laughter and they do laugh in a very physical way, a liberating way. In outwitting and humiliating the highest dignitaries of the state, both religious and secular, they are seen to have no fear of power, of prohibitions, of the sacred – the tale of *Musang Berjanggut* reads like a demolition of authoritative values and concepts.

'Laughter demolishes fear and piety before an object, before a world, making of it an object of familiar contact and thus clearing the ground for an absolutely free investigation of it. Laughter is a vital factor in laying down that prerequisite for fearlessness without which it would be impossible to approach the world realistically', wrote Bakhtin, the expert on laughter (Bakhtin 1981:23).

Reading the MB should make us realize that fearless laughter about power and sacredness does not necessarily lead to a radical reversal of all values. At the end of the narrative, the old order is still in control. The state's leaders have managed to cover up their embarrassing demeanour by generously granting bribes and titles. KA and DSAL, in return, silently agree not to spread the tale of how clerus and court were humiliated, and thus they join the spectacle which they first ridiculed: by choosing the appropriate words they become part of the very authority they initially laughed about. The Tale of the Bearded Civet Cat seems to suggest that laughter, no matter how vital and unrestrained, is eventually suppressed by authority and is nothing but a soothing safety valve which enables one to cope with a harsh society. The authoritative scheme of romance is maintained from beginning to end, from the proper education of the hero to the state's prosperity and justice. Fearlessness, it seems, did not really reverse the state of affairs, and neither secular nor religious authority is destroyed. Both cultural and literary traditions are maintained – the rhetoric of the past has gained another victory, the monologue of Power has preserved its superior control. Following Darnton, it could be argued that laughter has certain limits, that 'the tables turn back again once it has subsided', and that 'the trickster works within the system, turning its weak points to his advantage and therefore ultimately confirming it' (Darnton 1985:59).

Laughter, however, may be more than just the harmless irreverence of a single person; it could be regarded as the expression of freedom, the opposite of fear of authority. It should be realized that the hero and heroine could have easily killed the courtiers in their house, but apparently they did not see the point in doing so; they prefer humiliation and ridicule to violence: it makes more sense to degrade and question authority than to kill authority and make way for another authority. As a matter of fact, the tale seems to show that this humiliation is the most effective way to bring about movement and change: by assimilating laughter to the court, the Sultan makes sure that his state becomes prosperous and famous. The hero may eventually behave as grimly as the hero of a hikayat, yet there is no indication that laughter could not emerge once again among those who do not belong to Power, thus making for further movement. As long as there is authority, authority should be forced to formulate itself again and again, accepting laughter as a vital and dynamic supplement; a dialogue between the two may be the best guarantee for general well-being.

Safety valve or vitality? The Tale of the Bearded Civet Cat reads like a manifestation of that continuous tension between static rules imposed from above and the desire for change inspired from below (Clark and Holquist 1984:298). Rules are needed to give a community an identity, a stability, but too much emphasis on the abstract unchangeability of authority as the imposer of those rules makes it impossible to appreciate changes that may take place thanks to laughter. It is in this very laughter that the Tale of the Bearded Civet Cat reveals the weakness of those in Power: they vindicate themselves by an uncanny uneasiness, not to say distrust.

Mutual distrust among the courtiers, first of all. During their nocturnal escapade these prominent leaders of men curse each other for interfering in each others's private business ('why can I never enjoy myself without being disturbed by that crook!'), but faced with the possibility of being ridiculed in public they prefer to save each other from the shame of being exposed as the victims of a very mundane humiliation. The result is a perfect play that reads like the basic rule of Malay political life: religious and secular authorities keep up appearances toward outsiders, the commoners; in spite of conflicting interests they protect each other's name and contain each other's power. Actually, the play is more than perfect: those who try to disturb it are

eventually lured to join it. The embarrassment of the Sultan and his closest
associates is definitely silenced by a considerable sum of money, and the
transformation of KA from laughter to authority is completed when he and his
wife are granted beautiful titles and accept the Sultan's proposal to become the
leaders of the court. Now they, too, can play their part in this serious spectacle
in which those in power maintain their authority by keeping up appearances and
supporting each other. The court as a theatre. What audience would not laugh at
such a show?

There is yet another kind of uneasiness involved, and here we touch upon the
problem that every narrative more or less explicitly explores: the relationship
between language and reality, or rather between the referential and rhetorical
functions of language.

Let us begin with a closer look at the scene in which the bearded civet cat is
offered to the Sultan. KA arrives at the court to pay his respects – 'princes and
dignitaries and all the common people, both men and women, they all wanted to
see the bearded civet cat, they had never seen one before' – and tells the Sultan
that he has found the bearded civet cat His Majesty had asked for. Ordered to
have a look in the chest, the dignitaries, one after the other, loudly express their
astonishment to find the kadi inside, but when the leader of Islam threatens to
reveal their illicit visit if they dare to tell those present that he is in the chest,
they suddenly pretend ignorance of what a bearded civet cat looks like and
leave it to their Sultan to declare that there is indeed a civet cat in the chest, and
then to send it away. All who are present agree with His Majesty's
interpretation; they all accept his naming even though they all know that it is
not correct. This is the language of authority, the authority of language in its
grimmest form – those in power determine meaning: what counts is the play of
communication and not the search for words that as truthfully as possible
reflect reality.

Just like the others present, KA and his wife know that reality is different
from what the Sultan declares to be reality. No wonder that they wonder about
this uneasy victory of rhetoric.

Now, the Sultan himself feels embarrassed about his escapade and uneasy
about the rhetoric he had to display in order to silence subversive tales – as
though KA's laughter echoes in his ears. Eventually he summons the couple to
the court and gives them an authoritative explanation that covers his nocturnal
humiliation and its aftermath as a whole: he wanted to find out what the word
'woman' stood for, and he is satisfied with the result of his exploration: she is a
'real' woman. Her name, Dang Seri Arif Laksana, perfectly suits her – and that
is why she should be given another name, 'To Puan Lela Mengerna'.

Such is the logic of authority. Rhetoric in its grimmest form once again: create a word on the basis of tradition and expect reality to assimilate to it. This time, the couple fully support His Majesty's words – KA and DSAL are drawn into courtly discourse, thus making sure that Power will be challenged once again by referential discourse.

The Tale of the Bearded Civet Cat is full of such efforts to establish the appropriate link between the world and words, the protagonists being constantly in search of meaning. To formulate it in broader terms: there is a pervasive uneasiness about language.

The tale seems organized around two searches. First the search for a person who fits the word 'woman' (perempuan), then the search for the object that fits the term 'bearded civet cat' (musang berjanggut). The first is discovered to the satisfaction of everybody, the second is created by an authoritative decree. Realism versus rhetoric – a fine complementarity in which realism is the dominating factor because the search for the 'civet cat' is basically inspired by the search for the 'woman'.

The tale begins with the search for a 'woman' – no clarification is given of what that word stands for. The hero's primary aim is to challenge the court, authority. 'You have degraded the self-respect of all women in the state and, besides, you are lying to the people of this meeting, princes, menteri, hulu-balang', says his foster-father the Sultan. From his perspective, Kemala Arifin is lying indeed: he is speaking in terms which courtly rhetoric is unable to grasp and therefore should be overruled by way of a counter challenge: the hero should return within a year with his 'woman'. The boy pays a last visit to his parents, puts raw food – rice, spices, small fish, peanuts, and grated coconut – together in a bag and leaves. No girl is able to understand KA's intentions until he is invited to the house of DSAL, who is described as a 'woman' who is very language-conscious: she is 'wise and skilled, good in speaking and in understanding people's words'. In her wisdom she manages to separate the provisions and to prepare them in the appropriate manner. Finding the one who is able to turn the raw into the cooked has been one of KA's aims – and by doing this, DSAL raises his natural desires: she is not a 'female' but a 'woman'. On the way to her house, the boy has already spoken and behaved in riddles which puzzled his companion, DSAL's father – 'do you have a house without a kitchen?', 'this is a monkey's bridge', opening an umbrella in the middle of the jungle, using shoes in the mud. In this case, too, it is thanks to her intelligence and her capacity to understand words that the girl understands KA: she explains the meaning of his riddles to her father, who sighs that he himself does not have the *akal* (intelligence) that is needed. KA feels elated when he overhears their conversation and decides to marry her. His marriage proposal to her father is another riddle, but now the contact has been made, the father easily understands the meaning of his words. Effective communication about the world is possible now.

The marriage ceremony – it is a ceremony of village people, without the pomp and glitter of the court, but with the dung and the laughter of the common people – is concluded with another set of puzzles: the newlyweds test their understanding of the world by way of riddles in verse form. Metaphors and stilted phrases are transformed into down-to-earth words. The grasp of reality seems complete.

Back home, new riddles are waiting: KA's search for the meaning of 'musang berjanggut', which results in the dignitaries' search for the meaning of perempuan. Once again, the image of cooking – from raw to cooked – is used: the courtiers are kept waiting in the main room while DSAL pretends to be busy cooking in the kitchen – but in this trick, the food remains uncooked and natural desires are not satisfied. The search for the bearded civet cat fails, but it makes KA aware of the rhetorical use of language culminating in his acceptance of its authority. The search for the woman succeeds and makes the dignitaries aware of rude reality outside the court compound, outside court conventions, culminating in the Sultan's conclusion that she is truly, really (*sungguh sebenarnya*) a woman.

As already intimated in the summary above – a summary is never neutral – the tale of Musang Berjanggut reads like an uneasy version of romance. It does indeed follow the tripartite scheme of royal upbringing, adventures, and safe homecoming, but even in these main points of recognition the narrative creates uneasiness.

The hero's identity is unclear. He is said to be the son of a foreigner (*biaperi*), but in the second part is referred to as a palace orderly (*biduanda*) although at the same time he is the adopted son of the Sultan. Is Kemala Arifin a commoner, a courtier, or a prince who should be able to fly through the air spreading lightning and thunder? Ambiguous, in short, and therefore very suitable for playing a subversive role.

The hero's behaviour at court hardly fits in with the conventions which make us recognize this tale as a romance; he should not have taken the initiative himself and challenged the Sultan's wisdom, but, instead, should have waited for royal orders to be sent on a quest for something His Majesty was looking for. KA's subsequent search for a 'woman' is equally unfamiliar: no battles, no wonders, no violence, no misery. The hero's second search is even harder to recognize as a basic element of romance: he stays at home. And is there really a homecoming at all before he lives happily ever after?

In all, the Tale of the Bearded Civet Cat almost bursts out of its formal constraints, simultaneously exposing and subverting formal conventions with a parody-like vitality. The narrative construction is creaking in its seams like a neglected house, its content is pushing in all directions, eager to jump out of it, like a Sultan out of a commoner's house.

Haji Yahya tried to present the tale as a hikayat, just as he did with the other tales he was asked by the British to transform into writing. But even in this stilted form it is obvious that its place in the hierarchy of Malay narrativity is very low: the fillers of the romance scheme do not call up glittering courts, jewelled mountains, and battles against magical birds – instead they present a Malay house with an attic, kitchen, verandah, and aperture for dirt, rice fields, wordplays, and tricks. The stylized colloquial in which the tale must have been narrated – here and there traces of it have been preserved – could only have intensified the feeling among the audience that what was presented was not a past world, complete and self-contained, but the fragmented world of everyday life.

In this manner, the tensions which the protagonists face, torn as they are between the rhetorical and the referential function of language, are brought onto another level: the narrative tries to find allegiance with the world out there rather than with ancient literary traditions. In this attempt to break away from the formal constraints of romance, it appears to use language in order to get beyond language, inevitably turning to what we now call realism: it explores the rules of discourse that around the turn of the century – in particular thanks to newspapers and schoolbooks – would become accepted as the rules that govern the accurate representation of reality, leading to a conflict with traditions, 'clearing the ground for a free investigation of the world'.

The narrative could very effectively be read in its referential mode: it explores human experience and describes everyday life in a Malay village; yet to keep up a coherent and understandable form, it basically has to acquiesce in the imperatives of formal conventions so as not to fall into endless and inexhaustible series of descriptive details. Conversely, it could equally effectively be read in its rhetorical mode: it is clearly an example of romance, following the conventions in an intriguing manner, yet these conventions are constantly undermined by the narrative's pursuit of immediate reality, unattainable but attractive.

The conflict between and within these two modes of reading is personified in the conflict between the main protagonists. KA is the discoverer of meaning, challenging conventions, and the Sultan is the creator of meaning, confirming conventions. The fact that their relationship is an ambiguous one – KA is not the son of the Sultan and yet he is – is just another expression of the insoluble nature of this conflict. KA, protagonist of realism, is ultimately defeated by rhetoric: he is aware of the fact that the court operates on the basis of powerful rhetoric, successfully reveals its instability – and has himself willingly outwitted in the end. The Sultan, protagonist of rhetoric, has to make use of a realistic trick: the outcome of his nocturnal adventure makes him realize that the world does not always obey authoritative traditions and he has to lean on a realistic use of money and titles in order to make sure that traditions keep their authority. Thus the conflicting forces in the narrative compel its heroes to act in a way that is directly reverse to what could be expected from their (conflicting) nature. Conflicting modes of reading about conflicting characters whose doing contradicts their being. Pretty dazzling, altogether.

Let us return to where we started from, to laughter. KA laughs about the Sultan as much as the Tale of the Bearded Civet Cat should make us laugh about the constraints of norms. The Sultan is embarrassed about this fearless laughter as much as the narrative should make us feel embarrassed about the rudeness of its efforts to subvert its authoritative form. Laughter has a subversive potential – in ridiculing existent hierarchies it forms a counterpoint which, as Scott so convincingly argued in a context that is considerably wider than Bakhtin's literary context, may become either 'an institutionalized and harmless form of symbolic protest which strengthens the existing order'; or 'the normative focus of religious or political movements with an insurrectionary potential' (Scott 1976:233).

It seems a matter of perspective which of the two interpretations of counterpoint is given priority with respect to the situation in Malay communities around the turn of the century, the time the Tale of the Bearded Civet Cat was wandering around on the Malay peninsula and beyond. Either perspective runs parallel to an ideology that offers a distinct answer to the question whether an insurrection was taking place at that time, at that place.

In retrospect, it is not surprising that Winstedt and Wilkinson were not very interested in a 'rollicking farce'. They considered tales like the *Musang Berjanggut* as operating against the grain of the existing order, in every respect, and therefore not worth much attention. Such tales questioned the authority of hikayat. It remained beyond the control of writing. It was presented in a language that certainly differed from what the British wanted to impose as standard Malay. It contradicted the British idea of the Malay peasantry as blindly obedient to their rulers. Therefore, as far as these farces meant anything at all, they were just gross and harmless.

Now, it would be very hard indeed to show that the Malay peasantry of 1900 was on the fringe of a serious insurrection against its sultans, or against the British, for that matter. An insurrection, however, did take place in the field of language and literature. In the Malay-speaking communities of both the Dutch Indies and British Malaya, new genres of discourse emerged in forms that were strong enough to challenge the rules of tradition. The slow emergence of novels, newspapers, and personal poetry was the result of an increasing struggle for authority among the various forms of language under the pressures of print, the imposing presence of Westerners, the rise of Muslim modernism, the introduction of a money economy. The long-standing hierarchy within Malay narrativity was definitely broken, giving way to a situation of heteroglossia in which dialogues were substituted for a monologue and dynamics gained the upper hand over stasis within Malay culture.

From the perspective of this literary insurrection, orally performed tales like the Tale of the Bearded Civet Cat deserve much more attention than they have been given so far. In breaking away from the hikayat tradition, both newspapers and novels started out in pursuit of the world beyond words, and as such they continued a current in Malay narrativity that so far had primarily been explored by the voice of wandering storytellers. The fearless laughter of Kemala al-Arifin and Dang Seri Arif Laksana revealed the weaknesses of authority; in the long run it gave a strong impetus to the forces in Malay culture that were to bring about a radical reversal of values. That the fearlessness of the Malay-speaking people in British Malaya took a road that was so much different from that in the Dutch Indies is another story about fear, power, and language.[1]

Bibliography

Bakhtin, M.M.
1981   *The dialogic imagination; Four essays.* Edited by M. Holquist. Austin: University of Texas Press.
1984   *Rabelais and his world.* Bloomington: Indiana University Press.
Clark, K. and M. Holquist
1984   *Mikhail Bakhtin.* Cambridge/London: Belknap.
Darnton, R.
1985   *The great cat massacre and other episodes in French cultural history.* New York: Vintage Books.

[1] Special thanks are due to James Siegel, whose (unpublished) translation of the Acehnese version of the Musang Berjanggut was the direct inspiration for this essay.

Frye, N.
1957   *The anatomy of criticism*. Princeton: Princeton University Press.
1982   *The secular scripture; A study of the structure of romance.*
            Cambridge/London: Harvard University Press.
Scott, J.C.
1976   *The moral economy of the peasant; Rebellion and subsistence in
            Southeast Asia.* New Haven/London: Yale University Press.
Wilkinson, R.J.
1907   *Malay literature; Part 1, Romance; History; Poetry.* Kuala
            Lumpur: F.M.S. Government Press.
Winstedt, R.O.
1909   'Musang berjanggut'; *Journal of the Straits Branch of the Royal
            Asiatic Society* 52:121-72.
1969   *A history of Classical Malay literature.* London: Oxford University Press. [First edition 1939.]

N.G. PHILLIPS

Two variant forms of Minangkabau kaba

Poetic diction and oral literature are two of the many aspects of Indonesian literature on which Professor Teeuw has cast light during his career. I hope that this paper, which touches on those subjects, will not seem an inappropriate contribution to this symposium in his honour.

The aim of this paper is to give a provisional description of the form of two kinds of Minangkabau storytelling which have not so far been described, namely *dendang Pauah* and *rebab pesisir selatan gaya baru*, and to point out how they differ from texts of Minangkabau oral stories studied so far.[1] By texts of oral stories I mean transcriptions of performances, and these, as far as I know, are to be found in only three places: the two-volume *Kaba Minangkabau* published by the Pusat Bahasa (Jamil Bakar et al. 1979); Syamsuddin Udin's report on the *Kaba Anggun Nan Tungga Magek Jabang* (1979); and my own contribution on *sijobang* (1981). From these texts (with the exception of two in *Kaba Minangkabau* which I shall mention later) and the comments accompanying them we get the following picture of the form of oral *kaba*. They are made up of phrases or sentences about 8 or 9 syllables in length (what is usually known in Indonesian as *bahasa berirama, prosa berirama* or *prosa liris*). The diction is repetitive in several ways: in the use of pairs of synonyms (*korong kampuang, sabab karano*), and of parallelisms, where the sense of one line is repeated in the next, sometimes with the same grammatical structure; in the sense that the same action may be described more than once, for example, once when done and again when reported; and in the sense that the language is formulaic, that is, many elements, from phrases to whole scenes, recur, either unchanged or with some variation. In the case of *sijobang*, the formulaic nature of the text and its variability from one performance to another suggest oral composition on the lines of Lord's Yugoslav tales (Lord 1973), and it would

[1]   This paper is based on research done during a visit to West Sumatra in August and September 1984 funded by the School of Oriental and African Studies and the British Academy. I am extremely grateful to Drs Syamsuddin Udin of IKIP Padang for his kind help, without which the research might not have been possible. I am also deeply indebted to Sajoeti Rahman for his indispensable help in transcribing recordings.

not be surprising if the same held for the stories in *Kaba Minangkabau*. The diction of the kaba is also characterized by otiose epithets and lengthy terms of address. Finally, *pantun* are used in varying quantities for opening and closing sections of the story, and for dialogue and other purposes. Such, one might say, is the standard form of oral kaba.

Dendang Pauah

The first of the two non-standard kinds of kaba that I wish to describe in outline is dendang Pauah. Exactly in which areas of West Sumatra it is performed I am not certain, but the name, 'Song of Pauah', suggests a connection with Pauah, on the outskirts of Padang; and in *Kaba Minangkabau*, which includes one kaba from each of seven *kabupaten*, an example of dendang Pauah is chosen to represent the kabupaten of Padang-Pariaman (Jamil Bakar et al. 1979, II:335-427). Furthermore, it was in the Padang area that I recorded two performances of dendang Pauah stories in 1984, and the language of these stories has some features typical of the speech of Padang.[2]

The occasions in which dendang Pauah is performed are reported to be weddings and similar celebrations (Jamil Bakar et al. 1979, I:15, 20), and my limited experience confirms this. The singer, who is invited and paid, begins performing after *isya* prayers and continues, with breaks for rest and refreshment, until dawn prayers. He is accompanied by a *saluang* (flute) player, who maintains an almost continuous sound by means of circular breathing. Dendang Pauah stories are also commercially recorded in studios and sold on cassettes. The three stories which I have in this form are 4, 6 and 9 hours in length.

As regards the content of these stories, the four I know are all set in the 20th century, three before Independence and one after. All deal with ordinary people, their changing fortunes and family relationships; one tells, for example, of the daughter of poor parents who abandons them at her rich husband's instigation.

With regard to form, the most striking difference between dendang Pauah stories and most other kaba is that they are entirely in pantun, instead of being largely in bahasa berirama with pantun serving as an entertaining extra. The pantun are mostly 4 lines long, but there are also many 6-line verses and some even longer ones, including a few of as many as 20 lines. Most (88%) of the lines are of 9 syllables, the rest being nearly all of 8 or 10.

---

[2]   Dendang Pauah stories are metrically very like another kaba published in *Kaba Minangkabau*, named 'Bujang Pajudi' and said to come from the kabupaten of Solok (Jamil Bakar et al. 1979, II:265-334).

Performances

A performance begins with several minutes of solo saluang playing, after which the singer joins in with several long cries of *ai...* and one of *sawan* (perhaps *sauan*, short for *risauan*, sadness). He then (judging by the two performances I attended) sings introductory verses, which may last thirty or forty minutes, mentioning the reason for the performance and making complimentary references to the host and guests, before beginning the story proper. The host and main guests are also repeatedly addressed by name throughout the performance, usually in the *isi* (second half) of the pantun. (On commercial cassettes, the singer addresses the saluang player, the other singer,[3] or the listeners.) In sijobang, by contrast, it is only in the opening pantun that the audience is addressed, and then not by name but as *mamak* and *datuak* (sirs) or *tolan* (friends). In dendang Pauah the successive pantun are separated by breaks of five to ten seconds during which the saluang continues uninterrupted. Sometimes, too, there are breaks of a few seconds between lines of the same pantun, and often the singer pauses for several seconds before completing the last two syllables of a line, usually the final line of the isi, but sometimes that of the *sampiran* (first half). The aim may be to create a little extra suspense or attention, although the final syllables are often fairly predictable at that stage, and are anyway sometimes barely audible.

In the intervals between verses, members of the audience usually react with shouts and comments, the more heart-rending scenes evoking (it seems to me) especially loud responses. (This, according to a Minangkabau friend, shows not lack of feeling but appreciation of the storyteller's eloquence.) Audiences at sijobang performances react much less often, once the preliminary pantun are over and the story has got under way. Of the several tunes used in dendang Pauah, one called *lambok malam* (night dew), which is sung without saluang accompaniment, seems to be reserved for very emotional parts of the story and occurs only once or twice in the whole performance, lasting 10 or 15 minutes.

When the two performances I recorded came to an end just before dawn prayers, the story was not complete in either case; but although the fact was mentioned, it did not seem to matter very much to the audience. At the time I was surprised, as I had been told earlier that dendang Pauah stories took one night each. However, it has occurred to me since that dendang Pauah singers are not the only ones to present incomplete stories, for sijobang performances, too, consist of episodes from a larger plot, which may even be sung out of their

---

[3]   Two of the three dendang Pauah stories which I have on commercial cassettes are sung by a pair of singers, who take turns every hour or so. However, the two live performances I saw were given by a single singer.

'proper' order (Phillips 1981:28-9). A number of other facts also suggest that people do not listen to kaba primarily out of interest in the plot: the fact that on the paper wrappers of kaba on cassettes the buyer is urged to listen to all the cassettes, so that the story may be more clear;[4] the fact, which a shopkeeper told me, that if a kaba occupies ten or twelve cassettes people will sometimes buy only the first five or six and the fact that some cassette-kaba end, so it seems to me at least, rather in mid-story, as if the storyteller had been asked to fit his story into a certain number of cassettes and had not quite been able to. If it is not the overall plot that is the main source of entertainment, then it is presumably the quality of the language, the singing and the accompaniment as the story proceeds, and with dendang Pauah at least the frequent audience reaction suggests this very strongly.

Formulae

As one would expect of long metrical stories delivered without any reliance on written material, dendang Pauah stories, like sijobang and other oral kaba, are formulaic, in the sense that many elements, from lines and half-lines to whole scenes, are repeated either unchanged or with some alteration within the same pattern. In dendang Pauah this is most obvious in the sampiran of the pantun, where one soon notices the repetition of lines and especially half-lines from the singer's stock. For example, the line 'enggeran buruang katitiran' was used ten times in about 450 lines of sampiran (two hours of singing), 'ari manjalang pukua duo' five times,[5] and 56 other lines two or three times each. The number of recurring half-lines is even greater. The most frequently repeated initial half-lines in the sample (apart from 'enggeran buruang', with thirteen occurrences) were:

ari manjalang...	(12)	the time approaches...
pulang manjalang...	(7)	go home just before...
ka pulang ari...	(6)	will go home at...
manjalang ari...	(5)	just before...

These were followed in the second half of the line by formulaic patterns as:

pukua duo	2 o'clock
pukua anam	6 o'clock

---

[4]   In Indonesian the instructions, in one case, read: 'Supaya lebih jelas dengarlah kassettenya dari No. 1-4'; and in another case: 'Agar jelasnya isi cerita kaset ini anda dengarlah kaset cerita Pulau Punjung ini sampai tamat (4 kaset)'.

[5]   The frequent occurrence of *-an* and *-o* as final syllables in the sampiran reflects the many lines in the isi which end in *-an* or *-kan* suffixes and the words *juo, pulo* and *nyo*.

pukua limo	5 o'clock
pukua satu	1 o'clock
tenggih ari	the sun is high
patang ari	afternoon
tangah ari	midday

Place-names are much used. Thus the initial half-line

pagi-pagi ka...	early in the morning to...

or the pattern

tagak ka kelok...	stand at the bend...
tagak ka pasa...	stand in the market...
tagak ka ujuang...	stand at the end...
tagak ka simpang...	stand at the turning...

is followed by a four-syllable place-name such as Tanjuang Saba.

Another common pattern uses one place-name in each half of the line: *dari Solok ka Simpang Kandih* from S. to S.K.

All in all, the sampiran strike one as being put together from a fairly limited range of half-line and full-line patterns.

In contrast, the isi do not so quickly stand out as formulaic. In the two-hour sample, there is very little repetition of either speech or events in the story and therefore little need for the use of formulae. Nevertheless, a few full lines recur, for example

ado wakatu alang ari	upon a week-day

and a number of full- and half-line patterns emerge, like

bakato si As lambek-lambek	As said slowly
sudah minum abak turun	after drinking, father went out

in which the slots filled by *bakato*, *si As*, *minum*, *abak* and *turun* could all be filled by other words, as required by the story.

However, as the story unfolds and especially when one listens to three other stories sung by the same person, events begin to repeat themselves and the formulaic quality of both the diction and the plot becomes increasingly clear. For example, one of the stories I recorded contains two episodes in which someone falls ill and dies. Many of the phrases used in the two episodes are almost identical except for the names of the people concerned, the hero's father (*Abak*) and Javanese mother-in-law (*One* or *Nyai*). Here are some of the phrases:

nyo semba damam Abak tadi	Father was struck by fever
nyo semba damam One tadi	Mother was struck by fever
ubek lakek panyakik datang	when the medicine was applied the illness only increased,
Abak batambah kuruih juo	Father grew ever thinner
ubek lakek panyakik datang	when the medicine was applied the illness only increased,
Nyai lah batambah kuruih juo	Nyai grew ever thinner
babulan sakik ateh rumah	for months he lay ill at home,
tingga jangek pambaluik tulang	nothing remained but skin and bones
sabulan sakik ateh rumah	one month he lay ill at home,
tingga jangek pambaluik tulang	nothing remained but skin and bones
duo kali maangok gadang	he gave two great gasps,
Abak baimbau tak babuni	when Father was called he made no reply
sakali maangok gadang	she gave one great gasp,
One diimbau tak babuni	when Mother was called she made no reply

A noticeable difference between the use of formulae in dendang Pauah and sijobang, which the quotations above illustrate, is that in dendang Pauah formulae tend to be repeated with only the minimum necessary changes, whereas in sijobang formulae often recur in changed form, as a result of the substitution of a synonym within the same grammatical framework, in other words by using another member of the same formulaic system (Lord 1973:47-8). I suspect that this tendency to repetition rather than variation in dendang Pauah may be due to its almost total lack of parallelisms, which are numerous in sijobang and other oral kaba and may help to foster the verbal variation of formulae.

With regard to larger formulaic elements, the four dendang Pauah stories of which I have recordings (all by the same singer) contain many descriptions, varying in length from a few lines to 100 or more, of such scenes as eating, sleeping, dressing, a visit to the cinema, a journey by car, studying at school, sickness and death, burial and mourning. These descriptions recur in the four stories with enough similarity for it to be clear that they constitute a formulaic resource for the storyteller, as in sijobang and other oral literature. Such scenes naturally tend to vary from one occurrence to another, not only because different people and places are involved, but also because the singer may add, omit, lengthen, shorten or rearrange elements of the scene.

Variability

To get an impression of the degree of variability of dendang Pauah performances, I compared two performances by the same singer, Harun Rajo Bujang, of the opening verses (after preliminary greetings) of the story *Urang Silaiang*, one a recording transcribed in *Kaba Minangkabau* (Bakar et al. 1979:335-427) and the other recorded by me in 1984. As regards structure, the two versions of this passage are very similar: nearly all the elements of the scene are the same and they occur in nearly the same sequence. This is reminiscent of sijobang, which is quite stable as regards the structure of scenes, at least in the case of an experienced performer whom I recorded. As regards verbal content, an examination of the two versions shows that, out of 104 lines of *isi* in the transcription published in *Kaba Minangkabau*, 54 lines are exactly the same as lines occurring in the 1984 performance, 20 lines are similar but varied by the use of synonyms, and 29 are quite different. In contrast, in an admittedly short sample of sijobang only about 9% of the lines were exact repeats, about 30% were similar but varied, while as many as 60% were quite different (Phillips 1981:167-8). Thus, as regards verbal content, repeat performances of dendang Pauah are, according to this sample at least, about 70% similar while sijobang is only about 40% stable in this sense; and out of those similar lines in dendang Pauah a much higher proportion (54 out of 74) are exactly repeated, compared with sijobang. This is not surprising, in view of what was pointed out earlier about the characteristics of formulaic lines in dendang Pauah and sijobang. However, it is clear from looking at other parts of the story that the two performances are not consistently as similar as this sample suggests, and a large-scale comparison would possibly show a somewhat higher degree of variability.

Diction

The language of dendang Pauah is, on the whole, not as repetitive and wordy as that of sijobang and other 'standard' kaba. Ideas and phrases are sometimes repeated, perhaps for emphasis, as for example in a passage describing the hero's success as a shopkeeper (see Appendix I), but usually the story proceeds with very little repetition. Parallelisms, which abound in other oral kaba (they comprise about 37% of the lines in sijobang), are rarely heard, apart from a few well-known expressions like 'nasi dimakan raso sakam, aie diminun raso duri'. Pairs of synonyms of the korong kampuang type occur rarely; otiose adjectives (as in 'anjuang tinggi') and lengthy forms of address (like 'sutan pamuncak rang Piaman') are, I think, totally absent; and even phrases marking the beginning and end of a speech (like 'baru tadanga nan bak itu, manjawab

Abang Salamat'), which are normal aids to comprehension in other kaba, are quite often left to the listener's imagination in dendang Pauah stories.

There are, perhaps, two main ways of explaining the absence or rarity of these features in dendang Pauah, and both have to do with the pantun form. The first is that, because the isi of each pantun is a separate sentence, grammatically if not semantically independent of the preceding and following isi, if it is to convey a message in two or three lines it must be phrased in compressed language; hence there is no room for otiose adjectives or long terms of address. Secondly, to the extent that all the kinds of repetition mentioned in the preceding paragraph have practical, rather than aesthetic, functions (they serve to overcome interference, such as noise, and to reinforce the fleeting impact of the sung word) these functions are fulfilled instead, or at least made less necessary, by features of the pantun form, and by the manner in which the pantun are sung and listened to. For one thing, the relative meaninglessness of the sampiran frees the listeners' minds to attend to the message of the isi, while the preparatory rhymes of the sampiran perform the practical function of enabling them to hear more clearly the corresponding words in the isi lines. Communication between singer and audience may, I suggest, also be assisted by the isolation of each pantun from its context by several seconds of saluang playing (or, more effectively still, by several seconds of silence in the lambok malam passages); by the slow pace at which the pantun are sung (about 250 lines of isi per hour, compared with about 900 lines per hour of sijobang); by the flourish with which the last line of the isi is often delivered, as if it were the punch line of a joke, and, perhaps, the singer's practice of pausing before the last two syllables of certain lines, mentioned above as a possible attention-raising device; by the fact that some of the listeners are constantly being addressed by name and are expected to be aware of this and perhaps respond; and – partly as a result of this last – by the greater attentiveness of the audience, who are accustomed to making comments after nearly every pantun, compared to the less responsive sijobang audience.

To sum up, the main formal difference between dendang Pauah and the 'standard' kaba is that it is in pantun form. Like other kaba it is formulaic in language and composition, but the formulaic lines tend to recur with only minimal changes, rather than being varied through the substitution of synonyms. Dendang Pauah is almost devoid of the various kinds of repetition typical of ordinary kaba, but to the extent that these are aids to communication, their lack may be compensated for by features of the pantun form and by the manner in which the stories are sung and listened to.

Rebab pesisir selatan gaya baru

The second variant form of kaba to be discussed is known to me so far only from three commercially recorded kaba. All are by the same singer, Syamsuddin, who comes from Kambang in the kabupaten of Pesisir Selatan. Judging by other cassettes I have heard, I believe that this kind of storytelling is known as *rebab pesisir selatan*. (On Syamsuddin's cassettes the words *gaya baru* (new style) are added, but I am not sure whether this is recognized as a distinct form, or is more of a personal trademark.)

I have not yet heard a live performance, but Syamsuddin has told me that he is invited to sing at weddings and similar celebrations. He apparently performs without any written material. He accompanies himself on a violin held upright between the knees. On it he first plays an introduction, and thereafter provides a continuous accompaniment to the story, also filling in the gaps when he pauses for a few seconds after about every six or twelve lines.

Syamsuddin's kaba differ somewhat in both form and content from sijobang and other standard kaba, including the kaba chosen to represent Pesisir Selatan in Jamil Bakar's *Kaba Minangkabau*, 'Gadih Basanai', which is also accompanied on a rebab or violin. The main difference, apart from matters of form, is that Syamsuddin's stories are not traditional but composed by the singer himself, who claimed when talking to me to have composed about 20 such stories.[6] They are also set in modern times: people travel by Honda, jeep and aeroplane, and no aspect of pre-Independence life is mentioned. There are, however, traditional elements in the stories: in one story the hero studies with a *dukun* for two years before setting out on his adventures; the same hero is asked by his betrothed to return from his travels bringing prized objects; and the hero's and heroine's clothes are described in detail.

With regard to form, Syamsuddin's stories are in most ways very like standard kaba, but in a few respects show some interesting variety. As to metre, they consist largely of the same fairly regular approximately 9-syllable phrases. Pantun are used, as in standard kaba, for opening, closing and changing scenes, for dialogue, courtship and other purposes. However, Syamsuddin also employs pantun in a way which I have not encountered in other kaba: the sampiran, normally devoid of meaning, is used to list the names of places being travelled through, while the traveller's feelings of sadness, anxiety and so on are described in the isi. This use of pantun occurs in all of the three stories I have

---

[6] According to *Kaba Minangkabau*, new kaba created in recent times by the *tukang kaba* themselves are far less appreciated by the public than traditional kaba (Jamil Bakar et al. 1979, I:7).

on cassette, but is most prominent in *Merantau ke Jambi*, which contains three
long sequences of such pantun (17, 40 and 28 verses). Here is an extract from
one passage, in which the hero and his friends are travelling by bus to the
rantau, full of anxiety about their future.

Talampau kini Kapalo Banda	(the bus) had passed Kapalo Banda
masuak daerah Kudo-Kudo	it entered the area of Kudo-Kudo
di dalam atinyo susah	they were troubled in their hearts,
kampuang pabilo ka basuo?	when would they see their homes?
Talampao lai Kudo-Kudo	Kudo-Kudo was passed,
lah sampai di Tapan Ketek	they arrived at Tapan Ketek;
jo jantuang ati basangketo	they were full of anxiety
nan diagak kok tak ka dapek	lest they fail to achieve their aims.
Namun motor ka taruih juo	Still the bus went on.
Tingga daerah Tapan Ketek	Tapan Ketek was left behind,
lah masuak kini Tapan Gadang	now they entered Tapan Gadang
nan diagak kok tak ka dapek	if they failed to achieve their aims,
si tooh awak, kecek urang	people would say, 'You're stupid'.

Formulae

Like other oral kaba, Syamsuddin's stories are formulaic. Many lines, half-lines
and clusters of lines recur with varying frequency. Some common part-lines:

... (sa) maso itu	...at that time
sadang di untuang...	as for the fate of...
nan dibilang...	it is told of...
nan den bilang...	I tell of...
kini co iko di...	now this is what you must do...
sinan manjawab...	then answered...

Lines, and their variants, include:

indak ka kito rantang panjang	we shall not prolong (the story)
adolah pado satu ari	it was on one day
adolah pado satu malam	it was on one night
ari barangsua tenggi juo	the morning was passing
ari barangsua siang juo	midday was approaching
ari barangsua malam juo	evening was approaching
ari barangsua abih juo	night was approaching

co itu bana maso itu	so it was at that time
mandanga kato rupo itu	hearing such words

Recurring couplets, many concerning travel, include:

abih ari baganti ari	day succeeded day,
abih pakan baganti bulan	weeks turned to months
lah sarantang duo rantang	they travelled one stretch, two stretches
cukuik katigo rantang panjang	and completed a third long stretch
masin iduik, roda bageleang	the engine started, the wheels turned
kabuik bakaja di balakang	the dust chased behind
di ma panek sinan baranti	where they were tired they stopped
di ma patang sinan bamalam	where it was evening they spent the night
rem dipijak oto tagak	he trod on the brake, the bus stopped
masin mati pasisia turun	the engine died, the passengers got off

A good number of scenes of varying length also recur throughout the three stories. They include eating, sleeping, waking, bathing, praying, travelling, dressing, and walking gracefully (of girls). For example:

Sakalok lalok ari siang	He slept a little then day broke
bakukuak ayam manjagokan	the cock crew awakening him
ari siang lah jago lalok	when day broke he awoke
sudah mandi sudah sumbayang	he finished bathing and praying
inyo lah minum pagi-pagi	he had breakfast early
nyo pakai sarawa rancak	he put on smart trousers
nyo pakai baju nan elok	he put on a natty shirt
lah takilek cincin di jari	a ring flashed on his finger
lah mambayang arloji tangan	a watch could be glimpsed on his wrist
bakilek rupo sipatunyo	his shoes shone
malakok dasi di dado	a tie was pinned to his breast

It is clear from the above examples that, however modern the settings of the stories may be, much of the language is traditional, many formulae being part of a stock shared by older kaba.

Although I have not calculated the degree of formularity of these stories, it is plainly quite high, and I assume that Syamsuddin is another example of the oral poet in the Lordian sense.

Variant features

So far, so similar, on the whole, to standard kaba. But there are two ways in which Syamsuddin's stories differ quite noticeably from the norm. The first is that the singer imitates the voices of characters in the story, and occasionally other sounds. For instance, Syamsuddin mimics the seductive tones of a woman who tries to lead the hero astray in a 'Potiphar's wife' episode. Elsewhere sobbing voices are imitated, and in another instance the trotting of a horse pulling a *bendi* is suggested by the rhythm of the tune, while the sound of the bendi's bell is imitated by two pizzicato notes on the violin. Nothing of this sort is heard in sijobang, though it may occur in other styles of Minangkabau storytelling.

The second variant feature of Syamsuddin's stories is that, although they contain some repetition, they resemble dendang Pauah stories in containing hardly any parallelisms, paired synonyms or long vocative phrases. This characteristic, combined with a much higher proportion of action to dialogue than in standard kaba, makes for a comparatively condensed and fast-moving narrative, although the number of lines delivered per hour remains no higher than in sijobang, about 900. An example of a typical passage is given in Appendix II.

When asked about the lack of parallelism in his stories, Syamsuddin said that he purposely left out repetitions and unnecessary phrases and tried to speed up his stories because the recording company wanted him to use fewer cassettes per story. This is presumably from a wish to save on fees – Syamsuddin claimed to get Rp. 240,000 per cassette – and to make the stories more attractive to buyers. According to Syamsuddin, both this relative brevity of style and his use of mimicry were part of the gaya baru, and so was an avoidance of excessively local vocabulary in order to make the stories appeal to all Minangkabaus.

It would be interesting to know whether Syamsuddin employs a more redundant style in public performances, when there is no need to keep within four or five hours. But however that may be, and whether or not the relatively condensed style does in fact result from pressure by the cassette-makers, it does seem to me that the cassette medium makes possible a less redundant narrative style without a resultant loss of communication. For the clarity of studio recordings and the way in which a listener can play, replay, stop and start a cassette when and where he or she chooses – in short, treat it more like a book – surely help to make a very repetitive style of storytelling much less necessary.

That concludes a brief and in some ways provisional survey of two forms of

Minangkabau metrical narrative, the aim of which has been to draw attention to some of the formal variety which exists in that branch of Indonesian literature.

Bibliography

Bakar, Jamil et al.
1979   *Kaba Minangkabau.* Jakarta: Pusat Pembinaan dan Pengembangan
            Bahasa, Departemen Pendidikan dan Kebudayaan. 2 vols.
Lord, A.B.
1973   *The singer of tales.* New York: Atheneum. [First published Cam-
            bridge, Mass.: Harvard University Press, 1960.]
Phillips, Nigel
1981   *Sijobang; Sung narrative poetry of West Sumatra.* Cambridge etc.:
            Cambridge University Press.
Udin, Syamsuddin
1979   *Kaba Anggun Nan Tungga Magek Jabang; Suatu tinjauan dari
            sudut sosial budaya.* Padang: Proyek Pengembangan Bahasa dan
            Sastra Indonesia dan Daerah.

Appendix I

Tagak ka pasa Balai Alai	Straight on to the market at Balai Alai
ka ilia jalan Simpang Jati	downstream is the road to Simpang Jati
awak gombang bakadai pandai	he was handsome and a good shopkeeper
pokok kalebuik jua-bali	that's why trade was fast and furious
Banamo buruang katitiran	There was a bird called the ground-dove
inggok di ateh paku aji	it alights upon the fern
nyo beleang tunjuak di kadaian	he turned his fore-finger* in the shop
alah co ombak gadang ati	his happiness swelled like a wave
Limau puruik di dalam ladang	A lime grows in the field
ka ubek urang Tanjuang Saba	as medicine for the people of Tg. Saba
alah kalebuik naiak uang	the money piled up fast and furious
pokok murah tajua maha	he bought cheap and sold dear
Lubuak Aluang Balai Salasa	Lubuak Aluang and Balai Salasa
dibali udang tali-tali	*tali-tali* prawns are bought
pokok murah tajua maha	he bought cheap and sold dear
pokok kalebuik jua-bali	that's why trade was fast and furious
Ari manjalang pagi-pagi	It's just before early morning
masuak ka balai Pasa Solok	go into the market at Pasa Solok

babilang ribu si As tadi	As got many thousands
lah gadang labo dari pokok	the profit was bigger than the outlay

*Meaning obscure

From a performance of *Urang Silaiang* by Harun Rajo Bujang recorded in 1984.

Appendix II

Nan dibilang si Baharuddin	The one I tell of is Baharuddin
abih ari baganti ari	day succeeded day
awak ado di Sungai Panuah	he was in Sungai Penuh
maalun awak nak makan juo	of course he wanted to eat
ka nyo bali lapiak mingkuang	he bought a screwpine mat
diseo timbangan urang	he hired someone's scales
dibali lado jo bawang	he bought chilis and onions
inyo manggaleh ka di sinan	he traded there
maalun buyuang Baharuddin	as for young Baharuddin
abih ari baganti ari	day succeeded day
kadang tampak di Siulak Dareh	sometimes he was seen in Siulak Dareh
kadang tampak di Siulak Gadang	sometimes he was seen in Siulak Gadang
kadang-kadang di pasa Kayu Aro	sometimes in the market at Kayu Aro
kadang di pasa Sungai Panuah	sometimes in the market at S. Penuh
jo itu iduik tiok ari	that was his daily livelihood
abih ari baganti ari	day succeeded day
'bih pakan baganti bulan	weeks turned into months
kok untuak sakadar makan	as far as just eating was concerned
lai lapeh di Baharuddin	Baharuddin had enough
ati batambah sanang juo	he grew more and more content
namun Kambang takana juo	yet he still remembered Kambang
abih bulan baganti bulan	month succeeded month
barapo lamo Baharuddin di Sungai Panuah	Baharuddin was in Sungai Penuh for some time
lah tigo bulan maso itu	it was now three months
takana janji jo guru	he remembered his promise to his teacher
co itu buyuang Baharuddin	thus it was with Baharuddin
lah dilelang lado jo bawang	he auctioned his chilis and onions
timbangan sudah dipulangkan	the scales were returned
naiak oto kini di sungai Panuah	he got on a bus in Sungai Penuh

From *Merantau ke Jambi*, by Syamsuddin, recorded by Radio P2SC, Jakarta.

HENRI CHAMBERT-LOIR

Malay literature in the 19th century
The Fadli connection

Nineteenth century Malay literature has recently attracted quite wide attention. Specialists in traditional literature have unearthed, published and analysed travelogues and other texts which testify to a critical curiosity and a care for realism which are the marks of a new, 'modern' attitude. Of particular interest are the texts published by Skinner (1982) and Sweeney (1980). Skinner (1978) especially has devoted more detail to the impact on Malay literature of the encounter with the European mentality.

At the same time as the so-called 'classicists' were busy highlighting the cultural changes which took place in the course of the last century, the specialists in 'modern literature' for their part were questioning the notion of modernity and were pushing backwards the border of the modern. Well known are the efforts of Pramoedya Ananta Toer as early as the sixties, and now again after a gap of twenty years (1982), as well as a seminal article by Watson (1971), and more recently a huge bibliographical guide by Salmon (1981) that cannot but change everyone's view of modern Indonesian literature.

In the light of these various studies, not only do the limits and the periodization of both 'traditional' and 'modern' literatures have to be revised, but the notion of modernity has to be questioned, and the respective roles of the various ethnic communities must be re-evaluated. Moreover, literature as a cultural activity within a social context is receiving more and more attention, with a view to understanding the deep transformation which Malay literature underwent in the course of the 19th century.

This article is devoted to a special case of this transitional phase of Malay literature, a case which is set in one particular district of Batavia at the turn of the century, and which concerns written popular literature of an entertaining nature. This study has been prompted by the discovery of a close relationship between 26 Malay manuscripts (32 volumes) kept in the National Library in Jakarta (acquired by the Bataviaasch Genootschap van Kunsten en Wetenschappen in 1889 and 1899), ten manuscripts kept in the Leningrad section of the

USSR Academy of Sciences (acquired in 1912 from Dr W. Frank[1]), and seven manuscripts in the library of Leiden University (mostly from H.N. van der Tuuk's bequest).

The 26 manuscripts kept in Jakarta are signed in various and sometimes enigmatic ways. The most frequent signature reads Muhammad Bakir, the most complete is Muhammad Bakir bin Syafian bin Usman al-Fadli or bin Fadli.

The Leningrad collection is made up of ten items, two of which are signed Ahmad Beramka (B 2508 and B 2506) and another one in a more complete way Ahmad Beramka bin Guru Cit Safirin bin Usman bin Fadli (D 449). Based on comparison of the handwriting, I think at least two other manuscripts (C 1966 and D 450) are the work of the same scribe. Another manuscript is signed Safirin bin Usman (D 466). Lastly, one manuscript is signed Ahmed Mujarrab bin Guru Cit bin Usman bin Fadli (B 2507).[2]

As for the Leiden manuscripts, three items dated 1858 and 1878 are signed Safirin or Safirin bin Usman, another one dated 1888-89 is signed Guru Cit (according to Van Ronkel 1921:126-8; however, considering its date, it should probably be ascribed to Muhammad Bakir), another one dated 1870 is said to be the property of Ahmad Insab bin Safirin bin Usman bin Fadli, and the last two dated 1886 and 1888 are signed Muhammad Bakir.[3]

A study of the Jakarta manuscripts, a few years ago, led me to assume that Muhammad Bakir's father, Syafian bin Usman al-Fadli, was also called or nicknamed Cit (Chambert-Loir 1984:51). This hypothesis needs to be corrected. The Fadli family was active in writing and copying Malay manuscripts in the Pecenongan district, Batavia, from 1858 to 1909. Three persons were the main actors of this family enterprise, Safirin, Muhammad Bakir and Ahmad Beramka, but three other names are mentioned: Syafian, Ahmad Insab and Ahmed Mujarrab. Safirin is the one who is also named Guru

---

[1]   We know very little about Dr Frank: he held an official position (diplomat or counsellor) in the Middle East in the early years of this century. The Russian Imperial Science Academy bought eighteen Moslem manuscripts from him in 1904 (presently eleven Arabic and Persian manuscripts in the collection of the Leningrad Branch of the USSR Science Academy come from that lot). We may suppose that he resided in Batavia afterwards, where he acquired the Malay manuscripts now kept in the same library in Leningrad.

[2]   Moreover it seems to me, on the basis of the script, that the 80-page inset within manuscript D 446 may have been written by Muhammad Bakir. This is even more plausible because the inset contains a passage from the *Hikayat Sultan Taburat*, which is one of Muhammad Bakir's most voluminous works in Jakarta. The proper names mentioned in the inset are the same as those encountered at the end of Jakarta Ml 183D. The dates also fit, as Ml 183D is dated May 1887, whereas the inset is dated January 1888.

[3]   Cod.Or. 3245 (*Hikayat Cekel Waneng Pati*) is not 'copied by Dr v.d. Tuuk from a MS by Mohammad Bâqir' (Juynboll 1899:76-7): it is signed by and actually written by Muhammad Bakir himself in 1888.

Cit, and his name cannot be confused with Syafian (Syafiᶜan). At the end of one manuscript (Ml 183E:277), in a colophon in triangle shape, is specified the date of copying (15 January 1886) and the name of the copyist (Muhammad Bakir bin Syafiᶜan bin Usman bin Fadli), and, at the tip of the triangle, is added the name of Cit Safirin Usman. The fact that Muhammad Bakir could write these two names, Syafiᶜan and Safirin, with their quite different spellings, at the same time on the same page, clearly indicates that two different persons are meant. As both Syafian and Safirin are sons of Usman bin Fadli, they must have been brothers. Syafian's name is occasionally written in Latin characters in the reduced form *SPN* (Ml 183E:236). Similarly, Safirin's name is written *Sapiereen* and *Sapieren* (Cod.Or. 3221:21v, 100r). Therefore I will henceforth spell their names Sapian and Sapirin.

Muhammad Bakir makes two allusions (in Ml 183B and Ml 256) to his father's works, so Sapian must have produced manuscripts too. Unfortunately, none seems to have survived. According to a statement by Muhammad Bakir in one volume of the *Hikayat Sultan Taburat* (Ml 183D), Sapian died in 1885.

As for Sapirin's manuscripts, only five have been preserved. Their dates of composition range from 1858 to 1885. At the time of completing his *Hikayat Anak Pengajian* (Leningrad D 446), in February 1871, he wrote: 'The author of this story is Sapirin bin Usman Betawi, Kampung Pecenongan. The story was written at the time I was just recovering from a serious illness. This illness was caused first by a sickness which brought me close to death, second by the death of my son who was eight months old, third by the death of the child's mother, [fourth] by the death of my brother in the same year.' Furthermore he adds in a postscript in syair form: 'This I write as a consolation, Death has very much affected me, My son I hope will follow my path, I have only one son left'.[4] One year before, in May 1870, a writer, whom I assume to be Sapirin, had completed another manuscript (*Hikayat Maharaja Ganda Parwa Kesuma*, Cod. Or. 3241), which he stated to be 'the property of Ahmad Insab bin Sapirin bin Usman bin Fadli'. We may surmise that Sapirin was offering this manuscript to his newborn son, Ahmad Insab, and that this son is the one whose death he mourns in February 1871.

Sapirin seems to have had two more children: first Ahmed Mujarrab bin

---

[4]   'Yang mengarang ini hikayat Sapirin bin Usman Betawi Kampung Pecenongan. Pada masa mengarang hikayat ini pada tatkala baru bangun daripada penyakit yang amat payah, maka penyakit itu pertama sakit hampir maut, kedua sakit sebab ditinggal mati oleh anak laki-laki umur 8 bulan, ketiga sebab ditinggal mati oleh ibunya anak itu, ketiga [*sic*] sebab ditinggal oleh seorang saudara laki-laki pada tahun itu juga.' 'Hamba mengarang ini buat penglibur hati / Hamba dapat sakit payah sebab ditinggal mati / Anakku seorang harap jadi pengganti / Dapat cuma satu lagi anak laki-laki.' (D 446:260-1.)

Guru Cit, the copyist of *Hikayat Suwiting Batara Guru* (dated 1898), who may have been the only surviving son in 1870, and second Ahmad Beramka, who was writing around 1906-09. The similitude of the names of Ahmad Insab, Ahmed Mujarrab and Ahmad Beramka would support the hypothesis that they were actually brothers.

As for Sapian's son, Muhammad Bakir, a relatively large number of his works have reached us: 31 volumes kept in Jakarta, two in Leiden and one more in Leningrad, amounting to almost 7,000 pages. Muhammad Bakir was active during the years 1884-98. We have more than a hundred specimens of his signature, which developed through time. It is made up of some letters of his name together with the diacritical points of the name Cit (see reproductions in Chambert-Loir 1984:65-6). It is possible that he incorporated Cit's name in his own signature as a way of paying homage to his uncle, who may have been his master in the art of copying.

This biographical sketch is summed up in the following diagram:

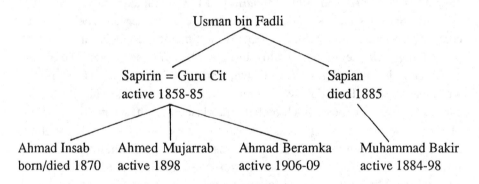

At the end of some of their manuscripts, Sapirin and Muhammad Bakir have added postscripts in syair form,[5] in which they may sum up the moral of the story and on occasion announce a following volume, they may ask their readers to take care of the manuscripts, or they may give some information about themselves. In the light of these syair it is clear that these manuscripts do not constitute a private library nor were they intended to be sold: they were copied in order to be rented out (at the price of ten cents per 24 hours). The Fadli family was running a lending library.[6]

---

[5]   This is not exceptional: compare Kratz 1977 and Iskandar 1981.

[6]   That one manuscript by Sapirin (*Hikayat Anak Pengajian*, dated 1871), and advertised by Muhammad Bakir around 1890, could be acquired by Dr Frank in Batavia around 1910, together with Ahmad Beramka's own manuscripts, is evidence that Ahmad Beramka inherited his father's and his cousin's manuscripts.

In seven manuscripts written between 1887 and 1896, Muhammad Bakir gives the lists of the texts he has for rent. If we compare these lists with each other and with the titles of the manuscripts we actually have, we can make up a list of at least 60 titles that Muhammad Bakir had for rent. And if we add now the manuscripts kept in Leiden and Leningrad, we reach some 76 titles (see the Appendix at the end of this article).

We know that manuscripts were loaned in many districts of Batavia (Iskandar 1981 mentions eleven kampungs in the northern part of the town), and we know that the manuscripts could travel from one district to another. This trade existed in other cities as well: to mention but two examples, a few manuscripts now kept in Jakarta come from a late 19th century lending library in Palembang (Kratz 1977), and as late as 1938 W. Kern was able to buy manuscripts in Banjarmasin from an old Chinese man, 'Babah Badak', who copied the manuscripts himself but whose trade was 'no more lucrative, due to lack of interest of the reading public for the old tales' (Kern 1948:544).

The case of the Fadli family is most unusual, however, considering the number of the titles we can still record and that of the manuscripts we actually possess. In his survey of the collection of Malay manuscripts kept at the Leiden University library, Iskandar (1981) has gathered information about owners of one or two items, which they loaned in order to earn some money. One or two manuscripts can hardly be called a library. Iskandar mentions only two examples of larger collections: one is that of a man who bequeaths 14 items to his son, the second is a note by Snouck Hurgronje 'to the effect that most manuscripts in that kampung (Pluit) were formerly owned by the former wijkmeester of that kampung' (Iskandar 1981:146-7). Therefore the Fadli family with its 77 items is unique.

Pecenongan was apparently a very active area in that respect, as not only were Sapirin, Muhammad Bakir and Ahmad Beramka running their lending library there, but three other owners and lenders of manuscripts at least lived in the same district, Utung bin Akir (Cod.Or. 3308 *Hikayat Amir Hamzah* and *Hikayat Raja Handak*, and Cod.Or. 3319 *Hikayat Marakarma*), Kiman (Cod.Or. 3195a *Hikayat Pandawa Lima*) and Ence Musa (Cod.Or. 3243 *Hikayat Dewa Asmara Jaya*). One more writer could even be part of the Fadli family, as he stayed in the same street as Muhammad Bakir, and his (almost illegible) signature seems to contain the name Cit (Jakarta, C.S. 137 *Hikayat Dewa Mandu*).

The Fadli collection provides us with a large number of works precisely dated and localized. We have a specimen of literature which was produced and consumed between 1858 and 1909. It is a popular literature, that is, a literature of entertainment intended for the lower social class, almost exclusive of any learned or specialized work. Moreover, in this specific case of a lending library run successively by two generations, there was direct contact between authors and readers, and we may surmise that there was some kind of interaction between them.

We know some scraps of Muhammad Bakir's biography from the postscripts he used to add to his works. The first manuscript we have by him, the *Hikayat Muhammadan al-Saman*, dates from 1884. It is written with great care, perhaps out of respect for the subject and probably also because Muhammad Bakir, who was still very young, was learning the craft of copyist under his father's or his uncle's guidance. When copying another religious text, the *Hikayat Syaikh Abdulkadir Jailani*, eight years later, he states that he is copying a manuscript written by his father.

He marries around 1890. In 1893 he states that he has a wife and two children. During those years, he has no other livelihood than his library, which means, if we believe him, that with the sole renting out of his manuscripts he earns a living sufficient for four people. But it is a hard life. In 1894 he explains his difficulties:

> 'I pay my respects to those who rent this story, and I let them know that the renting tariff is ten cents for one day and one night. Please have consideration for this, because I take much pain in writing and I spend a lot of lamp oil and paper for the sake of my children and my wife. Actually, I have had no proper job since my childhood and I get food and clothes from my uncle's charity. This is why I beg those who rent this story to pay the tariff of ten cents for a day and a night.'[7]

Yet three years later, in 1897, he says that he teaches religion to children ('tukang ajar anak mengaji'). His address is Pecenongan Langgar Tinggi, and it is probable that he was living in a *langgar*, where he also taught the children of the surroundings the reading of the Qur'an and the fundamentals of Islamic religion.

He had already sold part of his library to the Bataviaasch Genootschap in 1889. He sells a second lot of manuscripts in 1899. We have no more information about him after that year.

This is not much for a biography, yet the contents of his works give us some idea about his education. The great number of Arabic quotations in a few Islamic texts induce us to think that he knew rudiments of that language, some-

---

7   'Saya punya salam takzim pada yang menyewa hikayat ini, dikasih tahu wang sewanya sehari semalam sepuluh sen, lebih-lebih maklum sebab saya sangat berusahakan menulis dan bergadang minyak lampu dan kertas buat anak dan istri saya, boleh dibilang yang saya tiada bekerja dari kecil, menumpang makan dan pakai dari saya punya mama', maka itu saya minta kasihannya yang sewa ini buat sehari semalam sepuluh sen adanya.' (Ml 259:193.)

thing which fits with his occupation as a religious teacher. On the other hand, the literary genre he was probably most familiar with was that of wayang stories.

In the manuscripts he copied and especially in his own works, he inserted lots of details which are the stamp of his own personality: dates (which are dates of his copying) inserted within the narration, marginal notes, allusions within the text to contemporary events, sketches of objects or characters from the story, addresses to the audience, explanations of an archaic word, and so on. All those details, all those idiosyncrasies, give his library a style and a personality. It is clear that he deliberately insisted on that aspect, by character and by taste as a writer, but perhaps also with a view to keeping his readers. His customers knew that when renting a story by Muhammad Bakir they would have a certain kind of product, just like the readers of any popular novelist nowadays.

One feature of those stories is their humour: a simple and sometimes quite vulgar humour based on a variety of devices. A comic effect may arise out of contrast. This is the case with anachronisms: the *Lakon Jaka Sukara*, for instance, contains allusions to the Krakatau eruption, to Batavia beggars, to Gambir Square, to Kampung Cibubur, and to Dursasana perfuming himself with Cologne water. In another wayang story (*Hikayat Maharaja Garbak Jagat*), a war leader addresses his soldiers: 'Whoever retreats, his wages will be cut and he will be fired! Whoever is prepared to die will get a medal!'[8] In the same story, someone threatens to circumcise Durna. When analysing the *Sair Buah-Buahan*, Koster (1986) has demonstrated how the author was skilfully undermining the genres and patterns of traditional literature by the means of parody and irony.

These stories were intended to be read aloud and their humour is sometimes oral. This is the case with onomatopoeia[9] and again when the narrator reproduces the way of speaking (*pelo*) of a child or the accent of a Chinese.[10] Another type of humour, which is more relevant in the present context, is the way Muhammad Bakir creates a relationship between author, narrator,

---

[8]   'Siapa undur potong gaji dan dapat lepas, siapa yang berani mati dapat bintang.' (Ml 251:92.)

[9]   In one volume of the *Hikayat Sultan Taburat*, a war scene is the occasion for onomatopoeia which are written with thick letters: the weapons make 'cak cuk cuk', the broken bones 'kelatak kelatik kelatuk', the arrows 'serawat seriwit', the weapons knocking against one another 'gememprang gememprung', and the blows hit on the kings' bellies 'kedabak kedabuk' (Ml 183D:219).

[10]   In another volume of the same story, a Chinese ghost complains to his companion that his bride has been seduced by a castrator of cockerels (*tukang kebiri ayam*) who has bribed the girl's mother, and he goes on: 'My foltune is of the unlucky solt, let me mally another gil!' ('Peluntungan tiada bel-laku, bial-lah aku kawin sama olang lain saja', Ml 183C:119).

audience and characters of the story. First the author, that is, the individual signing the manuscripts with his name and known to his neighbours. In a number of manuscripts, Muhammad Bakir inscribes his name on the front page of the text, advertises the hikayat and syair he has for rent, signs again in the colophon, and speaks for himself in versified postscripts. He also inserts his signature in the text itself and however cryptic that paraph may be, it is a sign of authorship or at least of ownership that the reader could not ignore.

Secondly the narrator: he sometimes personally breaks in on the narration. When, for instance, a princess relates that she is an orphan, her listeners sob and cry, and the story goes on: 'Many tears were shed, and the narrator started crying as well, because his father died when he was still young and his mother did her best to comfort him so that he would not be heartbroken'.[11] He sometimes gives advice to the reader or comments on a scene. Thirdly the audience: the narrator may address them directly as, for instance, when having quoted a verse of the Qur'an, he adds: 'Oh you, my fellows who are sitting, please say Amin!'[12] Sometimes the audience seems to take part in the story: an extraordinary event is said to happen 'because the request of the gods was agreed, as well as the request of the mass and the request of those who are reading or listening to the story of Maharaja Garbak Jagat'.[13] At the beginning of the same story, Batara Narada sends Grubuk to earth and asks him to convey his greetings to the Pandawa and to the audience: 'and my best regards to your father Si Lurah Semar, and my best regards to those who are reading and listening'.[14]

And fourthly the characters: it happens in a few stories that they directly address the narrator, as if they were real, contemporary beings, dependent on the narrator's will, and at the same time free to protest against his creation. Once, for instance, when a princess has to part with her parents, one of her attendants exclaims: 'Oh my lady, so cruel is the narrator that he writes such a story. O stupid narrator, don't you know human suffering that you make my lady part from her father and mother!'[15] In another story (this time by

[11]   'Maka jadi bertangis-tangisan hingga pengarangnya jua turut menangis sebab dari kecil ditinggal bapak, seboleh-bolehnya dilipurkan hati ibunya jangan sampai kerusakan hatinya' (Ml 249:154).

[12]   'Hai sekalian saudaraku yang ada duduk, tolonglah berkata amin' (Ml 261:89).

[13]   'Daripada sebab keterima permintaan dewa dan batara dan keterima permintaan orang ramai-ramai dan keterima permintaan yang membaca atau yang menengar akan kabarnya Maharaja Garbak Jagat itu' (Ml 251:199).

[14]   'Dan salam takzimku pada bapakmu Si Lurah Semar dan salam takzimku pada yang membaca dan mendengar' (Ml 251:30).

[15]   'Aduh tuan, sampai hatinya orang yang mengarang ini akan membuat cerita yang selaku ini [...]. Hai pengarang yang bebal, tiada mengetahui sakit hati orang dibuatnya cerita tuan patik dipisahkan dengan ibu bapaknya' (Ml 259:94).

Sapirin), Sang Rajuna (i.e. Arjuna) himself is desperate and so he weeps: 'O you narrator, you have the heart to write this despair of mine. Who has written this? Who has been so cruel as to write that I should part with my beloved? O you narrator, why is your hand so rash that you write such a story, why are you so cruel as to fill my heart with pain? O narrator, this is enough, don't go on writing such things. I can't stand such pain. Change to another tale. Don't go on with this. May I recover from my illness. O narrator, who are you, and where do you stay, that you have the heart to make up such a story, so painful. You don't feel it, that's why you write whatever you like.'[16] Finally there are a few cases where some characters seem so peculiar and unexpected against the background of the story that it seems possible that Muhammad Bakir was drawing a comical portrait of some of his neighbours.

All these features reveal a very self-conscious author. Sapirin, and Muhammad Bakir after him, used to rephrase the formula 'by God's will' as follows: 'by God's will exerting itself on the narrator'.[17] The narrator occupies a privileged position between the Creator and the creatures. In the *Sair Buah-Buahan*, Muhammad Bakir explains the death of some characters by God's will (*iradat/kodrat Tuhan*), and at the same time emphasizes the power of the narrator over the narrative ('dengan takdir orang yang mengarang', Ml 254:88 st.3).

There is an ever-present play, in Sapirin's and Muhammad Bakir's works, on the ambiguous situation of the writer. Retelling classics, or framing new stories on no less classical patterns, they pretend to respect the rules of the game, they conform to known genealogies and schemes, they compose expected episodes and dialogues, then suddenly they create surprise by claiming their omnipotence and liberty as writers.[18] At the same time, we can detect a kind of familiarity between author and audience. Muhammad Bakir had his lending library at his own place,[19] and we can surmise that his clients lived in Pecenongan too and

---

[16] 'Demikian bunyi ratapnya, wah pengarang, sampai hatinya akan mengarang hal penyakitku ini, dan siapakah mengarangnya itu sampai hatinya mengarangkan aku dipisahkan dengan kekasihku? Hai pengarang, mengapakah lancapmu tanganmu akan menulis ceritera yang demikian sampai hatinya memberi pilu dalam hatiku. Ya pengarang, sudahlah jangan sampai hatimu mengarang seperti ini tiada kutanggung menahankan penyakit ini, marilah tukarkan kisah yang lain, janganlah dibuat yang demikian, mudah-mudahan sembuhlah penyakitku. Hai pengarang, siapakah engkau dan di manakah tempatmu sampai hatimu berbuat ceritera yang demikian alangkah sakitnya daripada engkau tiada merasakan jadi mengarang barang sekehendakmu.'(Cod.Or. 3241:116.)

[17] One example from Sapirin's *Hikayat Angkawijaya* reads: 'Maka dengan takdir Allah melakukan atas yang mengarang' (Cod.Or. 3221:6r).

[18] For a discussion of the question of authorship and authority on the basis of one work by Muhammad Bakir, see Koster 1986:88-93.

[19] In one manuscript he states: 'I rent out hikayat and syair, please come to my house.' (Ml 255:162.)

that he knew them all.

What sort of literature did these customers rent? It is what can be called an entertaining popular literature, and it is of a remarkable diversity. To give an idea of that diversity, we can arrange the 27 works of Muhammad Bakir in a few categories: first the five well-known stories which can be labelled as showing Indian or Indo-Javanese influence: *Hikayat Seri Rama, Hikayat Panji Semirang, Hikayat Cekel Waneng Pati, Syair Ken Tambuhan* and *Hikayat Indera Bangsawan*. A second group consists of seven wayang stories which might be original works by Muhammad Bakir himself. The third group is that of nine hikayat and one syair, most of which again are unknown elsewhere and could be Muhammad Bakir's own compositions: these are epics full of wonderful adventures which borrow elements from epics of Indian as well as Muslim type. A fourth group is made up of three typically Islamic texts (*Hikayat Syaikh Muhammadan al-Saman, Hikayat Syaikh Abdulkadir Jailani* and *Hikayat Bulan Berbelah*). And lastly two 'symbolic syair' (*Sair Sang Kupu-Kupu* and *Sair Buah-Buahan*) constitute an isolated group. According to an announcement in the *Sair Buah-Buahan*, Muhammad Bakir had twelve other similar syair for rent.

These 27 works, 22 hikayat and 5 syair, are typically traditional as far as titles and genres are concerned. So late in the 19th century, it is even rather surprising to find such a wealth of traditional literature still alive in a popular area of Batavia. Nevertheless a number of modern elements emerge from the mass of this traditional material.

The anachronisms and allusions to contemporary events which Muhammad Bakir inserts into his narratives tend to place age-old stories in a modern setting, or at least to question their setting in time. When, for instance, the letter of a king is dated 1 May 1897 (Ml 244:39), or when a prince is married on 9 September 1887 (Ml 249:264), this insistence on fictitious contemporaneity seems to make the characters to a certain extent current, and at the same time it deliberately raises the question of their fictionality.

There are more important modern tendencies in the psychology of the heroes and the realism of some scenes. Examples are to be found in an apparently original story consisting of two volumes: *Hikayat Nakhoda Asyik Cinta Berlekat* (Ml 261) and *Hikayat Merpati Mas dan Merpati Perak* (Ml 249).

In the first volume, the hero wanders from country to country as a trader. Being a prince himself, he does not seek the company of princes but that of merchants. He saves a princess and her parents from the attack of her suitors. (In one episode, the king, the queen and the princess disguise themselves to escape from their enemies: they hold empty bottles in their hands and pretend to be drunken sailors...) The hero, of course, eventually marries the princess, but he soon leaves her for new wanderings and he actually buys a village girl as a second wife. He pays all his wealth for her so that he is ruined. When after a while this second wife looks for the hero, she spends one night in a village occupied by *santri* (Islamic students) and, as she distrusts the santri who gives her shelter, she makes him drunk and makes a fool of him. We can see at once how matter-of-fact scenes from actual life find their place in the framework of a traditional narrative.

The heroes of the second volume, Merpati Mas and Merpati Perak, are the grandsons of the previous hero. Many of their adventures are reminiscent of episodes known from other hikayat and they are themselves perfectly conventional characters. But against this familiar background, a few surprisingly modern scenes stand out.

The kingdom has been totally destroyed by a tidal wave. Then, together with their parents, the two princes undertake to build a new city. Creating magic countries (*mencipta negeri kesaktian*) is a favourite trick of many a hikayat hero. By virtue of magical weapons, gifted kings can instantly produce out of nothing a fortified palace 'complete with walls and moats'. However, our two princes do not resort to magic, nor do they build a stereotyped stronghold. First they dig into the soil, looking for the remains of the former palace. They dig out gold and silver wares, jewels, money, precious stones, and the like, which they sell to the peasants of the neighbourhood, to a wealthy merchant (Hamdani), and even to a king. In that way they gather a real fortune. Then they buy from Hamdani a steamer which they load with building materials and they have a new town built according to a plan: a palace, a monumental gate facing the sea, several kampungs, a market, streets lined with trees, canals with bridges, mosques and schools. Agriculture is organized (rice, vegetables, fruit), capital is given to carpenters so that they can build up their trade, old men are appointed as *penghulu kampung*, and civil servants are chosen from among the most learned foreigners. Legal procedure is organized, the army is built up, and the four bravest, wisest and most honest men are selected as ministers. We have here something which is foreign to traditional literature, namely the outline of a utopia.[20]

This hikayat, like many others, contains many battle scenes. It is not particularly original in this respect. What is totally new is the depiction of a resting scene after the battle: when night has come, after the cease-fire, everyone occupies himself as he pleases. Some men take care of their horses, others

---

[20] See by comparison Lombard-Salmon 1972.

sing or smoke, some discuss the next day's tactics, some relate their own brave actions of the day. The wounded moan, some with a friend attending to them, some alone. The doctors look after the wounded and the crippled,[21] and the king promotes those who have distinguished themselves in the battle (Ml 249:222-4). In short, the scene is described with much realism and from the point of view of the soldiers, something which is certainly unusual in traditional literature.

Those few examples mark modern tendencies in Muhammad Bakir's works. However, it should be kept in mind that it is by contrast with the overall traditional character of the works that these tendencies are so striking.

Another characteristic involving contrast is the presence of a few Chinese elements. I have already quoted a passage where the Chinese accent was an object of mockery. In two other stories (both happen to be wayang stories), Chinese newcomers are also laughed at. In the story of Jaka Sukara, for instance, as the *panakawan* are quarrelling, 'people crowded to see the four brothers arguing because Lurah Semar's sons were speaking very rapidly like Chinese newcomers and everybody was laughing at them'.[22]

The single text where Chinese elements go beyond this type of scornful comparisons is the *Sair Buah-Buahan*. It is a composite text made up of three parts. The first is the one which gives its title to the poem, and it may be Muhammad Bakir's only text where typically Chinese words are used (Overbeck 1934:139). It is a 'symbolic syair' relating a love story between characters who bear fruit names. At the time of the marriage of the main characters, the young guests sing Islamic litanies to Chinese melodies.[23] The second part has only artificial links with the first. It is the story of a Chinese fellow, Baba Setiawana, who cannot stand the death of his wife and who eventually dies of grief.

About the categorization of this poem, Overbeck commented: 'The second poem may have had its origin in some local Chinese legend, and may even, to

---

[21]   The doctors take part in another scene: a warrior is brought back, thought dead. 'The doctors come immediately and inspect his body and his wounds. They hold his hand and find out that his pulse is still beating and his body is still warm. So they say "Don't bury him, he may still live."'(Ml 249:235.)

[22]   'Sekalian penonton pun jadi datanglah melihat keempat bersaudara itu berbicara karena sekalian anaknya Lurah Semar itu berbicara seperti Cina singkek dengan sambil berburu-buru maka jadi ramai orang tertawa padanya itu demikianlah adanya' (Ml 246:8). See also the expression 'bingungnya seperti Cina kebakaran jenggot' ('as puzzled as a Chinese whose beard is on fire', Ml 251:97).

[23]   'Demikian kata pengarang durjana / Ramai di luar anak muda yang bijaksana / Akan memalu pukul rebana / Mengadu dikir lagu Cina' ('So says the wicked writer / Witty youngsters were plenty outside / Playing the tabor / Competing in singing Chinese songs', Ml 254:51).

judge from the style, have already existed in the form of a shaer of local Chinese origin' (1934:143). Despite the 'remarkable coherence' of the whole poem (Koster 1986:85-6), Overbeck's view is somewhat supported by the way the manuscript itself is written: the last line of the first part (Ml 254:75) is written in the middle of the page and followed by Muhammad Bakir's signature, marking a clear break in the writing. But instead of a 'local Chinese legend', it may have been a syair written by a peranakan Chinese that Muhammad Bakir was copying in the second part of his poem, just as Ahmad Beramka was to do some years later. Besides, we must also consider the fact that Muhammad Bakir explicitly states that he is the author of the whole poem. Whatever the case may be, it is remarkable indeed that amidst 27 traditional texts, one should be a poem with a Chinese baba as its main character.

The comic hints at the accent of Chinese people when speaking Malay belongs to a type of humour known to every nation, by means of which a community emphasizes its identity by poking fun at outsiders. The Chinese episode of the *Sair Buah-Buahan,* however, could be a sign of the permeability of Malay literature, in this transitional phase, to peranakan literature.

Muhammad Bakir copied manuscripts for readers and listeners whom he knew personally. He addresses them directly in the postscripts which he has added to several of his works. The terms of address he uses supply us with information about the identity of his customers: he calls them *baba, nona* (male and female Chinese peranakan), *tuan, nyonya* (gentlemen and ladies, presumably European mestizos), *sahabat, kawan* (friends and mates), or *pembaca* (readers). At the end of the *Hikayat Seri Rama,* for instance, we find the following stanza: 'To the readers whoever they are, Peranakan and friends, Even more to you gentlemen, And to the wealthy'.[24] So it is clear that, as Iskandar has remarked (1981:149-50) for other manuscripts copied in Batavia in the same period, these texts were intended for Chinese peranakan and Indos as well as Indonesians.

Considering the terms of address in relation with the genres of the works, we could expect to classify the stories according to their public. But this proves to be erroneous: the Chinese are mentioned in Indian-like works, in wayang stories, in pseudo-Persian epics, and in symbolic syair. That is to say, only in a single category are they not mentioned, that of the typically Islamic works like the *Hikayat Muhammadan al-Saman.* But in fact nobody at all is mentioned in those texts, for Muhammad Bakir did not add any postscript to them. Therefore, what should be underlined is that the Chinese are not kept apart

---

[24]   'Pada pembaca juga siapa-siapa / Baba nyonya dan kawan-kawan / Apalagi pula pada tuan-tuan / Apa pula orang kaya hartawan', Cod.Or. 252:402).

from other groups: there is no literary category reserved for them and none from which they would be excluded.[25]

Let us now turn to Ahmad Beramka. Among the Leningrad manuscripts, there are five works that can be attributed with some certainty to him. In addition to their handwriting, these manuscripts show some formal similarities with regard to paper, binding and presentation. Apart from the collection of syair (B 2508), which will be examined below, the four remaining works are the following. First, another composite collection containing no less than 153 tales, summaries and short syair (C 1966). As in the collection of syair, the titles of the various texts are adorned with vignettes. A second item, dating from 1909, contains the first part of the *Hikayat Marakarma* (B 2506). A third one contains the second part of that hikayat together with a version of the *Syair Ken Tambuhan* (D 450). Finally, the fourth item, which was written between September 1905 and January 1906, contains an original poem which may have been composed by Ahmad Beramka himself, entitled *Sair Perang Ruslan dan Jepang* (D 449).

These titles are sufficient to show the mixing of genres. *Hikayat Marakarma* and *Syair Ken Tambuhan* are good examples of traditional literature. The collection of summaries and tales is more peculiar: its main source is the *Thousand and One Nights*, but it also contains summaries of Malay hikayat as well as original syair of a didactic nature. The poem on the Russo-Japanese war belongs to the quite extensive category of traditional war poems, with the important difference that it deals with a war far away from the Malay world, and at the same time it is part of a new type of literature inspired by the daily news.

The collection of syair has no less than 771 pages. It is made up of 15 syair copied one after the other without any obvious order. These poems are of very diverse length, from 37 to 2,440 stanzas. Most of them are accounts of more or less contemporary events, or at least they are presented as such ('yang betul sudah kejadian'). Five poems are not accounts of events: *Sair Abu Nawas* (still subtitled 'yang betul sudah kejadian di negeri Bagdad'), *Sair Baba Bujang dan Nona Bujang*, *Sair Anak Kwalon Atawa Ibu Tiri*, *Sair Kartu* and *Sair Capjiki*.

The ten other syair refer, or pretend to refer, to precise events mostly dating from the first years of this century: this is the case for the robbery of the Java Bank in 1902 (*Tuan Gentis di Betawi*), or the marriage of R.M. Tirta Adhi Surya in 1906 (*Sultan Muhammad Sidik Syah*), but it can also be said of the story of Nyai Dasima in 1813 which has recently been stated to be purely fictitious (Hellwig 1986:51 and note 8). The *Sair Nona Lao Fatnio* relates a love

---

[25]   Reference to 'a peranakan readership of an Islamic legend' can be found in a manuscript of the *Hikayat Raja Handak* copied in Semarang in 1797: see Kratz 1989.

affair which supposedly took place in Bandung in 1909, but its location is indicated in a rather evasive way: the second stanza reads: 'This is a true story, It happened this very month, The 15th of November 1909, It took place on the side of the street'.[26] This insistence on contemporaneity is the first apparent characteristic of these poems.

The events related are sensational enough: it is for instance a case of theft (*Tuan Gentis di Betawi*), a murder (*Lo Fenkui, Muhammad Saleh, Nyai Dasima*), the marriage of a Sultan's daughter (*Sultan Muhammad Sidik Syah*), or the adventures of a nyai (*Nona Lao Fatnio, Nyai Ima*). The variety of the characters is truly remarkable: they are Indonesian, Chinese, European and Arab. As regards the geographical setting, it is quite diverse too: action takes place in Batavia (4 poems), in West Java (3), in East Java (1) and in the Moluccas (2). Only the five syair not related to events are not localized (with the exception of *Abu Nawas*, of course).

We know that this manuscript, as well as the others in the Dr Frank collection in Leningrad, were bought in Batavia before 1912. As the manuscript seems to have been written at a stretch, and as one of the syair was most probably composed in November 1909, we can conclude that the manuscript was copied between 1909 and 1912. What is more difficult to establish is whether it was composed at that time, or merely copied from one or more models, and also whether Ahmad Beramka was its author or only the copyist.

Ahmad Beramka signed eight of the fifteen syair: the first five and the last three. He does it in a brief and succinct way, without any address to the reader, nor any postscript, as his father and his cousin used to do. Yet there is no reason a priori to distrust him on that point. Nor does it mean that he is not the author of the poems he did not sign. Perhaps an analysis of his style could cast some light on that subject.

If we examine the poems signed by him, two tendencies become apparent: first a propensity for overloading the lines and lengthening them up to 19 syllables, secondly the tendency to utilize the same rhymes over and over. Ahmad Beramka of course has no monopoly of these tendencies, which belong to any poor or hurried poet. However, some repetitions from one poem to another lead to the assumption that this could be a stylistic feature of Ahmad Beramka.

Within the *Sair Nona Lao Fatnio*, for instance, which is signed by Ahmad Beramka and which is very short (40 stanzas), more than half of the stanzas (24 out of 40) are built on three suffixes (*-nya, -an, -lah*) and on one rhyme eight times repeated (*itu/tentu/waktu/situ*).

---

[26] 'Ini sair yang kebetulan / Sudah kejadian di ini bulan / Lima belas Nopember 1909 / Di mana tempat di pinggir jalan' (p. 751).

Another short poem, which is not signed, *Sair Baba Lo Fenkui*, presents the same characteristics: more than half of the stanzas (28 out of 53) are built on four rhymes, which are again the three suffixes *-nya*, *-an*, *-kan*, and the repetition of *itu/tentu/waktu/situ*. Twenty other stanzas are built on five other rhymes with slight variations, which means that the greater part of the poem (48 stanzas out of 53) is built on only nine rhymes with an extremely frequent repetition of the same words at the end of the lines. In the play upon 'variation within identity' there is not much variation here!

If we look now at a longer poem (492 stanzas) which is not signed (but it is incomplete at the end), *Sair Sultan Muhammad Sidik Syah*, the analysis of the first 200 stanzas shows that 192 stanzas out of 200 are built on fourteen rhymes only, or better, that 66% of the stanzas are built on five rhymes, which once again are suffixes (*-an*, *-kan*, *-nya*, *-lah*) and the quartet *itu/tentu/waktu/situ*.

It is in this poem too that we find immoderately long lines such as the following:

'Karena menyambut tuanku putri empunya warta
Penganten mengadap di kamar penerimaan ibu suri
Kira-kira setengah jam penganten duduk depan ibunya'.

Besides this collection, Ahmad Beramka has signed a 2,747-stanza syair, namely *Sair Perang Ruslan dan Jepang*. An analysis of two sequences of 100 stanzas each shows the same tendency: 59% are built on four rhymes (suffixes *-an*, *-kan*, *-nya*, and the syllable *tu*), and 76% are built on seven rhymes only.

However, the last two poems of B 2508 (*Sair Kartu* and *Sair Capjiki*), which are signed by Ahmad Beramka, show the reverse features: rhythm, economy and diversity. The great majority of the lines are made up of four root-words with a clear pause, and the rhymes are not repetitive to the same degree.

I would be inclined to think that rhyme paucity is characteristic of Ahmad Beramka's own compositions, with the consequence that *Sair Baba Lo Fenkui* and *Sair Sultan Muhammad Sidik Syah* may be attributed to him, and conversely that *Sair Kartu* and *Sair Capjiki* are not his own works, even though he has signed them.

A comparison with other texts, printed for that matter, may also shed some light on the authorship of Ahmad Beramka's poems. Moreover it gives some insights into the nature of that literature.

Most of Ahmad Beramka's syair are known via other printed versions. The only ones which are not are the following: *Sair Hasan Mukmin di Tanah Jawa* (the story of Kasan Mukmin's rebellion in East Java in 1905; see Kartodirdjo 1978:80-6), *Sair Sultan Muhammad Sidik Syah* (the account of Tirta Adhi Surya's marriage to the Sultan of Bacan's daughter in 1906), *Sair Nyai Ima* (which is also set in the Moluccas) and lastly *Sair Abu Nawas* (of which we know only a prose version).

The eleven other titles also exist in published versions. His third syair, for instance, entitled *Sair dari Muhammad Saleh yang betul sudah kejadian di Betawi Meester Cornelis* and signed by him, has the same subject as another syair which was printed with the title *Sair Moehamad Saleh dan Moehamad Bentol (jang telah boenoe sa-orang Arab di Meester Cornelis lantaran perkara oetang)*, but this book is not to be found any more: it is only known through advertisements (Salmon 1981:383).

Let us take as an example the comparison of two poems by Ahmad Beramka with syair printed in the same period, in order to estimate the freedom of creativity of the respective authors, and to get a clearer picture of the type of literature Muhammad Bakir's cousin was devoted to.

First the *Sair Tuan Gentis di Betawi yang sudah kejadian 22 Nopember tahun 1902*. This 236-stanza long poem, signed by Ahmad Beramka, relates the unsuccessful robbery of the Java Bank at Batavia on 22 November 1902. The robbery was organized by a 27-year-old Dutch man named C.M. Gentis, who had arrived at Batavia two and a half years earlier. He succeeded in seizing a bag containing 110,000 guilders, but thanks to the bravery of the bank employees, he was forced to leave the money and run. He was eventually arrested near Bogor and, one year later, he was sentenced to 15 years' detention.

We do not know when Ahmad Beramka wrote his syair, but it cannot be after 1912. It happens that F. Wiggers and a Chinese author who signed Y.L.M. did publish ten years later, in 1922, a syair about the same subject entitled *Sair Java Bank di rampok*, which is twice as long as Ahmad Beramka's poem and far more detailed. The comparison of the two texts proves that, despite their respective dates, Ahmad Beramka copied three fifths of his stanzas from those by Wiggers and Y.L.M. (or perhaps from a model used by these authors). The choice, the transformation and the restructuring of the narrative would deserve to be studied in more detail. Suffice it to say for the time being that, in the case of the *Sair Tuan Gentis*, Ahmad Beramka composed his poem by drawing most of his material from an already existing work, but at the same time he accomplished a careful and personal work of reorganization.

It would be totally misleading at this point to speak of plagiarism. When copying almost word for word some 150 stanzas, Ahmad Beramka was working as a copyist just as when he copied, and signed, the *Hikayat Marakarma*. But when reordering those stanzas and completing them with 90 original ones with a view to creating a new narrative, he was working as a modern author.

It happens that the enigmatic Chinese author Y.L.M. and Ahmad Beramka have another text in common: the twelfth poem in Ahmad Beramka's collection, *Sair Baba Lo Fenkui pachter afiun di Banjarnegara*, is 53 stanzas long only, and it is not signed. It deals with the same subject as that of a syair published in book form in 1903 by Y.L.M.: *Boekoe sairan dari tjerita jang betoel soeda kedjadian di Poelo Djawa dari halnja satoe toean tana dan pachter opium di Residentie Benawan bernama Lo Fen Koei* (Batavia, 1903, 88 pp.).

The story is the same, but in this case the two poems have no formal relationship: the printed book is ten times longer than the manuscript and the two poems do not share a single stanza. Y.L.M.'s poem is probably an adaptation of a.prose story published the same year by Gouw Peng Liang, who drew his information from the journal *Bintang Betawi*. This last book was entitled *Tjerita jang betoel soeda kedjadian di poelo Djawa dari halnja satoe toean tana dan pachter opium di Res. Benawan, bernama Lo Fen Koei (terpetik dari soerat kabar Bintang Betawi)*.

The story is that of a lecherous wealthy Chinese who does not hesitate to have a man imprisoned under false accusation when he covets that man's wife. He even goes so far as to order the murder of the wife of a man who is in his way. When the crime is discovered, he commits suicide.

It is not possible to state whether Ahmad Beramka based his own poem on his personal knowledge of the events, on the news published in *Bintang Betawi* or another journal, on the prose story by Gouw Peng Liang, or on the syair by Y.L.M. Here again we have a poem inspired by a criminal affair of the first years of this century, but this time Ahmad Beramka's work seems to be original. It was not rare at that time for the same subject to be handled by several authors one after the other.

Ahmad Beramka's language too is comparable to that of his contemporary fellow writers. It belongs to that variety of Malay spoken in the big cities which was the vehicle of popular literature before the standardization initiated by Balai Poestaka (Salmon 1981:115-22). Ahmad Beramka is less Jakartan than some of his contemporaries. It is striking, for instance, that when adapting stanzas from Y.L.M.'s *Sair Java Bank di rampok*, he systematically replaced *tra*[27] by *tidak* or *tiada* and the suffix *-in* by *-kan*.

Balai Poestaka novels would not only promote a concern with 'good language', but they would also introduce psychological analysis. Ahmad Beramka's syair belong to a literary genre which, perhaps because it draws its substance from current events, pays more attention to the realism of facts than

---

[27] This word is not in dictionaries, which record only *terada*. The word *tra* occurs also, for instance, in the two *Sair Njaie Dasima* published in 1879 (Hellwig 1986:53).

that of characters. Be it the crimes of Lo Fenkui or the love affair of Nona Lao Fatnio, depiction of the characters almost does not exist.

The best example of this feature is the *Sair Sultan Muhammad Sidik Syah,* which relates in great detail the marriage of Raden Mas Tirta Adhi Surya to the daughter of the Sultan of Bacan. Now that we have a long and excellent biography of Tirta Adhi Surya (*Sang Pemula* by Pramoedya Ananta Toer, 1985), we read the poem in expectation of a contemporary portrait and appreciation of this illustrious figure. But nothing of the kind is to be found in the poem: we learn everything about Tirta's costume and time schedule, but his portrait is limited to the cliché 'In Java nobody was his match'. In this sense, and despite its modern setting and language, this syair is purely traditional.

This poem, as we have seen, is not signed. It does not seem to exist elsewhere than in Ahmad Beramka's collection and it is therefore possible that Ahmad Beramka is its author. When between 1909 and 1912 Ahmad Beramka undertook to write this 771-page manuscript, he may have copied poems that he had written previously; he may also have composed at that time the 15 poems one after the other. In any case, it seems probable that he is the author of the 15 poems – the author as the term was understood at that time, that is, he retold in verse news items already known to his contemporaries, drawing his material from the newspapers or from the works of his fellow writers, and occasionally he borrowed from them part of their works.

The most conspicuous feature in this regard is the identity of his fellow writers. Of the ten titles which Ahmad Beramka shared with books published by other writers,[28] all the writers concerned are Chinese peranakan, with the exception of Wiggers, who is the co-author of the *Sair Java Bank di rampok*.[29]

Printed literature at that time, which became a source of inspiration for Ahmad Beramka, was for a great part written and published by the Chinese. We have a good example here of the interpenetration (or should we say the identity?) of the so-called Chinese-Malay literature and the Malay one. The literature produced by the Chinese was not isolated, even if it had some characteristics of its own. It was one of the most active agents of the modernization of Malay literature. In the case of Ahmad Beramka, some of the 'Chinese-Malay' works were assimilated and incorporated into a collection intended for a mixed Batavian public.

---

[28] The most well-known example is that of the *Tjerita Njai Dasima* by G. Francis, first published in 1896: two syair were published afterwards, one by Tjiang O.S. in 1897, the other by Lie Kim Hok the same year (Salmon 1981:26, 127; Hellwig 1986).

[29] A second exception could be M. bin Moehamad Sentol, who published in the thirties a tiny volume (*Roepa-roepa Sair rame*) including a syair entitled *Orang maen kartoe*. Yet this author is registered in Salmon's bibliography (1981:252).

Realism has a deep-rooted tradition in Malay literature, especially in syair form. A number of poems relating contemporary wars in great and accurate detail have been edited, one of the earliest being the famous *Syair Perang Mengkasar* (Skinner 1963), and we know that topical compositions were sung at the courts of Aceh and Patani in the early 17th century,[30] to mention but two examples.

What is new in Ahmad Beramka and his fellow writers' works is the social and geographical scope of their topics: the main characters of their stories are mostly common people from various ethnic groups. Everyday life comes to the fore. Murders, sentimental affairs, robberies, insurrections become material for literature. The fate of a Sundanese nyai in the Moluccas, the tribulations of a Dutch thief in Batavia, or the mischiefs of a Chinese trader in Java are deemed worthy of a syair. Writers pay attention to what happens anywhere within the borders of the Indies. Literature becomes a literature of news. This phenomenon is partly provoked by the emergence of the press, which brings to the view of the public sensational events previously beyond its horizon. People become curious about what is happening hundreds of miles away, they become conscious of being part of a certain community larger than that of their family, district or town.

Muhammad Bakir's unreal stories, with their heroes endowed with superhuman faculties, give way to the news items and the everyday-life characters of Ahmad Beramka. This 'news literature' focuses not on characters, however, but on facts. Despite the titles, which are frequently personal names, acts and not actors are described. Literature has to be informative and entertaining as well, and the ultimate aim is moral: the stories provide the public with examples, usually negative ones. Whereas traditional literature puts forward ideal models of behaviour and social values, the new type of reading presents models *not* to be followed.

These radical changes in mentality were shared by the authors and their audience alike. In the case of the Fadlis' library, the public may have had a particular type of influence on the authors. The situation was no longer that of (traditional) public oral performances by professional storytellers, and it was not yet that of (modern) individual reading. The manuscripts were rented by individuals who read them aloud for an audience. Yet the authors were still in

---

[30] The French merchant Augustin de Beaulieu attended an entertainment at Sultan Iskandar Muda's palace in 1621, where 15 or 20 women were singing the sultan's conquests (Lombard 1967:142). The *Hikayat Patani* records the name of a few compositions of the Patani opera troupe around 1640, including accounts of the wars of Malacca against the Portuguese and Johor against Jambi (Teeuw and Wyatt 1970:115-6).

direct contact with the public. The readers came to the author's house and we may surmise that they questioned him about the contents of the stories, and that they opened and had a look at the various books on the shelves before choosing a title. It is probable also that the owners of the library would not have entrusted somebody unknown with a manuscript. In other words an exchange took place. The author was subjected to comments and criticism; he had to answer questions; he knew immediately what was liked or disliked, which genres were more in favour than others; he knew whether his jokes had provoked laughter,[31] whether his adventures had excited passion, whether he had been able to charm his public, or whether he had to modify his stories and his style; he could see what was most favoured: hikayat or syair, long or short texts, wayang stories or epics. His living was actually dependent on the response he would prove able to give to his customers' demand. In brief, the public was in a position to influence the production.

The evolution of literary taste and values which we can observe within the corpus of the manuscripts produced by the Fadlis reflects cultural transformation. With Sapirin bin Usman, Muhammad Bakir and Ahmad Beramka, we have an example of the transition between tradition and modernity within a limited milieu localized in time and space. The very few works by Sapirin that have survived show an extremely self-conscious author writing edifying tales and wayang stories for an Islamic audience. Muhammad Bakir proves to be a very productive and imaginative writer. All his works (almost 30 in number) are traditional by genre, but incongruous insertions in this traditional framework testify to a care for rationalism, a concern for realism, and a consciousness of conflicting values. Ahmad Beramka is less talented than his older cousin. His works belong to both traditional literature and the new type of reading which was growing at the turn of the 19th century under the leadership of Chinese authors.

Two types of literature coexist side by side in the family library produced by the same writers and read/heard by the same public. The *Syair Ken Tambuhan* and the poems about nyai and murderers were enjoyed by the same audience at the same time. Elements of modernity emerge in different ways in the three authors' works. Traditional genres are still ever-present, but in the span of fifty years we can see the transformation process at work which will lead to modern literature.

---

[31]   A few scribbles in the margins of some manuscripts reflect the spontaneous reaction of a reader: more than once it is the protest of someone shocked by an erotic scene or word.

Bibliography

Braginsky, V.I. and M.A. Boldyreva
1977   'Opisaniye malayskih rukopisey v sobranii leningradskogo otdeleniya Instituta vostokovedeniya an SSSR' (Description of the Malay manuscripts kept in Leningrad), in: B.B. Parnickel (ed.), *Malaisko-indoneziiskie issledovaniya; Sbornik statei pamyati akademika A.A. Gubera*, pp. 131-67. Moskwa: Nauka.

Chambert-Loir, H.
1984   'Muhammad Bakir: A Batavian scribe and author in the nineteenth century', *Review of Indonesian and Malayan Affairs* 18(Summer):44-72.

Hellwig, T.
1986   'Njai Dasima, een vrouw uit de literatuur', in: C.M.S. Hellwig and S.O. Robson (eds), *A man of Indonesian letters; Essays in honour of Professor A. Teeuw*, pp. 48-66. Dordrecht/Cinnaminson: Foris. [KITLV, Verhandelingen 121.]

Iskandar, T.
1981   'Some manuscripts formerly belonging to Jakarta lending libraries', in: N. Phillips and K. Anwar (eds), *Papers on Indonesian languages and literatures*, pp. 145-52. London: Indonesian Etymological Project; Paris: Archipel.

Jamilah Haji Ahmad (ed.)
1981   *Hikayat Sempurna Jaya*. Kuala Lumpur: Dewan Bahasa dan Pustaka.

Juynboll, H.H.
1899   *Catalogus van de Maleische en Sundaneesche handschriften der Leidsche Universiteits-Bibliotheek*. Leiden: Brill.

Kartodirdjo, Sartono
1976   *Protest movements in rural Java*. Kuala Lumpur: Oxford University Press.

Kern, H.
1948   'Uit de verslagen van Dr W. Kern, taalambtenaar op Borneo, 1938-1941', *Tijdschrift voor Indische Taal-, Land- en Volkenkunde* LXXXII 3-4:538-47.

Koster, G.L.
1986   'The soothing works of the seducer and their dubious fruits: interpreting the Syair Buah-Buahan', in: C.M.S. Hellwig and S.O. Robson (eds), *A man of Indonesian letters; Essays in honour of Professor A. Teeuw*, pp. 73-99. Dordrecht/Cinnaminson: Foris. [KITLV, Verhandelingen 121.]
Kratz, E.U.
1977   'Running a lending library in Palembang in 1886 A.D.', *Indonesia Circle* 14:3-12.
1989   'Hikayat Raja Pasai: a second manuscript', *Journal of the Malaysian Branch of the Royal Asiatic Society* 62-1:1-10.
Lombard, D.
1967   *Le Sultanat d'Atjéh au temps d'Iskandar Muda, 1607-1636*. Paris: Ecole Française d'Extrême-Orient.
Lombard-Salmon, C.
1972   'Société peranakan et utopie: deux romans sino-malais (1934-1939)', *Archipel* 3:169-95.
Overbeck, H.
1934   'Malay animal and flower shaers', *Journal of the Malayan Branch of the Royal Asiatic Society* 12-2:108-48.
Ronkel, Ph.S. van
1921   *Supplement-catalogus der Maleische en Minangkabausche handschriften in de Leidsche Universiteits-Bibliotheek*. Leiden: Brill.
Salmon, C.
1981   *Literature in Malay by the Chinese of Indonesia: A provisional annotated bibliography*. Paris: Maison des Sciences de l'Homme.
Skinner, C.
1963   *Sjaᶜir Perang Mengkasar (The rhymed chronicle of the Macassar war) by Entji' Amin*. 's-Gravenhage: Nijhoff. [KITLV, Verhandelingen 40.]
1978   'Transitional Malay literature, part I: Ahmad Rijaluddin and Munshi Abdullah', *Bijdragen tot de Taal-, Land- en Volkenkunde* 134:466-87.
1982   *Ahmad Rijaluddin's Hikayat Perintah Negeri Benggala*. The Hague: Nijhoff. [KITLV, Bibliotheca Indonesica 22.]
Sweeney, A.
1980   *Reputations live on; An early Malay autobiography*. Berkeley: University of California Press.

Sweeney, A. (ed.)
1980   *The Tarikh Datu' Bentara Luar Johor.* Berkeley: University of
            California Press.
Teeuw, A. and D.K. Wyatt
1970   *Hikayat Patani; The story of Patani.* The Hague: Nijhoff. 2 vols.
            [KITLV, Bibliotheca Indonesica 5.]
Toer, Pramoedya Ananta
1963   *Realisme-sosialis dan sastra Indonesia.* Djakarta: Prasaran di
            FSUI. [Jakarta, stencil, 1980.]
1982   *Tempo Doeloe; Antologi sastra pra-Indonesia.* Jakarta: Hasta
            Mitra.
1985   *Sang Pemula.* Jakarta: Hasta Mitra.
Watson, C.W.
1971   'Some preliminary remarks on the antecedents of modern
            Indonesian literature', *Bijdragen tot de Taal-, Land- en Volken-
            kunde* 127:417-33.

Appendix

THE FADLIS' LENDING LIBRARY

The Jakarta National Library collection of Malay manuscripts contains (at least)
25 titles from Muhammad Bakir's library (among which only one was not
copied by Muhammad Bakir himself). At six different times between 1887 and
1892, Muhammad Bakir made up lists of manuscripts he had for rent. 15 titles
on those lists are not to be found in the Jakarta collection, but two of them are
now kept in Leningrad. Another list of 14 syair is added in verse form at the
end of the *Sair Buah-Buahan.* In the same poem, some characters read eight
traditional texts which seem to be part of Muhammad Bakir's collection as well,
as three of them are actually preserved in Jakarta and Leningrad.

By putting together these various pieces of information, we obtain a list of
61 titles which most probably were part of Muhammad Bakir's lending library
around 1890. The seven manuscripts kept at the Leiden University library, and
the ten manuscripts kept at the Leningrad branch of the USSR Academy of
Sciences were more or less simultaneously part of the Fadlis' lending library in
Pecenongan.

MANUSCRIPTS KEPT IN JAKARTA

1 Hikayat Agung Sakti, Ml 260 (also in lists).
2 Hikayat Asal Mulanya Wayang, Ml 241 (also in lists).
3 Hikayat Begerma Cendera, Ml 239 (also in lists; the only manuscript not written by Muhammad Bakir).
4 Hikayat Gelaran Pandu Turunan Pandawa, Ml 253 (also in lists).
5 Hikayat Indera Bangsawan, Ml 245.
6 Hikayat Maharaja Garbak Jagat, Ml 251 (also in lists).
7 Hikayat Merpati Mas, Ml 249 (also in lists).
8 Hikayat Nabi Bercukur, Ml 256-2.
9 Hikayat Nakhoda Ashik, Ml 261 (lists: Hikayat Isma Tuturan Nakhoda Sunkar bi'l-Malih).
10 Hikayat Panji Semirang, Ml 177.
11 Hikayat Purasara, Ml 178.
12 Hikayat Seri Rama, Ml 252 (also in lists).
13 Hikayat Sultan Taburat, Ml 183 and 257-259 (also in lists).
14 Hikayat Syah Mandewa, Ml 243 (cf. no. 28).
15 Hikayat Syahrul Indera, Ml 242.
16 Hikayat Syaikh Abdulkadir Jaelani, Ml 256-1 (also in lists).
17 Hikayat Syaikh Muhammadan al-Samman, Ml 250 (also in lists).
18 Lakon Jaka Sukara, Ml 246.
19 Sair Buah-Buahan, Ml 254.
20 Sair Cerita Wayang, Ml 248.
21 Sair Ken Tambuhan, Ml 247.
22 Sair Sang Kupu-Kupu, Ml 255-2.
23 Sair Siti Zawiyah, Ml 255-1.
24 Seribu Dongeng, Ml 240.
25 Wayang Arjuna, Ml 244.

OTHER TITLES ADVERTISED IN MUHAMMAD BAKIR'S LISTS

Hikayat Anak Pengajian (Leningrad D 446 no. 70).
Hikayat Raja Sebudak (Leningrad D 668: Hikayat Raja Budak no. 74).
26 Arjuna Mangunjaya (perhaps the same as no. 25).
27 Dongeng yang Bagus (perhaps the same as no. 24).
28 Hikayat Damarjati Anak Syah Mandewa (cf. no. 14).
29 Hikayat Jaya Lengkara.
30 Hikayat Mashudulhak.
31 Hikayat Nur Hadan.
32 Hikayat Pandawa Sakit.

33   Hikayat Seratus Satu Ceritera (perhaps the same as no. 24).
34   Hikayat Siti Hasana.
35   Hikayat Sungging Sukar Sumpira.
36   Hikayat Tamim ad-Dari.
37   Hikayat Taskhir Tukang Kas.
38   Sair Abdul Muluk.
39   Sair Ibadat.
40   Sair Palembang.
41   Sair Perang Pandawa (perhaps the same as no. 20).
42   Sair Zainal Khair Tanda Islam.

TITLES ADVERTISED AT THE END OF SAIR BUAH-BUAHAN (no. 19)
43   Sair Anggur dan Delima (no. 19).
44   Burung Bayan dan Nuri.
45   Jeruk Jepun dan Manis.
46   Laler dan Nyawan.
47   Nyamuk dan Agas.
48   Sair Binatang Hutan.
49   Sair Bunga-Bungaan.
50   Sair Jangkrik dan Gangsir.
51   Sair Kakap dan Tambera.
52   Sair Kembang Ros.
53   Sair Kuyan-Kuyan.
54   Sair Rinum Sari.
55   Sair Sang Capung (perhaps the same as no. 22).
56   Tawon dan Kumbang.

OTHER TITLES QUOTED IN THE SAIR BUAH-BUAHAN (no. 19)
     Hikayat Merpati Mas (no. 7).
     Hikayat Raden Cekel (no. 62: Hikayat Cekel Waneng Pati).
     Hikayat Sultan Taburat (no. 13).
57   Hikayat Bidasari.
58   Hikayat Raja Bermadewa.
59   Hikayat Raja Pandawa (perhaps the same as no. 4).
60   Sair Kembang Merambat (perhaps part of no. 19).
61   Sair Nasehat.

MANUSCRIPTS KEPT IN LEIDEN
62 Hikayat Angkawijaya, Cod.Or. 3221 and 3244 (Sapirin, 1858).
63 Hikayat Cekel Waneng Pati, Cod.Or. 3245 (Muhammad Bakir).
64 Hikayat Maharaja Ganda Parwa Kesuma, Cod.Or. 3241 (property of Ahmad Insab, 1870).
65 Hikayat Sempurna Jaya, Cod Or. 3247 (Cit Sapirin bin Usman, 7878).
66 Hikayat Sempurna Jaya, Cod.Or. 3246 (Muhammad Bakir, 1886; edited by Jamilah Haji Ahmad 1981).
67 Kitab Nukil and treatise on tawhid, Sn. H. 75 (Guru Cit, 1888-89).

MANUSCRIPTS KEPT IN LENINGRAD

The Dr Frank Collection
Hikayat Sultan Taburat (80-page insertion in D 446; fragment of no. 13).
68 Collection of 15 syair, B 2508 (Ahmad Beramka).
69 Collection of 153 short pieces, C 1966 (Ahmad Beramka's handwriting).
70 Hikayat Anak Pengajian, D 446 (Sapirin bin Usman).
71 Hikayat Marakarma I and II, B 2506 and D 450 (Ahmad Beramka).
72 Hikayat Marakarma, C 1967.
73 Hikayat Miraj Nabi Muhammad, B 2510.
74 Hikayat Raja Budak, D 668.
75 Hikayat Sanghyang Batara Guru dianyaya oleh Semar, B 2507 (Ahmed Mujarrab).
76 Sair Ken Tambuhan, D 450 (Ahmad Beramka's handwriting).
77 Sair Perang Ruslan dan Jepang, D 449 (Ahmad Beramka).

Contents of Ahmad Beramka's collection of Syair (no. 68)
a Ini Sair Tamba Sia Betawi yang sudah kejadian di Betawi pada tahun 1851-1856, p. 1.
b Ini Sair Tuan Gentis di Betawi yang sudah kejadian di Betawi 22 Nopember tahun 1902, p. 273.
c Ini Sair dari Muhammad Saleh yang betul sudah kejadian di Betawi Meester Cornelis, p. 299.
d Ini Sair Nyai Dasima yang telah sudah kejadian di Betawi pada tahun 1813.
e Ini Sairnya Hasan Mukmin di Tanah Jawa yang betul sudah kejadian perang sabil di Gedangan pada 19 Juni 1905, p. 417.
f Sair Sultan Muhammad Sidik Syah di Bacan yang tatkala mengawinkan anaknya Putri Fatimah pada bangsawan Jawa Raden Mas Tirta Adi Surya yang betul sudah kejadian pada 8 Februari 1906, p. 426.

g   Inilah Sair Nyai Ima yang betul sudah kejadian di Tanah Maluku itu, p. 481.

h   Ini Sairnya Abu Nawas yang betul sudah kejadian di negeri Bagdad, p. 501.

i   Ini Sair Baba Bujang Nona Bujang, p. 653.

j   Sair Nona Kimgiok Nio istrinya Letnan Cina The Kinggi gila komidi bangsawan namanya Sitingshan adanya.

k   Ini Sair Anak Kwalon atawa Ibu Tiri, p. 731.

l   Sair Baba Lo Fenkui pachter afiun di Banjar Negara, p. 744.

m   Sair Nona Lao Fatnio di Bogor yang betul sudah kejadian di Bogor 15 Nopember 1909, p. 751.

n   Sair Kartu, p. 756.

o   Sairnya Capjiki, p. 760.

YUS RUSYANA

Literary uses of folkloristic materials in Sundanese novels

I. The study of folklore in literature

Folklore and the novel are both verbal arts. Although there are differences between them, and some of these are supposed to be in opposition to each other, it turns out that they can merge: folklore can merge into the novel. This is very interesting in several respects.

Firstly, for folklore scholars and observers, novels and other literary works are a printed source alongside magazines, newspapers, local histories, pamphlets, almanacs, and diaries. Although in these sources folk traditions observed or heard by the writers are not noted word for word, they are important for the collection of folklore. The most compelling reason, as stated by Dorson, is that the concept of fieldwork dates only from the early 19th century, so that in order to provide historical antecedents for contemporary specimens of oral and material culture, the folklorist must comb earlier records. Then comes the question of how to locate, identify, and evaluate the quality of folklore in a vast labyrinth of printed words (Dorson 1972:466).

Secondly, it is interesting to note that imaginary folklore is blended within the novel, which is born within the convention of realism. This is an example of the merging of two 'opposing' types of literature: oral-written, imaginary-realistic, old-new. It is interesting to see how the novelist manipulates folkloristic materials, and how the materials are transformed by the writer's creativity and the conventions of the novel.

Thirdly, it is also interesting that folklore did not die with the birth of the new genre and the coming of printing technology. What happens is that folkloristic materials survive in the novels and are spread by the medium of printing. In other words, folklore still survives in a society that is already using the technology of printing. It is important to note that by mentioning that folklore still survives one does not mean to restrict folklore to only a dead survival from the past, because, as has been stated by Dundes, the folklore of social protest and the folklore of computers demonstrate convincingly that folklore is a living aspect of the modern world (Dundes 1975:33-4). Moreover, because of the close relationship between literature and folklore, this particular phenomenon requires more attention from scholars of literature.

Considering that the topic is related to folklore as well as to literature, a theoretical basis for the two is needed. Folklore and literature are part of the verbal arts so that there is a close tie between folklore and literature, and the same can be said of the science of folklore and literary study (Propp 1984a:5-6). Methods of literary analysis can be used to explore the genre of folklore, its structure, its device of poetical language, and to find the most distinctive poetics of the artistic beauty of folklore. But because there are differences between folklore and literature, literary analysis by itself is unable to explain them, and for that purpose historical study and ethnography are needed to explain the genesis of folklore and its early development (Propp 1984a:9-15).

The problem discussed in this article is not the study of folklore in its broad sense as described above, but concerns only the study of folklore in literature, so that it limits itself to the same basis as the science of folklore and literary study, by keeping in mind Dundes's warning that the study of folklore in literature cannot be expected to advance as long as folklorists identify without interpreting, and literary critics interpret without identifying folklore sources (Dundes 1980:213). Note also Culler's reminder (in Teeuw 1984:142) that to engage in the study of literature is not to produce yet another interpretation of *King Lear* but to advance one's understanding of the conventions and operations of an institution, a mode of discourse.

To get a picture of how folkloristic materials are used in Sundanese novels, the following steps have been taken: 1. to identify a possible folkloristic element or form occurring in Sundanese novels and to identify its sources; 2. to differentiate which are folkloristic elements and which are the work of the novelist, including the changes made by the novelist to the folkloristic elements; 3. to analyse text and context of the folkloristic elements to uncover their structure and why they are used on a given occasion in Sundanese novels; and 4. to interpret the use of folkloristic elements within the conventions of the novel.

The Sundanese novels to be used in this discussion were all published before World War II, the time of the birth and early development of the novel in Sundanese. They are:

Joehana, *Tjarios Agan Permas* (AP – The story of Agan Permas), 1926.

R. Memed Sastrahadiprawira, *Tjarita Mantri Djero* (MD – The story of an official in the royal household), 1928.

R. Memed Sastrahadiprawira, *Pangeran Kornel* (PK – Prince colonel), 1930.

Mohamad Ambri, *Boerak Siloeman* (BS – Spirit), 1932.
Mohamad Ambri, *Ngawadalkeun Njawa* (NN – Offering the soul), 1932.

II. *Existence of folkloristic materials in Sundanese novels*

According to their type, folkloristic materials used in Sundanese novels are: narratives (myth, legend, folktale); other folklore elements such as *uga*, *cacandran, totonden, tabir mimpi,* and *paribasa*; and old forms of poetry. Their place in the novel can be divided into folklore as a basis or major part of the plot of the novel, folklore as a minor part of the novel, and folklore as small elements scattered throughout the discourses of the novels.

Folk narratives as a major part in the novel

There are Sundanese novels using old folk narratives as the basis of their plot: the whole sequence of the novel is based on folk narrative. A clear example of this is *BS*. Included in this type are *NN* and *PK*.

BS uses the tale of *dedemit* and *siluman* (spirit) and the tales of *kajajaden,* which are very common in Sundanese folklore. The story of dedemit is a folktale in which its hero is a siluman whose role is to punish people who break a prohibition or tradition in a certain place, while in kajajaden the hero is a man who later becomes a ghostly animal (Rusyana and Raksanagara 1978:51). The whole plot of *BS* is similar to that of the story of siluman and kajajaden. The main character in *BS* breaks the prohibition on going to the *jamban* (a place for washing and bathing) at dusk: pregnant women and virgins should not go there; the prohibition says: 'ulah ka cai sereupna', meaning 'do not go to the water at dusk'.

The plot in *BS* is as follows: Nyi Asmanah, a girl, loves a siluman that enters her imagination as Prince Arjuna (one of the five Pandawa heroes). Her love for the siluman is so great that she refuses the love of a young man who offers to marry her. Her odd love grows stronger, so that she abandons the life of an ordinary human being and follows the call of the siluman, loses her human consciousness, and so becomes a siluman herself.

It is very possible that this story comes from folklore, because stories of a human being becoming a siluman and various prohibitions on virgins are well known in Sundanese folklore. Moh. Ambri, the writer of *BS*, knew the stories very well, and has collected folklore in his *Dongeng-dongeng Sasakala* (volume I), which contains folktales, legends, and myths. In his story *Munjung* (to serve the siluman), folktales, legends, and myths are constructed in frames, using the conversations of nightwatchmen as the frame. In *BS* folklore is moulded into a long story as if it truly happened, although the characteristics of a tale are still found: it is full of imaginary elements, such as a human being entering the siluman world.

The other novel using folklore as its major part is *NN*. Before presenting the main plot of the novel, the story of the main character's ancestors is introduced. Viewed from the structure of the story, this part has little to do with the main plot. As in any other folktale, it does not present details of characters, place, or time, but lays more stress on the actions of the main character. *NN* has several sub-plots: a sub-plot with Datawardaya as its hero, a sub-plot with Walia as the main character, and a sub-plot with Sarimaya as heroine. In the first sub-plot, which as a whole can be accepted logically, Ajengan Datawardaya listens and comprehends the conversation between two snakes that are going to kill Walia. In tradition there is what people call *aji dipa*, by which a human being can understand the language of animals. There is also an incident in a dream world in which Datawardaya dreams of meeting his late wife, who gives him advice. The two incidents are decisive in the first sub-plot. They are not impossible in a folktale. In the second sub-plot, in which the main character is Walia – which as a whole gives the impression of really happening and has logical sequence – there is a miracle: the walking-stick inside the house suddenly buds. This part is symbolically important in this sub-plot. In the last sub-plot, with Sarimaya as the hero, there is also a miraculous incident: the journey of Sarimaya's soul to heaven, her meeting with other souls and angels, and her coming back to life.

From the interrelation of imaginary elements it is clear that *NN* uses materials from folklore. It is also mentioned on the book-cover that Moh. Ambri is not so much an author as an adapter. The folktale with Japara as a setting at the beginning of the Islamic era in Java (around the 16th and 17th century) apparently uses folklore as its source, very probably Javanese folklore.

Another novel, *PK*, seems to be using old tales too. The story about Pangeran Kornel (or Pangeran Kusumah Dinata), the regent of Sumedang (1791-1828), with his ancestors, has been spread as folklore, besides the written form of old literature called *babad*, namely the *Babad Sumedang*, written by Raden Aria Adipati Martanagara (1921). In *PK* it is also stated, in the part which relates the building of a road at Cadas Pangeran, that the writer has collected folklore. As a person who worked for the government and had a great interest in historical events, it is understandable that R. Memed Sastrahadi-prawira, the writer of this novel, knew folklore and old stories about the life of the aristocrats of Sumedang and the Sundanese in general. In folklore, events concerning the regents of Sumedang are told. In the *Babad Sumedang* there is a part which tells about the experiences of Raden Jamu, the son of the regent of Sumedang, who had to run away from his birthplace, and who after overcoming every obstacle managed to come back and become the regent of Sumedang.

Folk narratives as a minor part in the novel

Besides the use of folk narratives as a major part there is also the use of old tales as minor parts in Sundanese novels, that is, where the folk narratives are found among other parts of the novel.

The story of Aji Saka in MD

This story found in Sundanese folklore may come from Javanese sources. The story is about the Javanese-Sundanese alphabet *hanacaraka*. Aji Saka orders one of his servants, Ki Sembada, to guard his kris with the order that it may not be given to anyone but Aji Saka himself. Long afterwards, after Aji Saka has become king, he remembers his kris and orders another servant of his, Ki Dora, to fetch it. Ki Sembada is not willing to give the kris to the messenger because this was the order of the king himself. And so they quarrel and fight each other until the two faithful servants die. Aji Saka comes to the place and realizes his mistake. To commemorate the incident he writes down sentences which turn out to contain all the letters of the alphabet. This is the origin of the hanacaraka.

The story is recounted in *MD* at the time when Raden Yogaswara, the hero, is receiving his education from his father. The older man teaches him to work hard and to maintain good behaviour. While he is learning to read and write his father tells him the story, which he discusses with his son in a dialogue. The father uses the story relating the attitude of Ki Sembada and the carelessness of the king. This is meant by the father to develop Yogaswara's self-reliance. It is meant to prepare the young man for facing obstacles in later life. *MD* describes the conflict between right and wrong, where Yogaswara is on the right side; he has to face many kinds of tests, often endangering his own life. So the theme of the folktale is similar to the theme of the novel as a whole, and in particular similar to the fate of his father, who suffers because of the carelessness of his king.

The story of Kiai Gede Pamanahan in MD

This story comes from Javanese folklore and tells about Kiai Gede Pamanahan, who drinks the coconut-water served by the wife of his friend. His friend leaves the coconut-water untouched when he goes to work in the hope that he will be able to finish up all the coconut-water in accordance with the prophecy that the descendants of whoever drinks up the water will become king of Java. Later it turns out that the son of Kiai Gede Pamanahan, Sutawijaya, becomes king of Mataram.

This story is found in *MD* in the part which tells about Sutawijaya's army from Mataram being involved in a campaign to take over neighbouring kingdoms, including Nagara Tengah where the main character is serving.

This story seems to say that Nagara Tengah should surrender to Mataram because that has been prophesied. This war with Mataram is related to the test that Yogaswara has to face as commander of the army in battle, and also in facing the slander that he has had an affair with one of the king's concubines while the king was in Mataram.

The story of Cadu Ngadahar Lubang (taboo on eating eels) in MD

This story is about Dalem Nagara Tengah when he wants to go into the woods to escape from the army of Mataram. His troops cannot go on because of a big flood, so that they have to wait on the bank of the river while the enemies are approaching. They see a floating log. The log suddenly forms a kind of bridge so that the Dalem's men can go across safely. When the enemies walk on that bridge the log sinks and they are all killed. When they get to a safe place, some of the Dalem's followers find that they have the skin of an eel on their soles. Since that time they and their descendants decide that eating eels is taboo.

This incident has an important role in saving them from the enemy. Why is this fantastic story used? The writer seems to be trying to show that the followers of the Dalem are protected by their ancestors. This is meant to maintain the honour of the Dalem, who is also deferred to by the writer. He shows that the Dalem does not deny his duty as a hero, namely to fight the enemy. Here he escapes on the demand of his people so that they will not be killed in the war. This is an effort of the writer to maintain the honour of the defeated.

This kind of folklore, which in Sundanese is called *pacaduan* (taboo), is very common. It gives the reason why people or a group of people consider that eating something or doing something is taboo.

The story of Pangeran Gotama in MD

This story displays influence from outside. It tells about Prince Gotama, who is protected by his father so that he will not see the real life of his people. One day he sees an old man, a sick man, and then a dead man. He is curious to know about them, and then he asks what all of them are, and if such suffering will also happen to him. The answer is yes, that suffering is unavoidable. The prince contemplates this life and realizes that life is transient and full of suffering. To be free of this, people should do good and avoid doing evil.

This story is told by Raden Yogaswara, the hero in *MD*, on a silent night on a hill to two of his guards. He tells the men that life in this world is short, so that people had better prepare for life in the next world. The two guards are impressed by his story, so much so that they reveal the secret that they have been ordered by Raden Anggataruna to kill Yogaswara. In this way the hero is saved, so that later Yogaswara can free himself from the accusation of having had an affair with one of the Dalem's concubines.

The story of Aki Kahir in PK

This is a story about Aki Kahir, a well-known teacher of martial arts. He is a teacher of the aristocrats in Cianjur. One day he is made to fight an expert in martial arts from Macao. For a long time a fight of life and death goes on, but finally Aki Kahir wins. Aki Kahir is well known as the founder of the Cimande martial arts. This legend in *PK* is used to describe the cultural background of Cianjur, which in the 19th century was one of the cultural centres of Sunda. People there were interested in studying religion, culture, and the martial arts. To this place goes Raden Jamu, the hero in *PK*, to seek protection from Dalem Cianjur, who later gives him a good position. The story of Aki Kahir in *PK* is not told as a legend but is presented as a real event at that time.

The story of Bagus Rangin in PK

The legend of Bagus Rangin or the battle of Bantarjati is closely related to a historical event, the people's rebellion in Cirebon under the leadership of Bagus Rangin against the Dutch colonial government. Pangeran Kornel as the regent of Sumedang takes part in putting down the rebellion. This legend in *PK* is meant to picture how the hero always has to pass several tests, one of them being to crush the rebellion, and that he can do the job very well. This legend is presented as a real event in history.

The story of Pangeran Dipanegara in PK

This legend is related to the historical Diponegoro war. Pangeran Diponegoro leads a military campaign to preserve morals and defend truth. The regent of Sumedang is ordered by the colonial government to lead the regents' legion to protect the border. This story in *PK* shows how the main character always gets assignments or tests and is able to finish them well. This legend is presented as a real event at that time.

The story of 'Misdeed against parents' in AP

Imas, who later changes her name to Agan Permas, is the concubine of a Dutch tea-planter. She used to be poor. Her mother, after a long search, finally hears about her daughter. When they meet, the mother recognizes the daughter, but the daughter pretends not to know her mother and sends her servant to drive the woman away because Imas is ashamed of having a poor mother.

This part in *AP* is in fact an application of an old story with new characters and setting. In Sundanese folklore there is the story of an ungrateful child who denies his parents; one of them is that of Dalem Boncel, a very poor boy who later becomes a regent. He denies his parents so that later he becomes sick and dies.

The story of 'The mother who falls in love' in AP

Imas, the concubine of a Dutch tea-planter, falls in love with a young man, one of the clerks on the plantation. Later she finds out that the young man is her own son. She is terribly shocked, falls down, has a concussion, and dies.

This story, which is found in AP in the part that tells about Imas who is now freed from suffering and lives in luxury and then forgets herself, reminds us of the legend of Sangkuriang, the young man falling in love with a woman who later turns out to be his own mother. In Sangkuriang it is the son who falls in love, while in *AP* it is the mother. This seemingly opposite event can be considered not contradictory: if the story of Sangkuriang is viewed as a projection, as Dundes has done with the story 'Love like salt' (Dundes 1980:215), then the Sangkuriang tale is a projection of a mother who falls in love with her son, as in the story in *AP*.

Uga, cacandran, totonden, tabir mimpi, paribasa

Sundanese novels also use other folkloristic elements.
1. *Uga*, an expression containing a prophecy of what will happen in the future. For example, Sutawijaya from Mataram will win a victory in the war as prophesied in the *uga* (*MD*).
2. *Cacandran*, an expression containing a description of a place and the prophecy of its future condition. Some examples: *Bandung heurin ku tangtung*, 'Bandung overcrowded by people', *Sumedang ngarangrangan*, 'Sumedang is like a tree shedding its leaves', *Cianjur katalanjuran*, 'Cianjur is overdoing it'.
3. *Totonden* is a description of how the signs of nature are considered to influence the life of man. For instance, the coming of a comet or thunderstorm is considered to presage a historical event such as war and upheaval (*MO*).
4. *Tabir mimpi*, 'interpretation of a dream', in which the dream reflects an event in the future for someone. For example, Raden Jamu feels that he will

have problems from intrigue, and this is already reflected in his dream of being heated by fire.

5. *Paribasa*, 'proverb', is found throughout Sundanese novels including those from outside, like Javanese (*MD*).

These folkloristic elements are used to depict place, time, and cultural background relating to the events happening in the novels, and are sometimes also an element in the plot.

Forms of old verse

In Sundanese novels verses are often found in the middle of prose which in other respects has the form of a novel. In *PK*, for example, there are parts in the form of fixed verse called *guguritan,* which is usually sung. For instance, the opening contains a description of true honour in *asmarandana,* the description of a journey in *kinanti,* a letter in *dangdanggula,* and a picture of the beauty of Bogor town with the image of the kingdom of Pajajaran and a quotation from poetry in dangdanggula which is well known in Sundanese culture, in the *Guguritan Laut Kidul* (Ode to the South Sea), which is still sung today (Kalipah Apo 1921).

III. *Contact between two conventions*

Conventions of folklore and of the novel

Folklore and the novel each have their own conventions. For the basic discussion of this article it is necessary to present some aspects of these conventions.

Folklore has its own means of facing reality; among others, it does not use the connection of cause and effect, but has its own way of perceiving space and time and of considering something as real or not (Propp 1984a:10). In this way the picture of reality in folklore is different from that in the novel.

The novel, with realism as its defining characteristic, strives to imitate reality, and in this effort the formal realism of the novel allows a more immediate imitation of individual experience set in its temporal and spatial environment than other literary forms (Watt 1957:32).

Aspects of some conventions of folklore and of the novel will be discussed below.

Relation in the story

In the folktale the relation is not cause-and-effect. A reason – or, to use the language of poetics, motivation – is not required for actions. Units of the tale follow one another, but it is not necessary for this succession to be motivated; the units can follow one another according to the principle of agglutination; in other cases the action is based on pure chance (Propp 1984b:25-7).

In the novel the relation between one unit and the other is a causal relation. This is seen in the plot. The novel's plot is distinguished from most earlier fiction by its use of past experience as the cause of present action: a causal connection operating through time replaces the reliance of earlier narratives on disguises and coincidences, and this tends to give the novel a much more cohesive structure (Watt 1957:22).

Character

In folktales many of the characters have no name, and their outward appearance is rarely described: what is important is their actions. Their characterization is not individual but stereotypical, and sometimes represents a social position. All characters are either good or bad, an 'average type' does not occur in folklore. Everyone is assigned a role in the narrative and there are no extra characters, so folklore tends to have only one protagonist (Propp 1984b:27-9).

In the novel, which pays attention to particular individuals, there is particularization of character, for example by giving a proper name to show a particular identity. This is an effort to show that the novel is a full and authentic report of human experience (Watt 1957:18, 32). There are usually several characters in the novel, within the complexity of human interrelations.

Place

In folklore there is also a setting, because the action is always performed in space. But because the focus is on action, it only focuses on empirical space, that is, on the space that surrounds the hero at the moment of action and not on the surrounding environment; there is no attempt to portray the reality of the surroundings (Propp 1984b:22).

The novel, on the other hand, pays attention to place and attempts to describe its details. There is an effort to show that the novel is a full and authentic report of human experience. Also, the characters of the novel can only be individualized by being set against a background of a particularized place. A detailed picture is painted of both natural and interior scenery, in an attempt to put people wholly in their physical setting (Watt 1957:26-7).

Time

There is an element of time in folklore, and the unity of space is inseparable from the unity of time. But, like space, time in folklore cannot admit interruptions. Pauses do not exist. In folklore there is only empirical time, measured not by dates, days, or years but by the personage's action. In its awareness of time, folklore reflects the pre-agricultural stage, and its designations of time are therefore always fantastic (Propp 1984b:24-5).

In the novel, on the other hand, time is of the utmost importance. The novel has interested itself much more than any other literary form in the development of its characters in the course of time. Time is very important in defining the individuality of any subject. The characters of the novel can only be individualized if they are set against a background of particularized time. Also, the plot of the novel unfolds over the course of time, thus past experience is seen as the cause of present experience (Watt 1957:21-2).

Form of existence
Folklore works never have an author but are transmitted by word of mouth. They exist only when two agents are present, the performer and the listener, opposing each other directly. The performer does not create the work by himself, but has heard about it before; the performer, however, does more than simply transmit the work to another person. The performers do not repeat their text word for word but introduce changes into them. What is important is the fact of changeability of folklore compared with the stability of literature (Propp 1984a:6, 8).

Novels, as literary works, have an author. They are transmitted through writing. A novel, once it has arisen, no longer changes. The novel also presupposes two agents, the author and the reader. A novel is immutable, but the reader always changes, so that the reading and comprehension changes. There is no possibility for the readers to introduce any changes to suit their own personal taste or the views of their age (Propp 1984a:6-8).

These are several aspects in the conventions of folklore and the novel. Other aspects, like the use of language, will not be discussed here. In the above comparison it is evident that there are several differences between folklore and the novel. It is interesting to see what happens when folkloristic materials come into the novel, so there is contact between the conventions of the two.

Results of contact between folklore and the novel

Inclusion of convention: elaborated folklore in the novel
In the use of folkloristic materials as the major part of the novel, one of the means is to place the material in the framework of a story which describes real life, and in that story the folktale is then used critically, by saying that 'it is only folklore'. This is the case in *BS*.

In *BS* the realistic story is only a small part – the beginning and the end of the novel – and serves as the framework in which the folktale is placed. Folklore itself acquires certain features as the result of the application of the conventions of the novel.

From the narrative view, the novel *BS* consists of two layers: the first one is told by an omniscient novelist presenting Iyem, her mother, her husband, and Uncle Ijan. They are involved in a very interesting conversation. The second layer is told by Ijan as the performer and the other characters as listeners. He is telling the story about Nyi Asmanah becoming a spirit. This second layer is the major part of *BS*.

From the viewpoint of the reader of the novel, there is a sequence of distance from the reader: reader-novelist-Ijan-(Sarpiah from whom Ijan heard the story)-Nyi Asmanah (the heroine of the story). The first layer is closer to the reader than the second. The first layer gives the impression of real life. The second gives the impression that it is only a folktale. Viewing it from the impression of reality, the folktale can be divided into two parts: the first, the event when Nyi Asmanah runs away from home, gives the impression that it is real or a realistic plot; the second, the story when Nyi Asmanah becomes a spirit, does not give the impression that it happens in reality, as it has a mythical sequence or plot. This second layer very probably comes from folklore. Plot, characters, space, and time in the second layer have partly been moulded according to the conventions of the novel, and the rest remains as folklore, namely the part containing the fantastic world of spirits.

There are many characters: in the first layer five, and in the second fourteen. They are characterized by giving them names, a description, and expressions through dialogue and actions. This is especially the case for the characters in the second layer, which comes from folklore. In the characterization the writer focuses his attention on the physical appearance of the characters. But, by describing their physical appearance, he also gives only a glimpse of their inner being: the development of Nyi Asmanah's soul from her childhood, when she enjoys wayang performances and falls in love with Arjuna, up to the time when she runs away from home because she feels she is being called by Arjuna, is not fully portrayed. In describing the characters in a certain event, the writer succeeds in portraying them as living individuals, and these individual characters give an impression of their age and environment: simple people in the village living in a past age.

The background of the story is also described. The space in the first layer, a modest house in the village, is only briefly described. On the other hand, the space in the second, the world of the spirits, is elaborately portrayed: the parks, gardens, streets, buildings with their beautiful furniture, sculpture, the square, trees, baths, and the gorgeous court. In the first layer the function of the space is merely to describe where the dialogue takes place and it pictures a similar situation in a village, while the portrait of the world of spirits is used to create an appropriate atmosphere.

A sense of ancient time in the novel is created by descriptions of customs and traditions of long ago.

The writer of *BS* has tried to present folklore in the midst of real village life and has applied the conventions of the novel, and yet he still treats it as folklore. As a novelist his attitude toward folklore is expressed by its narrator: we may not believe in anything of which we are not sure of the truth.

Substitution of convention: folklore for the novel

Another way of using folkloristic materials as the major part of the novel can be considered as a further step by the writer, and can be categorized as literary invention based on literary folklore. There has been a further movement away from the source folklore, although its composition may elaborate a plot known in the tradition. This is found in the novel *NN*.

There are two sequences of plot in this novel: the plot with Ajengan Datawardaya as the hero, and the plot with Walia. In the first story the sequence of events is as follows: Datawardaya is looking for a perfect man as the husband of Sarimaya. He finds one who meets his standard: someone with a perfect voice. But afterwards he is in doubt. He cannot make up his mind. Then he uses a different standard and tries to find someone of Sarimaya's choice. Datawardaya looks once again, and again he is not sure. Finally he makes up his mind and takes a risk. His decision turns out to be right. In this plot there has been a conflict in Datawardaya: the conflict between his decision and the risk he has to take.

In the second plot, with Walia as the hero, the sequence is like this: as someone who has been cursed and has sinned, Walia tries to find true knowledge so that he can be forgiven. In his journey to seek forgiveness he faces obstacles arising from his own lust. Later he manages to develop his own good desire, and although he has not found self-assurance he becomes submissive. Because of Allah's grace he finally becomes a virtuous man.

In fact there is yet another sub-plot, with Sarimaya as the heroine. She is looking for a good husband, finds him, makes up her mind, and leaves her fate in the hands of God, so that she is even willing to sacrifice herself.

The events in the plot of Datawardaya are all common, and they are probable and logical, except certain parts. The same can be said of the plot of Walia, and of Sarimaya too. In the plot with Sarimaya the events come in a logical sequence, except for the journey of her spirit to heaven where she meets with other spirits and angels, and later she comes to life again.

In this novel the physical and mental development of the characters are treated equally. The behaviour of Ajengan Datawardaya and Walia is understandable as their inner struggle is well portrayed.

Viewed from the angle of the story as a whole, the story is panoramic, but its main plot is dramatic because the focus is on Walia's inner struggle and Datawardaya's doubts.

In general the characters are human beings; besides them there are two snakes and the angels – 18 characters in all. The characterization is done by giving names (often the meaning of these names can be traced etymologically), by making descriptions, by making pictures according to *firasat* (extrasensory power), by self-revelation through the character's own words and dialogue, and their actions. Both their inward and outward behaviour are described. The characters are typical: Datawardaya, Lembana, and Sarimaya are people from religious families: knowledgeable, virtuous, and generous. They are of the devoted religious type. But Datawardaya is portrayed as a rounded personality, with anxiety and indecisiveness. Walia is more of an individual character: he has physical appearance and an inner character. Different from the static character of Datawardaya and Sarimaya, Walia is a dynamic character. In characterizing the heroes and heroine, the novelist has succeeded in bringing them to life.

The setting in *NN* is the town of Japara; also Bombay, Jakarta, Cirebon, Pamanukan, Demak, and Ampel, places related to the characters, are mentioned. A detailed description is presented of houses, buildings, verandahs, godowns, gold vaults, mosques, and stables. There is also a description of the natural environment: the angry sea, the coast of Kalimantan, the mouth of the Ciliwung River, floods, forests, and graveyards full of shrubs. A place of the spirits is also mentioned, but without portrayal. All are sensory portrayals that function to evoke similarity or an illusion of the place where the event takes place, while the others are expressions of the character's mind. The time of the event is not mentioned in terms of year, but the writer says it happened at the time when Islam had not been long in Java. Thus it suggests that the story happens in the 16th century. The time it uses is realistic, not fantastic.

It can be concluded that the writer of *NN* has applied the conventions of the novel to the material he works with, but he leaves certain parts still as in folklore, especially those concerning the mind and world of the characters.

Integration of convention: folklore into the novel

Another way of using folkloristic materials as the major part of the novel is to integrate folklore into the novel fully, as in the novel *PK*. Here two plots are merged, one with Dalem Patrakusumah and Demang Dongkol, the other with Raden Suria as the main character.

The first plot is as follows: Demang Dongkol incites Dalem Patrakusumah to suspect a Sumedang aristocrat. Dalem Patrakusumah frees himself from the intrigue and discharges the Demang's troops, and takes Raden Suria, the Sumedang aristocrat, as his son-in-law. Demang intrigues again and tries to kill Suria. Dalem loses his son-in-law and his relations with the Sumedang aristocrat are cut off. Demang Dongkol spies on him and reports his mistakes to the Dutch. Dalem is discharged from his position as regent of Sumedang.

The other plot begins with Raden Suria suffering from slander; he is patient and careful, the slander dies away, he becomes the son-in-law of Dalem Patrakusumah; slander and intrigue again, but he tries to avoid them carefully; safe from intrigue and assassination, he becomes head of a *cutak* (district), and later regent. In this position he is assigned several tasks which he carries out very well so that he receives high honour.

The two plots are intertwined, except in parts of the second plot where some tasks are repeated. Elements in the plots are logically related, causally and also in the related actions of the characters, so that units are realistically related. The events, although not of everyday life, are not fantasy. The inner feelings and actions of the characters are both described. The portrayal of inner motivation is mostly that of the antagonistic Demang Dongkol. An interesting physical description is the deer-hunt at Tegallicin and a martial arts contest against the Chinese; even more interesting is the moral struggle when Dalem Sumedang confronts the Dutch Governor-General Daendels.

There are more than 29 characters. Characterization is done by giving names, which also shows the status of the persons; by describing physical appearance, behaviour, and attitude; by giving statements and reactions of other characters; by expressing characters through dialogue; and by presenting their actions. The characters are described by their inward and outward behaviour. The characters are of the typical and static type, and Raden Suria is a set character with good ideals suitable to an aristocrat. Demang Dongkol, on the other hand, is a static individual.

PK has Sumedang as its setting, where the hero lives. Other places are Limbangan (Garut), Cianjur, Bantarjati (Cirebon), Bogor, and Yogyakarta. In describing the setting the writer describes its environment, history, and social culture, including folk traditions. The places of action are a house or other buildings and their surroundings. The condition of the houses and other buildings, such as the mosque and the regent's residence, is only mentioned, not described. On the other hand, natural surroundings are described in detail, like nature and the atmosphere of Sumedang, the hunting ground of Tegallicin, the night atmosphere of the places that Raden Suria passes when he escapes: the moonlight, the song of the birds, the mountains, fields, and meadows, the coffee plants in blossom, the geographical condition of Cianjur, and so on. The natural environment as a background is presented in the form of sensory impression, reaction, and association, and functions to give depth to the events, besides portraying them; in other parts it evokes feelings and atmosphere.

The time of the novel *PK* is the 18th century, when the regencies of Sunda were under the Dutch government. It is explicitly stated that the time is between 1775 and 1828. The time is realistically presented in year, month, and day.

So, in *PK* the folkloristic materials which are the main part of the novel have been fully integrated into the conventions of the novel. The plot and events are all in keeping with the conventions.

Preservation of convention: folklore in the novel
When folkloristic materials are only a small part in the novel, they are not changed conventionally. They are still treated as folklore, and retain their original characteristics; in this way the folkloristic text is presented in its context, and it is said exactly how, when, where, to whom, and by whom the story is uttered on a given occasion, so that the texture fits the context. This kind of use of folkloristic materials can be considered as a preservation of folklore in printed sources, namely in a novel, and is handed down in this way. It is possible that it also continues orally, as commonly happens.

The stories preserved are: 'Aji Saka', 'Kiai Gede Pamanahan', 'Taboo to eat eels', 'Prince Gotama' (all in *MD*), 'Aki Kahir', 'Bagus Rangin', 'Prince Dipanegara' (in *PK*). In the stories 'Ungrateful child' and 'The mother who falls in love with her son' in *AP* the folklore plot is used in the novel. Also included in the preserved elements are: uga, cacandran, totonden, interpretation of dreams, proverbs, and other forms of old verse.

In fact, in everyday life folkloristic materials are alive and used even in the educated community, so that it is not strange that a novel containing a full and authentic report of human experiences should have these elements.

IV. The creativity of the author: transforming folk imagination into literary work

In the discussion above it was clear that there has been contact between folklore conventions and those of the novel, with certain consequences. Folklore has been elaborated, substituted, and integrated with the conventions of the novel. A change of the materials has taken place because of the conventions of the novel. By comparing some aspects of the conventions of the two genres, in fact, one can predict what interference may result from the contact. But what actually happens and how it happens are determined by another factor, which is unpredictable: the creativity of the novelist. Novelists have a free hand: they may accept or refuse, wholly or partly, and they may add or take away. Also, how an author puts the material into reality, into a world of creativity, depends wholly on him or her. The following part of this article is an attempt to trace, where possible, what has happened to the folklore as a result of the writer's work.

Arranging the story into a plot

Do Sundanese novels use folklore as materials for the story only, or do they work them out further into a plot? Plot is a sequence of events, but these events should be arranged into a structure of cause and effect. It turns out that some novelists have arranged the stories into plots, as in *PK*. In this novel the writer is able to construct a plot that can evoke maximum emotional effect. This is also true with the writers of *BS* and *NN*.

Thus, in using a tradition that they know, the writers of Sundanese novels have found a new way of weaving traditional elements or adapting them to the demands of realistic illusion.

In the plot the writers have created conflicts, both physical and mental. In *PK* there is the physical conflict between one character and another, and between a character and his inner self. In *BS* there is a conflict between the conscience of a human being and the call of a spirit. In *NN* the conflict is in a man who tries to fulfil his responsibility in life. Most of the conflicts end happily: the victory of human hope.

Characterization

The writers have worked out the characterization intensively, as is evident in *PK* and *NN*. The characters are depicted in the third person, and the writers act as omniscient novelist. In *PK* and *NN* the characters as third persons are in direct relation with the writers and readers, while in *BS* (the second layer) they are in a more distant relation to the writer and reader.

And so, because of the creativity of the writers, the heroes and heroines have names, character, religious identity, and social status as belonging to the aristocracy or as commoners. They are involved in human relationships, with different nuances of feeling. The writers describe their condition, physical as well as mental and moral, and create their dialogue, their behaviour and actions.

Description of place and time

The writers portray the place where the actions take place: they give a detailed description of houses, buildings, and surroundings, not only to identify the place of events, but also to create a similarity to reality, to support characterization, to build up atmosphere, and even to become a decisive factor for the characters. The writers also link all the events with a particular time, and give a picture of a certain time.

Assigning a theme

It is the writer who assigns a theme as an important basis in the structure of the novel. In *PK* the main theme is 'egoic', namely that in this life people always have to face difficulties and obstacles as a test; the one who works well and conscientiously is one who passes the tests. A good person can overcome all his or her problems, and is always ready and alert to face trials.

In *NN* the writer takes a spiritual theme: a perfect person is the one who scores high in religion, ethics, knowledge, aesthetics, and economy. In searching for truth the theme is: searching for knowledge is looking for truth, because of the urge to know, and all of these are only because of God's will. In *BS* the writer has *kasilumanan* (the spectral world) as theme: someone who is attracted by her imagination or imaginary world and refuses reality will be tempted by the spirit.

Performing the folklore

The writer has done his job as performer of folklore through the characters who tell stories, such as in 'Aji Saka' and 'Taboo on eating eels'. As a performer he not only tells the story as he has heard it, but also makes some changes to fit conditions in the context of the novel.

Expression of attitudes

In the novel the writer's attitudes are mirrored. They reflect the writer's way of thinking and feeling. In *BS* the writer, who has a taste for realism, tackles in a descriptive way the life of people in the villages, which is full of suffering. He describes the problem as it really is, without adding to it or diminishing it. But as a writer he is critical: he expresses his opinion on the superstition of the village people. In *PK* the writer considers aristocrats as a moral ideal: it is the aristocracy who have the chance to excel in morality, because they have the power. But if they do not fulfil the tasks or function of the aristocracy they will meet their downfall. In *NN* the writer puts forward his concept of a perfect person: it is a rounded whole consisting of several aspects: moral behaviour, knowledge, economy, artistic accomplishment, nobility, and a good body or appearance.

Creating composition to evoke the illusion of reality

Above all, the writer has absorbed and assimilated the materials into a form, and what previously is folk imagination becomes a composition that can evoke the illusion of reality. *PK* and *NN* have attained the level of good literature, which can evoke the illusion of reality, or in other words fulfil an aesthetic function.

In conclusion, Sundanese novelists have used folkloristic materials and transformed them into works of literature by using their creativity and taking account of the conventions of the novel.

V. Closing remarks

Based on the previous discussion the following notes can be put forward.

In Sundanese novels there are elements that can be identified as folkloristic materials, in the form of narratives and other elements, such as uga, cacandran, totonden, interpretation of dreams, proverbs, and old verse, both as a major part in the plot of the novels and as a minor part scattered throughout their discourse. The texture and text of the folkloristic materials have undergone adaptation to suit their context in the novel.

There are differences between the conventions of the novel and those of folklore, as seen in the relation between parts of the plot, characterization, description of place and time, and their form of existence. In Sundanese novels, contact between two genres has resulted in the placement of elaborated folklore within the novel, substitution of the folklore for the novel, integration of folklore into the novel, and preservation of folklore in the novel.

By considering the conventions of folklore and the novel, Sundanese writers have produced new works using their creative freedom in such a way that the folkloristic materials they draw on have also undergone changes. The writers have moulded the stories into a plot, have worked on the characterization of the dramatis personae, have made a description of place and time, have presented themes as a unifying principle in the structure of the novel, have expressed their own attitudes, and have made changes to the text in order to fit into their context, so that a new composition evoking the illusion of reality then emerges. As a consequence of the contact between the conventions of folklore on the one hand and of the novel on the other, combined with the creativity of writers in their work, certain transformations in the folklore found in Sundanese novels have taken place.

Bibliography

Ambri, Mohamad
1932   *Boerak siloeman, Sasakala panganten awewe teu meunang ka tjai tengah poë*. Weltevreden: Balai Poestaka.
1932   *Ngawadalkeun njawa*. Weltevreden: Balai Poestaka.
1944-46   *Dongeng-dongeng sasakala*. Djakarta: Balai Poestaka.
Apo, Kalipah
1921   'Dangdanggoela Laoet Kidoel', *Volksalmanak Soenda* 3:240-6.
Dorson, Richard M.
1972   'The use of printed sources', in: Richard M. Dorson (ed.), *Folklore and folklife*, pp. 465-77. Chicago: University of Chicago Press.
Dundes, Allan
1980   *Interpreting folklore*. Bloomington: Indiana University Press.
1975   'The study of folklore in literature and culture: identification and interpretation', in: Allan Dundes, *Analytic essays in folklore*, pp. 28-34. The Hague: Mouton.
Joehana
1926   *Tjarios Agan Permas*. Bandoeng: Dachlan Bekti.
Martanagara, Raden Aria Adipati
1921   'Babad Soemedang', *Volksalmanak Soenda* 3:209-33.
Propp, Vladimir
1984a   'The nature of folklore', in: Anatoly Liberman (ed.), *The theory and history of folklore*, pp. 3-15. Minneapolis: University of Minnesota Press.

1984b   'Folklore and reality', in: Anatoly Liberman (ed.), *The theory and history of folklore*, pp. 16-38. Minneapolis: University of Minnesota Press.

Rusyana, Yus and Ami Raksanagara
1978   *Sastra lisan Sunda; Ceritera karuhun, kajajaden, dan dedemit.* Jakarta: Pusat Pembinaan dan Pengembangan bahasa, Departemen Pendidikan dan Kebudayaan.

Sastrahadiprawira, R. Memed
1928   *Tjarita mantri djero.* Weltevreden: Balai Poestaka. 2 vols.
1930   *Pangeran Kornel.* Weltevreden: Balai Poestaka.

Teeuw, A.
1984   *Sastra dan ilmu sastra; Pengantar teori sastra.* Jakarta: Pustaka Jaya.

Watt, Ian
1957   'Realism and the novel form', in: Ian Watt, *The rise of the novel*, pp. 9-34. Berkeley: University of California Press.

C.W. WATSON

Religion, nationalism, and the individual in modern Indonesian autobiography
Hamka's Kenang-Kenangan Hidup

Any doubts which we might have had about the appropriateness of autobiography as a subject of literary criticism have now surely been dispelled by the recent work in the United States, to which we owe the demonstration that autobiography is not only a literary genre with specific characteristics which make it amenable to modern literary critical approaches, but that it also shares certain fictive conventions with other genres, above all lyrical poetry and the novel, which qualify it to be considered from the same perspectives as these other modes of self-expression. The attention to autobiography has also been stimulated by the reaction against the New Criticism – noted among others by Professor Teeuw – which has led critics once more to turn to biographical information as an integral element of critical interpretation. In this respect Wimsatt's important article on 'The Intentional Fallacy', often considered the definitive statement of the New Critics in their rejection of authorial interventions in interpretation, has been stood on its head to show that Wimsatt's strictures, far from being as clear-cut as he had intended, open up new sets of critical possibilities in relation, not so much to the superficial meaning of a text, but to the analysis at a more profound level of what are variously labelled sub-texts, 'différances', critical absences, and so on, in which not only marginal minutiae and syntactic peculiarity, but also intellectual biographies make vital contributions.

There is, then, no longer a need to preface a critical study of an autobiography with an apologetic defence of the enterprise. The argument which justified the new critical attention, which in its time had proceeded from dissatisfaction with the intellectual inchoateness of earlier histories of autobiography – although to the observant even these contained seeds of the new hermeneutics, deriving in some measure from Dilthey's interest in autobiography as self (and species) interpretation – has now in its turn been displaced by a worried metacritical insistence on trying to distinguish autobiography as a genre with specific formal properties of structure. The most immediate way of establishing that structure has appeared to be through recalling the original descriptive ethnography of autobiography, but holding that earlier tradition at a distance by an appeal to the new critical advances in historical and anthropological methodology.

Thus these new taxonomists of autobiography distinguish among acknowledged autobiographies with the aid of an historical and anthropological calculus. In such a reckoning, for example, Augustine's *Confessions* is taken as the first example of autobiographical writing, not because it is the first text in which the writer refers to himself, but because it is the first in which the object of the study, its focus, is the unfolding development of the writer's ego. Holding this to be the single significant criterial innovation within an ongoing cultural tradition, the criticism poses the question, why was it, if we concede this primacy, that the *Confessions* was written when it was? And, as we might have expected, an answer is provided in terms of a paradigm which describes the impact of Christian theology on the self-consciousness of the European individual made aware for the first time in his history of his personal responsibility for his own salvation. In this way, tautologically defined, autobiography can only be written in the context of a certain theodicy, with the corollary that as the theodicy comes to be challenged and modified as a consequence and cause of historical change, so too the accidental features of autobiography change. Plotting the progress of intellectual development within an historical context allows the criticism then to account for the rise of modern autobiography, this time with Rousseau's *Confessions* as the first example of a totally self-referential individualism.

Similarly struck by the peculiarity of the text's self-reflection but less concerned with charting the history of the genre, other critics, sharing the historian's assumptions that the emergence of the form is peculiar to a certain moment in European historical development, have suggested that autobiography is unknown to other cultures, where a consciousness of individual self is submerged within a cosmic view of the nature of life which allows no significance to individual experience. Following this view, the numerous non-Western autobiographies which exist from the nineteenth century must be considered not as products of a traditional concept of self, but as the consequences of encounters with Western civilizations, which, either in the form of creating a demand for the autobiographical narrative, or through the indirect imposition of an alien cultural awareness, lead to the formation of an innovatory intellectual context which makes the writing of autobiography possible.

The problems of genre definition need not, however, restrict analysis to questions of history and anthropological interpretation. One influential line of discourse commencing with the *differentia specifica* of autobiography, which for our purposes here we might define as the writing of narrative essentially true, in the events of which the writer has participated, have examined the variations on this *pacte autobiographique* and the different literary conditions and conventions under which it obtains, again after finding origins in pre- and praeter-autobiographical narrative.

Implicitly accepting many of the arguments, then, in relation both to the historical and cultural specificity of the autobiographical form and to the stylistic peculiarity of autobiographical narrative, writers on Malay/Indonesian autobiography have been at pains to deny any continuity between the texts they consider and what they regard as traditional literature. In insisting in this way on a rupture between a traditional world-view and a modern Western-influenced self-consciousness, they implicitly undermine the authenticity of the writing. Works have been written for colonial patrons or government publishing houses, or have been modelled on Western autobiographies, hence we cannot accept their claims to be genuine autobiographies.

Paradoxically, however, as literary critics turn to the history of ideas and anthropological descriptions to substantiate the European uniqueness of the autobiographical form, historians and anthropologists, themselves learning from different schools of literary criticism and from their own reflections on the intellectual premises of their disciplines, have come to question those very paradigms on which those classifications and demarcations depend. There is now much less certainty among historians and anthropologists concerning those classic divisions on which earlier generations of scholars relied so heavily: no one now thinks of using notions of a soul of the primitive, or disjunctions between mediaevalism and the Renaissance thought, or the old division between Classicism and Romanticism. Even as first-step heuristic devices, these concepts appear to have outlived their usefulness; furthermore, this new scepticism even calls into question the most recent of the *grandes theories* designed to replace older models.

In so far, then, as one can identify from among anthropologists and historians – and it is worth observing that frequently it is now difficult to distinguish one from another – a common purpose, it is that both are now concerned with the elaboration of continuity: no longer the significance of historical and cultural-intellectual turning points, but the continual evolution of forms impervious to what were for earlier generations the watersheds of historical change. This emphasis on continuity is also reflected in critiques of autobiography.

Dissatisfied with the increasingly formalistic distinctions between autobiography and fiction, several of the more recent critics have preferred to work with the notion of self-representation, and this has allowed them to consider works such as *The Prelude, Portrait of the Artist, Sons and Lovers,* as also engaging in a form of the *pacte autobiographique.* The logic of such a procedure immediately commends itself once it is conceded that on the one hand, as novelists frequently remark, the fiction of a novel is irredeemably rooted in personal experience, and, on the other, equally irretrievably, autobiography follows a method of composition and organization which is essentially fictive – in as much as the progress of the protagonist can never replicate the arbitrariness and uncertainty of the life as it was lived.

Accepting, then, these new imperatives, both those relating to our understanding of the history of other cultures and those which urge us to seek within the variations of form clues to the interpretation of self-consciousness, one can discern in the texts of modern Indonesian autobiographies themes and preoccupations which, while being specific and local in their reference to Indonesian events, places and personalities, also contain elements which at a general level of abstraction link with universal modes of autobiographical writing, both offering confirmation of certain structural forms – in which cases it should be stressed that they do not simply reproduce European models – and at the same time, providing sufficient substance of an original kind to warrant the modification of our concepts of autobiographical structures and the cultural determination of self-consciousness.

There can be no doubt that for Indonesians born before 1930 the crucial life-experiences took place in the years between 1942 and 1950, that is, the three-year period of the Japanese occupation, followed by revolution. Reading the autobiographies and the fictions relating to those years, the memoirs of political figures and the novels and short stories of the men of letters, one perceives that whatever the kaleidoscopic heterogeneity of their experience of turbulence and disorder, two issues gave a shape and, consequently, purpose and significance, to personal vicissitudes. The first was a growing recognition of Indonesianness, a sense of national identity, and the second, an intensive education into the minds and hearts of people at a supra-local level. Sometimes, as in the case of Hamka, as we shall see, this second issue evolving into a principle of organizing experience, also led to greater self-awareness and hence purposiveness; for others, however, the experience contributed only to cynicism.

That it is a growing awareness of nationalist self-consciousness, a sense of being a citizen of a nation, no longer simply a member of a localized territorial, or at best a regional, grouping, is to be discovered not so much from the conscious reference to nationalist issues or the deliberate discussions of various regionalisms, although these do exist, and again, nowhere so demonstratively as in the writings of Hamka, but in the selection and organization of subjects for description. The orientation of the writing is essentially outward, inasmuch as the writer describes public events, often events in which he was not a participant, but which had a significance for him, but a significance not so much personal as communal. And even in relation to those local events in which the writer did participate, the purpose of the description is rarely to exploit the occasion for a revelation of the developing character of the individual, but to celebrate the historical moment as yet one more stage in the triumphal advance to ultimate success. Only rarely does the writing turn inward and take as its subject the hero himself, since implicitly – at least in autobiographical hindsight – the hero has, during those years at least, no personality, no sphere of private intimacy, detachable from his public performance.

But it is the other focus of the autobiographical writing of those years which interests me in relation to Hamka: the sense of *Umwertung aller Werte*, of a world turned upside down in which the move away from established routines and into an unfamiliar milieu often led to a personal crisis in which one's values become constantly sharpened as a consequence of colliding with a range of others. And here, in the interstices of graphic descriptions of public episodes, one finds inserted the personal anecdote, the revelatory experience, which having been selected for recording and preservation is described in sufficient detail to render the reader aware of the poignancy of the event for the hero. The movement of Indonesian autobiographies, then, is this irregular shuttling backwards and forwards between public event and private experience, the consciousness of the individual perceived as having been bred from both, although in the ultimate analysis, it is to be noted that both sets of experience occur in public, not private space.

Before going on to look at the case of Hamka as an illustration of the autobiography which constantly negotiates the space between public events and personal response to them, it is worth pausing to indicate what other possibilities there might have been, since the experience of reading autobiography can often delude the reader into ignoring the absences of the text. One of the notable absences is any but the most perfunctory mention of domestic life. Not only is the experience of passion and emotion excluded – that one might have expected from the difficulties of transcending the cultural prohibitions against such exposure – but so too is any reference to family and intimate friends. This absence is the more striking if one recalls that in a number of autobiographies of childhood it is precisely the emotional intensity of those years which finds expression in the context of memorable episodes associated with peers and members of the family. One is thus left with the impression that adulthood for Indonesian autobiographers inevitably entails an abandonment of that private absorption in emotional experience and an entry onto the stage of public service. At least this is the impression from the formal autobiographies, most of which, it must be conceded, have been written by those who have had careers within the public service. For such as these, their public identity has become their self-identity, hence the unwillingness to mar the image and the desire to justify their actions.

This reluctance to display emotion, a cultural trait of course most frequently associated with the Javanese *priyayi* but also found as an ideal among other groups of Indonesians, prohibits the kind of revelation of weakness, that openness, of which Rousseau's *Confessions* is the first example. (Though at times, one might argue, Pramoedya Ananta Toer's autobiographical works come close to this dramatic honesty. In this latter case, however, the disguise of these works as fiction throws up other questions of interpretation which cannot be considered here.) The failure, then, to find accounts of the *homme moyen sensuel* in the autobiographical literature is at least partly to be expected – and there are of course exceptions. A further notable absence is, however, less easily explainable in terms of a conscious suppression from public view of an emotional life, and that is any account of religious experience.

For anyone acquainted with European autobiographies it is noticeable that many of the greatest autobiographies are concerned precisely with religious experience, and at the risk of appearing over-schematic one can point to three types of such autobiography: those which deal with the rejection of religion in youth and the gradual discovery of God in adulthood, the example here is Augustine's *Confessions*; those which deal with the passionate embrace of a conformist religion in youth and its gradual relinquishment – one thinks here of Gosse's *Father and Son* – and, finally, the autobiographies which deal with the experience of God – think of St. Theresa's *Life*. Now clearly, to interpret these autobiographies one has to set them in the context of a history of religious ideas in order to understand both their significance for the intended readership of the autobiographies, and also for the writers themselves. Equally, however, one has to consider why Indonesian autobiographies which deal with religious experience take on very different forms.

It is possible to find equivalences or parallels in Indonesian literature with the types outlined above, but usually not within what we would immediately recognize as autobiographies. For example, the personal experience of God is well known to us in the poetry of Indonesian mystics, in the writings of Hamzah Fansuri, for example, and this tradition persists most remarkably in modern literature in the poetry of Amir Hamzah. Similarly, the experience of liberation from narrow conformism is vividly described in Achdiat K. Mihardja's novel *Atheis*, which is commonly thought to contain autobiographical elements. And as for the work which dwells on the rejection of religion in youth, there are suggestions of this in Hamka's autobiography. On the whole, however, it is the absence of any account of personal religious experience which strikes one in reading modern Indonesian literature, and in a country where the celebration of religion is so central to social life this requires some explanation. We can obtain some help here if we look briefly at African autobiographies.

Camara Laye's autobiography *L'Enfant Noir*, beautifully translated by James Kirkup as *The African Child*, describes the early years of an intelligent boy brought up in a traditional Muslim environment in Guinea. One of the central episodes in the book is the account of the boy's circumcision. Now it is noteworthy that in his description of the ceremony and the accompanying rituals surrounding the event, the Islamic significance of the ceremony is never mentioned. On the contrary, what is stressed is the importance of the ritual for creating a sense of identity within a peer group and an awareness of initiation into adulthood. It is clearly for the boy the most important of the *rites de passage* of childhood, to be compared in emotional intensity with the secular tie of leaving home for the first time. Another African example which indicates the significance of circumcision in this respect is to be found in Ngugi's novel *The River Between,* where again the ceremony makes a profound impact on the psychological and emotional consciousness of the hero.

Readers of Indonesian and Malay literature will immediately recall identical scenes from their reading: Pramoedya Ananta Toer's short story *Sunat*; Ajikik's story with the give-away title *Aku Telah Dewasa*, Hamka's autobiography and numerous other minor examples. In all these works, as in *The African Child*, we find that it is the social rather than the religious significance of the occasion which is highlighted. Without wanting to make too much of this coincidence at this point, I would suggest that the attention given to circumcision offers a clue to the understanding of contemporary religious experience in Muslim Indonesia which allows us to perceive why, even in religious autobiographical writings, by which I mean works such as Hamka's *Kenang-Kenangan Hidup*, Saifuddin Zuhri's *Guruku*, Darman Moenir's autobiographical novel *Bako*, the ecstatic experience of a personal God plays such a relatively minor role. And before offering a tentative explanation it needs to be stressed that I am not arguing that there is something quintessentially Islamic which makes the experience of God fundamentally or qualitatively different from the experience of other religions, or that there is an essentially Indonesian or non-European quality to that experience. My argument applies solely to the contemporary manifestation of the experience which is a product of a complex historical evolution involving the cultural and historical peculiarities of the experience of Muslims in Indonesia over the last hundred years.

Being a Muslim in Indonesia means participating in the religious rituals of Islam and abiding by specific Islamic prohibitions. Above all, the practice of Islam requires abstaining from pork and some commitment to fasting, and to a lesser degree it means participating in the Friday prayer and observing the five daily prayers. In addition, for men it means being circumcised. The reward for undertaking the minimal requirements is acceptance by and into the local social community, the penalty for absolutely rejecting Islam is social alienation. Very few people opt for the latter, and if they do, they invariably move away from their community of origin. It is, however, only a minimal commitment which is required and local communities are, or at least were until recently, tolerant of unorthodox beliefs, ranging from heterodox forms of Islamic devotion to membership of the Communist Party. The stress, then, is on conformity to ritual prescriptions, not to a specific theology, nor even to Islamic laws, although of course religious teachers try to inculcate an awareness of and a commitment to the latter. Conformity, then, indicates membership of a community, and strict adherence beyond the conventional minimum indicates visible membership of a specific subset of the community. There are, however, other religious subsets, in particular those associated with religious political parties, where the emblem of membership is not always strict conformity, but the acceptance and practice of certain social attitudes only loosely associated with Islam: for example, the wearing of European dress. The degree to which a person conforms to Islamic practice then is a consciously recognized form of self-identification, a public symbol of commitment. Not that this explains entirely the commitment of the devout to the five prayers, which are usually privately observed, and which certainly do indicate more than superficial conformity. On the whole, though, the practice of Islam is a this-worldly affair.

There is of course a tradition of Islamic mysticism in Indonesia, but over the past one hundred years this tradition has been under attack and in Sumatra at least it has almost disappeared or gone underground. With the emphasis on orthodoxy, conformity to ritual prescriptions and adherence to a moral code, the spiritual resources of the religion to provide psychological and emotional sustenance have been neglected, and have been replaced by secular satisfactions which have received a religious gloss: participation in politics, success in one's career and the accumulation of wealth, provide goals for individuals for which religious sanction and approval are only important after the event. The autobiographies provide confirmation of this view in their detailing of what are essentially secular careers, to which by way of comment and reflection token religious sentiments are attached in a way never satisfactorily integrated into an account of the significance of personal experience.

The absence, then, of a spiritual dimension to religious autobiographies can be explained in historical terms. In the following account of Hamka's autobiography the argument must be taken as read, since I do not refer to it again. Instead I have chosen to look in detail at what is clearly the central episode of the autobiography around which the narrative has been structured: the crisis which occurred in Hamka's life at the end of the Japanese occupation. Before going into detail, however, some preliminary remarks are required on Hamka and on the composition of the autobiography.

When he died in 1978 Hamka was the most well-known religious figure in Indonesia. He was above all an outstanding self-publicist. He had for years been an active journalist and was also a popular novelist. His novel *Tenggelamnya Kapal Van der Wyck* was arguably the most popular romantic novel of the thirties and forties, its judicious mixture of sentiment, romance, and home-spun morality finding a very wide appeal. In the fifties and sixties he had turned himself, if not into a religious scholar, at least into a popularizer of Islam, working through his journal 'Panji Masyarakat' to disseminate religious news relating both to Indonesia and the wider Muslim world, as well as giving religious instruction of a fairly straightforward nature. To the same end he embarked on a comprehensive exegesis of the Koran, which through his distribution and marketing outlets became widely known throughout Indonesia. It was, however, in the sixties that his stock as a religious figure rose, primarily as a consequence of his imprisonment by Soekarno for being hostile to the latter's style of government. This spell in prison turned Hamka into a focal figure for the modernist Islamic opposition to Guided Democracy, hence after the fall of Soekarno it was hardly surprising that Hamka's rehabilitation became symbolic of the revival of modernist Islam. Capitalizing on this symbolic status which Hamka had now assumed, the New Order Government of Suharto, to enhance its credibility with Muslim groups, went out of its way to court Hamka, and as the Indonesian expression has it, 'memberi dia angin' – gave him room for manoeuvre and helped to promote him officially through the media as a religious figure who met with their approval.

The culmination of this process of legitimation came when Hamka was invited to head the new Majelis Ulama, the Council of Religious Scholars, which the government had set up in 1973. Several people advised him against accepting the appointment, fearing that the Council would be merely a rubber-stamping body for government pronouncements and by associating himself with it Hamka would lose credibility while lending support to a regime which was by that time increasingly identified as hostile to Islam. Hamka did in fact accept the appointment, although he withdrew from the Council in later years. At his death his reputation was very high, not only in Indonesia, but also in Malaysia, where he was frequently invited to preach. At present his memory is still revered. 'Panji Masyarakat' continues to publish under the editorship of his son, and his books are still popular and are constantly reprinted. In a collection of essays intended as a reassessment of the man one or two writers were critical of him, but the criticisms are not shared by the mass of the public (Nasir Tamara, Buntaran Sanusi and Djauhari 1983).

Kenang-Kenangan Hidup was written in 1950 when Hamka was 42. Its writing satisfies a double audit: one historical, one personal. The Indonesian Revolution was just over and it was a time both for recording the history of that revolution, documenting both the events and the leading personalities, in which task his own individual interpretation, perhaps the first of many synoptic accounts, was offered of the progress of a movement which had come to a triumphant conclusion. In this sense the autobiography, where Hamka locates himself if not at the centre, at least in the thick of the action, is constructed teleologically, the events being described in an ordered concatenation leading inexorably to the ultimate achievement. There is no sense of fortuitousness, no arbitrary extraneous description; an implicit purpose is seen both to underlie events and Hamka's role within them. At the same time, however, the achievement of independence celebrated in the autobiography implies an openness in relation to the future of the nation. What will happen next is unknown, unconsidered, beyond speculation. The rhythm of the narrative which has had as its recurring theme the growth of a nationalist consciousness and the realization of that consciousness in significant events is constructed from the portraits of influential personalities and from the description of ideas and institutions which have contributed to the final achievement. Nothing in that ordered configuration looks beyond independence to future possibilities. Even in the later editions of the autobiography where the writer, having lived through the post-independence years, is now in a position to appreciate the limitations of a narrative constructed around that final point, and consequently qualifies earlier assessments, in particular in relation to the character of Soekarno, these fresh additions are insufficient to eradicate the strong definition of the original patterning.

At the same time, however, by contrast, the progressive evolution of the hero's personality, which has been developed in the narrative parallel to the disclosure of the trajectory of nationalism, avoids this negative finality, and deliberately juxtaposes the end of the historical process with the start of a new career for the hero, pregnant with potential because it is securely attached to a new sense of self-awareness. At the end of the book Hamka is made to reflect on his career to date, and this reflection mirrors and condenses the whole autobiography at the same time as it makes explicit the underlying purpose of its composition. His conclusion is that his career to date has been a series of false starts, some more successful than others. He has been a teacher, a journalist, a writer, a leader of the Muhammadiyah and a politician, but in none of these does he feel that there has been a proper consummation of purpose. At his shoulder, haunting him, is the figure of his father, the great religious teacher, and now impelled by a sense of vocation which he has all those years tried uneasily to shuffle off, he makes the decision that he will postpone the fulfilment of that vocation no longer. He will strive to emulate his father, and the visible correlative of that decision is his transferring to Jakarta, where after the failures of his experiences in Medan and Padang 'fresh fields and pastures new' offer themselves for his conquest.

In his evaluation of the past, then, Hamka organizes his account of national events from the perspective of a potential which has been achieved, and the selection and judgement of events are conditioned by their contribution to that realization of potential. In reflecting on his own position, however, the orientation is not backward into his history, but forward towards what can now be done after the settling of accounts with himself. The historical moment of that stock-taking is the establishment of the nation, but for Hamka himself the moment of significance is the decision to move geographically and spiritually to a new terrain.

Despite the appearance of openness in the account of the life-history – in contrast to the closure of the interpretation of national history – it is important to recall that the structuring of the personal story is equally fictive and programmatically designed, in the sense that the arrangement of episodes and the way they have been plotted and mapped to form a coherent whole is the product of a conscious creative purpose. As critics of autobiographies have frequently observed, the semblance of spontaneity in autobiographies belies an organized, well-modulated patterning, since the very act of self-reflection required in composing an autobiography involves the imposition of a creative stamp on the flux of experience. Paradoxically there can never be autobiography, only biography, since the writer is through the experience of self-reflection always a different person from the one being described. Realizing this, then, one of the tasks of any critique of autobiography must be to expose and explore in relation to specific texts that tension, distinctive of autobiography, between the appearance of authentic self-representation and the controlling and decisive purpose of the writer.

The autobiography was originally published in four small volumes totalling about 950 pages. The style of the writing and the organizing principles which determine the contents of the work differ significantly from one volume to another. The first volume covers the author's childhood from his birth in 1908 in Maninjau in West Sumatra to his return from the haj pilgrimage in 1926 and his marriage in 1929. In tone it is very much an autobiography of childhood with affectionate reminiscences of well-remembered episodes; at the same time it conveys the sense of a *Bildungsroman* as the hero advances in maturity from one educational experience to another. The choice of narrative persona is revealing. The book commences in the first person, using the term *aku* – what might be called the demonstrative first-person, as opposed to the more outwardly deferential *saya* – but after a few pages this changes, as though the writer were uneasy with his own assertiveness, and the narrative slips into the third person, *dia*, a transition made so abruptly that on first reading I had to return to the text to satisfy myself that the referent of *dia* was in fact the hero of the autobiography. Later, again as though himself conscious of the awkwardness of using a potentially ambiguous *dia*, the persona is changed to *kawan kita*, our friend, later still *pemuda kita*, our young man, an easy enough transition in Indonesian/Malay, where there exists a widely spread linguistic convention of using third person forms for self-reference. In the second volume the mode of address changes once more, this time to *Bung Haji kita*, our Brother Haji. An analysis of these various shifts in self-identification, particularly when coupled with an unusual convention followed in the later volumes where on occasion the writer consciously adopts the persona of biographer directly addressing his subject, would, I suggest, offer valuable insights into Indonesian conventions of reading. The complexity of the assumptions concerned with the relationship of writer to reader which these stylistic shifts imply lead one to speculate what the culturally specific conventions of communication operating here might be, but such a study is beyond the scope of the discussion here.

The second volume dealing with the period between 1930 and 1942 differs markedly from the first, in so far as the chronicling of Hamka's life is interspersed with set essays, on adat, on *kaba*, on being a writer, which bear no relation to the autobiography. This introduction of short essays and poems is also accompanied by a shift away from personal anecdote to a description of achievements. As someone has noted, childhood autobiographies are indistinguishable in that the subjects of the works are children whose actions as children are not seen as reflecting the special status which the writers acquire in adulthood. On the contrary, such autobiographies are celebrations of the eccentric whimsy and fantastical imagination of the child. By contrast, autobiographies of adults who have become public personalities are often written as a record and justification of actions and decisions. Hamka's autobiography shows a very conscious awareness of this principle of organization, and from the second volume it is the public actions which are seen as requiring description and explanation to the exclusion of private emotion.

This tendency to develop the public persona of the hero becomes more pronounced in the third and fourth volumes, which deal with the period of the Japanese occupation and the Revolution, and it is in these later volumes that the two narratives of the history of the individual and the history of the nation become critically and inextricably interwoven. Whereas prior to 1942 the account of Hamka's life and his various undertakings in the fields of education and journalism had been associated only peripherally with the nationalist movement, touching it tangentially at various points through his participation in the Muhammadiyah and through his occasional, almost fortuitous meetings with nationalist figures in Yogya and, briefly, with Soekarno in Benkulen, now the record of events and actions in which he plays the major role are associated centrally with the life of the nation. Medan becomes the symbolic microcosm of Indonesia under the Japanese, and Hamka, himself, the exemplar of the Indonesian patriot caught up in the maelstrom of events on which he imprints his personality and his ideas: individual and nation fuse in a portraiture which despite its particularity is to be taken as a representative of Indonesian life in those years.

The increasing sureness with which this identification of the hero with historical moment and the intensity with which it is pursued should, however, make us reflect who it is that is urging the reader to accept this view of events. At one level it is clearly Hamka the writer of 1950, who, looking back at the period, is artfully orchestrating the description to build up to an appropriate climax; at another it is Hamka the autobiographer, faithfully trying to recollect not only the sequence of events, but the emotional and psychological atmosphere of the times; at a third level the writing records the perceptions of Hamka the man, as he experienced them in living through that period. If we can retain in our consciousness a simultaneous awareness of these separate perspectives which influence the unfolding of the narrative, then our reading of the anticipated climax when it arrives is doubly enriched, since what occurs is an unexpected reversal of our expectations. After the defeat of the Japanese, it is dramatically revealed that Hamka is regarded as a traitor who had sold his country to the latter and who must now be socially and politically ostracized. The significance of this unexpected outcome affects the reader exactly in proportion to the levels of consciousness at which the narrative has been read up to that point: Hamka the hero of the narrative, Hamka the writer, Hamka the autobiographer and Hamka the respected religious authority all merge, and yet remain distinct at the point of evaluation. Crucially, too, at this instant, a space emerges between the personal and the national histories which over the course of the final volume of the autobiography will be progressively exploited to allow the hero to disengage from that existential commitment to the nation's destiny in which he has been so disastrously involved, and to emerge distinct and intact when the process is complete.

At the beginning of the fourth volume, however, the space is still barely visible: a mistake, an error of individual judgement has been made, but despite the bitterness of rejection the hero is still convinced of the centrality of his role. Acting on this conviction, Hamka moves to Padang determined to rehabilitate himself, participating in public life more cautiously and circumspectly than before, but still confident of his association with the political destiny of the nation. At this stage in the narrative, however, the attempt to distinguish the interpretations of writer and autobiographer becomes highly problematic.

As the description proceeds, however, it becomes clear that in the very act of winning back not only his self-respect but also the public acknowledgement of his contribution by leaders of the revolutionary movement, Hamka, reassessing the social and political circumstances of the time, comes to feel that his proper role is not in politics. Consequently, gradually withdrawing from official positions, while nonetheless using different occasions to demonstrate his commitment to the Revolution, he increases that distance between himself and the national destiny. At the completion of the autobiography, then, the reader has been prepared for the separation of Hamka from the political life of the newly independent nation. While rejoicing in the successful outcome of the revolutionary struggle, to which he has made important contributions, he leaves it to others to share out the political cachets, while he goes off to Jakarta to begin a new life as a religious scholar.

The decision to move to Jakarta must also be set in the context of another theme which, although it is only explicitly touched on from time to time in the autobiography, must clearly be considered an explanatory key to understanding Hamka's personality: the relationship of Hamka to his father. The beginning of the autobiography opens with the mysterious words of the father at the birth of his son, 'Sepuluh tahun' (Ten years), and it transpires that the words refer to the father's desire to make of his son a religious scholar whom he intends to send to Mecca for ten years to further his education. The recounting of this incident, highlighted as it is by being put at the start, establishes immediately for the reader the autobiographer's consciousness of the spiritual bond between father and son, and a sense of religious vocation. In the years of adolescence which follow, that bond of intimacy between father and son weakens as a consequence of his father's repudiation of his mother, which brings in its wake Hamka's rejection of paternal authority. Nonetheless, the bond endures and at points throughout the narrative, although there is no suggestion that the two ever regain the warmth of the relationship of childhood, there is an indication of the father's increase of stature in his son's eyes over the years. The father's death in Jakarta just before the end of the Japanese occupation forecloses the possibility that the two will come to a mature mutual understanding, and is thus a cause of grief, yet at the same time it liberates Hamka from the implicit challenge and competition which his father, living, posed for him. If at the end of the Revolution, then, he decides to follow in his father's footsteps and devote his life to religious education, he no longer need feel the baleful and critical eye of his father attending his actions.

The journey to Jakarta is, according to this interpretation of the narrative, a real and metaphorical return of the prodigal: real in the sense that it is a pilgrimage to his father's grave, and in this respect also an imaginative return to the atmosphere of childhood evoked at the commencement of the autobiography; metaphorical, in that it represents a decision to take up the mantle which his father had left for him, thus returning from the secular world of journalism and politics to the world of religious scholarship which he had temporarily abandoned.

Important as this theme is in determining the structuring of the text of the autobiography, however, it operates almost at an unconscious level of which both writer and reader are only occasionally aware. The major critical event of the narrative is, without doubt, the error of judgement at the defeat of the Japanese, and it is this which shapes both the text and the creation of the persona of the subject of the autobiography, and it is this shaping, finally, which calls for comment.

Hamka as Lord Jim and Marlow

At the age of 42 in 1950, even from the evidence of the autobiography, there was no ostensible reason for Hamka to have written his autobiography. His achievements till then had been modest: some success as a sentimental novelist, a local reputation in Sumatra for his journalism, and a certain rhetorical style, highly prized in a society where oral traditions still flourish. He was only a minor figure in the pantheon of nationalist heroes of the revolution, one who had some acquaintance with the great and the good. If this was his self-appraisal, then, there was none of the obvious justifications for the autobiography: there are no great triumphs to celebrate, no popular curiosity concerning a well-known public figure needing to be satisfied, no extraordinary personal experience to be described. And yet there is a sense, at least at the commencement of the book, that one has to do here with a strong personal ambition which is overcoming successive vicissitudes with a conviction of ultimately achieving greatness. With that greatness not yet achieved in 1950, however, the reason why Hamka, especially in the context of a culture which considers 42 a relatively young age, should have chosen to write an autobiography is puzzling.

One approach to the puzzle lies in our regarding Hamka as Marlow to his own Lord Jim. For Jim, one recalls, the crucial episode in his life-history is the desertion of the pilgrim ship, the *Patna*, crucial for three reasons: because it destroys for Jim his previous self-esteem, because it is an event which haunts him and requires from him a constant rehearsal and analysis of the circumstances of the occasion; and finally because it determines the future course of Jim's life, reoriented as a consequence of a new self-appraisal. Of course it takes Marlow to bring out these implications and significances, acting as he does both as narrator, and, at a more subtle level, Jim's conscience. The narrative pivot of the story, then, is the charge of cowardice levelled at Jim and his angry, baffled, awkward sense of guilt. The reader's own estimation of the situation is controlled and informed by the inclusion of the preceding and subsequent history of the action, which places the event in a context in which the moral dilemma can be properly interpreted.

It is Marlow (ultimately, Conrad) who selects, arranges, and comments upon the actions to put the reader in possession of the facts. Following the analogy it is Hamka, the writer, as Marlow, who performs a similar function for us in the autobiography, and he is doing it in the same omniscient fashion as the creative writer of fiction. In so far, however, as this is not a novel, but autobiography, the creative organization of the text must also be regarded as both work of self-analysis and an apologia.

Here the crucial episode is Hamka's ostensibly craven response to the defeat of the Japanese, and the superficial cowardice of his flight from Medan to Padang which had such profound consequences. Within the ordering of the text there is sufficient internal evidence to identify this episode as the central one, but if additional confirmation is required it is available in the insertions of the later editions of the work, where a different Hamka, the nationally respected religious figure of the early seventies, comments on the self-analysis written in 1950. Chapter 21 of Volume III in the 1973 edition of the book is entitled 'Mengulang kenangan (setelah 30 tahun kemudian)', 'Recalling memories (thirty years after)', and it begins (p. 257):

> Penderitaan dan percobaan yang berat itu telah saya alami 30 tahun yang lalu, tahun hijrah 1364. Waktu itu usia 37 tahun, sekarang 67 tahun. Tetapi terus terang saya katakan bahwa percobaan Ramadhan 1364 atau Agustus sampai Desember 1945 itu adalah yang paling hebat dan paling besar dalam kehidupan saya.

> Those difficult sufferings and trials I endured [note here the use of the first person, *saya*, in contrast to the third person in which the original narrative is related] thirty years ago in A.H. 1364. I was then 37; I am now 67. But in all honesty I can say that these trials of Ramadhan 1364 or August to December 1945 were the gravest and the most significant of my life.

By any reckoning, therefore, the drama of Hamka's reaction to news of the Japanese surrender must be regarded as central to the composition of the autobiography. The writing serves two purposes: it is at once a real attempt on Hamka's part to come to terms with a critical experience, the consequences of which had caused pain and suffering, but the dynamics of which he could only understand through the creative liberation of expressing them in the coherent form which a narrative imposed upon them, and at the same time it is an attempt to explain and extenuate for the reader – as Marlow did with respect to Jim – the actions of the man Hamka who committed the gross error of judgement.

The easy response to the account, though to my mind it is facile as much as easy, is to read it as exculpation. That this is ultimately a superficial reading can be demonstrated by those passages in the work where Hamka the hero is the subject of the gentle irony of Hamka the autobiographer. The best example of this is in Chapter 11 of Volume III in which Hamka, returning from a visit to Jakarta and putting various proposals to the Japanese Governor (the Tyokan), fondly imagines that the latter will appoint him Head of the Department of Religious Affairs, a new post, from which he will be able to exercise a commanding authority over political developments in Sumatra. The extravagant illusions and expectations of the hero are built up over two and a half pages in which his own sense of self-importance is humorously described as taking over from a proper sense of reality. When the decision of the Tyokan is made, indeed creating the new position, but not awarding it to Hamka, it is not the reader who is surprised at the outcome, but Hamka, who is thus mildly ridiculed.

These passages of self-depreciation, then, predispose the reader to accept as authentic the analysis of the critical episode when it occurs later in the same volume. In addition, another important set of events which occurred during the occupation, the confrontation between the Muhammadiyah, the *Kaum Muda* ('Young Generation') party, and the established religious scholars of the East Sumatran courts, representatives of the *Kaum Tua* ('Old Generation'), over the proper ritual form of prayer, in which Hamka suffered a humiliating defeat, described in Chapter 15, also prepares the reader for the emotional and psychological charge which will accompany the more substantial defeat of his ambitions.

As it is described, the impending defeat of the Japanese is anticipated, but at the same time expectations have been raised to almost fever pitch, by the Japanese promise of 'Independence for Indonesia within a short time', that an end is in sight for foreign domination, and that under independence those who had been working in the Japanese-controlled councils would be the ones to exercise authority in the new administration. What transpires in fact, however, is devastating for Hamka.

> Dengan muka muram, campur benci, campur dendam, Nomura berkata: 'Perang sudah habis.Tentara Nippon terpaksa berhenti perang! Amerika menjatuhkan bom, bikin binasa negeri Nippon. Sumatera ini mau diambil Inggeris!'
>
> Barulah dia melongo! Mulutnya boleh dilalui lengau dengan tidak usah minta permisi lebih dahulu. Hal yang ditunggu telah datang! Tetapi menyebabkan dia melongo juga. Sebab tidak di-sangka2 secepat itu. Disangkanya agak 6 atau 7 bulan lagi [...]
>
> Kemerdekaan! Kemerdekaan! Bagaimana jadinya? Ditengah jalan dia singgah minum di kedai Tionghoa, terlalu haus, panas!
>
> Radio berbunyi. Maklumat Gunseikanbu dari Bukittinggi. Isinya sama dengan keterangan Tyokan tadi. Jepang telah mengakui tunduk kepada Empat Bangsa, yaitu Inggeris, Amerika, Rusia dan China. Wah bukan main gembira segala orang China.
>
> Kegembiraan itu meluap keluar, tidak tertahantahan. Mereka tidak lagi menyembunyikan perasaan. Ber-salam2an, ada yang bersorak sorai, dan orang Nippon yang pada waktu itu belum masuk kandang berjalan ditepi jalan raya me-nyisih2. Adapun Hamka sendiri, tengah minum itu, bila masuk seorang Tionghoa melihat kepada dadanya, mereka se-akan2 mengejek. Ya, benar-benar mengejek, bukan se-akan2. Lekas2 dibayarnya harga minumannya dan pulang. Ada apa didadanya? Mengapa orang2 Tionghoa tadi mengejek?
>
> Tanda anggota Syu Sangikai!

Masih dijalan, tanda itu telah dibukanya, disimpannya sebab dari mas!
Dia teringat lagi: 'Kemerdekaan!'
Sampai dirumah dinyatakannyalah kepada isterinya bahwa Jepang telah kalah. Dia
bersedih, dia menangis! 'Mengapa menangis?' Tanya isterinya.
'Bagaimanalah jadinya kemerdekaan Indonesia? Putus perhubungan kita dengan
Jawa. Radio dari sana tidak bersuara lagi! Berhenti semua!' 'Khabarnya Sumatera ini
akan diserahkan kepada Inggeris. Orang Nippon sendiri yang mengatakan kepadaku!'
    Kemerdekaan! Tidak tentu apa yang akan diperbuatnya sehari itu. Dari tangis
ketangis. Dia duduk sebentar dirumah. Sebelum menghapus air mata, dengan tidak
mengingat bahwa dijalanan dia akan bertemu dengan orang banyak, dikayuhnya pula
sepedanya, menuju Gunseibu. Hendak menemui Tyokan. Tyokan tidak 'sebesar'
kemarin lagi. Dia diterima oleh seorang manusia Jepang biasa, yang kemarin bergelar
Tyokan, yaitu Tuan Nakasyima-Yah dimuka Nakasyima San dia bertanya sambil
menangis 'Bagaimana kemerdekaan tanah airku, tuan? Saya hendak ke Jawa tuan!
menemui pemimpin saya Sukarno!'
    Lama kemudian baru dia tahu, bahwa disa'at itu dia sudah mulai 'kurang beres'.
Tyokan memberi isyarat kepada juru bahasanya dengan sudut mata. Dan dia 'dihantar'
baik-baik keluar.
    Dia pulang lagi kerumah. Seketika buka puasa, makannya tidak sempurna. Sampai
di Jalan Kamboja tempat orang-orang Muhammadiyah berkumpul hendak sembahyang
terawih, pidatonya sehabis taraweh pun tidak tentu lagi ujung pangkalnya.
    Sebetulnya tidaklah diingatnya lagi, apa yang terjadi dikelilingnya. Tidak
diperhatikannya muka kawan2nya yang sudah agak tercengang melihat perubahannya.

With an expression which combined uneasiness, hatred and vengefulness Nomura
said: 'The war is over. The Japanese army has been compelled to cease fighting!
America has dropped a bomb, it has destroyed Japan. Sumatra will be taken over by
Britain.'
    Then for the first time his jaw dropped! His open mouth would have allowed a fly
to enter without asking permission first. What he had been waiting for had come. But
it had also caused his jaw to drop. Because he hadn't thought it would be as quick as
that. He had reckoned on it being six or seven months more [...]
    Independence! Independence! What would happen to it? On the way, he stopped
for a drink in a Chinese shop; he was very thirsty, hot!
    The radio came on. An announcement of the Gunseibanku from Bukittinggi. The
content was the same as the information that the Tyokan had just given. Japan had
surrendered to the Four Nations, Britain, America, Russia and China. And weren't the
Chinese pleased, all of them.
    Their pleasure spilled over, uncontainable. They didn't disguise their feelings any
more. They kept shaking hands, some even shouted for joy, and the Japanese, who at
that time had not yet been confined, walked by the side of the road avoiding people.
As for Hamka, he was in the middle of having his drink, when a Chinese came in and
looked at his chest. They appeared to be scoffing at him. Indeed they were scoffing,
there was no 'appearing' about it. Hurriedly he paid for his drink and went home.
What was it on his chest? Why had the Chinese scoffed at him?
    It was his badge of membership of the Syu Sangikai [regional advisory council].
Still in the street the badge was taken off, and kept, because it was of gold.
    He remembered again: 'Independence!'

Arriving at the house he told his wife that the Japanese had been defeated. He was depressed; he cried! 'Why are you crying?' asked his wife.

'What will happen with Indonesia's independence? Our communications with Java are cut. There are no radio transmissions from there! Everything has stopped. They say that Sumatra will be surrendered to Britain. The Japanese themselves said it to me!'

Independence! He didn't know what he should do that day. He continued to cry. He sat for a while in the house. Without drying his eyes, forgetting that on the way he would meet several people, he got on his bike again and pedalled to the Gunseibu. He wanted to meet the Tyokan. The Tyokan wasn't as grand a person as he had been the day before. He was received by an ordinary Japanese person who yesterday had held the title of Tyokan, Tuan Nakasyima Yah. In front of Nakasyima San he asked weeping: 'What will happen to the independence of my country, sir? I want to go to Java, sir. To meet my leader, Soekarno.'

It was only a long time afterwards that he understood, that it was then that he had begun to act strangely. The Tyokan gave a sign to the interpreter out of the corner of his eye. And he was politely shown outside.

He went home again. It was time for breaking the fast, he didn't eat properly. When he arrived at Jalan Kamboja where the Muhammadiyah assembled for the *tarawih* prayer, even his talk after tarawih was confused.

In fact he didn't know what was happening around him. He didn't observe the faces of his friends surprised to see the change in him.

The description begins unremarkably, indeed almost as though introducing further satirical criticism. The word *melongo* – to be open-mouthed – is essentially comic, in contrast to the neutral expression *mulutnya menganga* meaning the same thing. And the humour is reinforced by the notion of a fly not asking permission and able to fly in and out, an adaptation of a standard cliché to describe open-mouthed wonder. As the writing proceeds, however, it is the unusual strained circumstances which are emphasized, and the humour is all but forgotten. The sentences which follow (not quoted above) are all short and abrupt, simple sentences with no subordinate clauses. 'He returned home. At home he found a letter of summons from the Tyokan. Hurriedly he got on to his bike with the solid tyres, straight to the Syu Sangikai building. He found that the meeting had just begun. They were all there. The Sultans too had sent representatives. He found a place to sit.' The sense of a series of events following each other in quick succession, and the lack of coherence to the happenings implied by the absence of subordinate clauses or linking conjunctions, is made even stronger in the Indonesian, where the uninflected verbs fail to denote even some chronological order. Everything occurs vividly in the historic present, thus rendering the experience more immediate.

Psychologically unprepared for what is now happening around him, Hamka thinks of the promises of Independence. The anaphoristic 'Kemerdekaan! Kemerdekaan!' directly reflects his state of mind. It is this thought which keeps recurring to him in the midst of the pieces of information which assault him one after the other: first the soldier's statement, then the Tyokan's official announcement, next the reply to his question informing him that Soekarno has proclaimed independence. So far, however, the news and the events are impersonal; what has occurred is at an abstract remote level, and the implications for his own personal position have not yet been considered. Up till this point it is not so much a description of his own involvement which is being presented, but an account of the atmosphere of the time, not confessions but a memoir, a representative recording of events. This rhetorical style shifts, however, in mid-paragraph. The description changes from being a recording of historically significant events to an analysis of his own personal experience. The rhetorical question: 'What would happen to it (independence)' is abruptly followed by the sentence: 'On the way he stopped to have a drink in a Chinese shop', and the reader is consequently invited to suspend his interest in national history and contemplate the plight of the hero.

The incident in the shop which follows dramatically shocks the hero into a consciousness of his own peculiar position in the changed circumstances, and the progressive introspection of the writing at this point, although still conducted in the formal style of an objective narrative of events, carries the reader further away from the external situation to an evaluation of the behaviour of the hero. There had earlier (p. 117) in the description of the progress of the occupation been an intimation that those who had co-operated with the Japanese in their administration of government were regarded with suspicion and hostility by some sections of the population. Now that hostility is being brought into the open, and Hamka recognizes for the first time the precariousness of his position. At this point, however, the reader is moving with the autobiographer beyond the self-consciousness of the hero. The latter circumspectly removes the badge, but instead of allowing this gesture to be symbolic of a conscious and deliberate rejection of his past collaboration with the Japanese, the autobiographer deliberately undermines any such significance being attached to the action by describing the careful manner in which the badge is pocketed because it is gold. Thus although writer and reader are fully alerted to the moral quandary in which the hero is placed, the latter himself is only half aware of a problem, and this failure of recognition consequently compounds his guilt.

The manner of this disclosure, it seems to me, reveals something about autobiographical style in general at the same time as it directs our attention to peculiarly Indonesian cultural conventions of critical analysis. Written in the first person an autobiography at this point would probe the psychology of the hero in an attempt to make explicit what it was that the hero was thinking about, what was passing through his mind. In a third-person autobiography, however, this is not possible without impairing the convention of the third-person style, and thereby breaking the pact between writer and reader. If the psychology of the hero is explored, then the reader's response is to suspend belief in the convention, and either regard the work as fiction, with an omniscient author creating a character and his psychology, or, taking the exploration to be evidence of the autobiographer's commitment to self, regard the analysis as special pleading, self-justification. Either way, the honesty of the account is impugned, called into question and prone to rejection. Here we are at the limits of third-person autobiography. And yet the third person is, in terms of Malay-Indonesian oral culture at least, the obvious and acceptable form which autobiography must take. In traditional literature, that is, where the conventions of oral presentation obtain, the narrator of a story or the poet, when he mentions himself, always does so in a self-effacing fashion, calling into question his own ability, and again enforcing this modesty by reference not to his individual self, the ego of the writer, but speaking of a third person, usually *hamba*, the servant, an insignificant third person, one of many. We have already seen how Hamka himself at the start of the autobiography seems to have trouble with the use of *aku* and quickly moves into the third person, and how at times clearly finding this procedure irksome he employs other strategies (notably the spurious interview) which will allow him to retain the first person at certain points.

But if this third-person convention which appears so limiting has been imposed by one set of cultural norms which do not allow the writer to explore his own individuality through introspection and self-presentation, another set of conventions does make possible self-critical analysis through oblique reference. Such oblique reference is commonly accepted within Malay/Indonesian society where it is denoted by the concept of *sindiran*. Sindiran is a socio-linguistic convention which allows one to criticize another indirectly, but as sharply as one would wish. Since direct criticism is only rarely permissible among adults, because of what might loosely be termed considerations of 'face' which are in turn predicated on a complicated network of assumptions concerning interpersonal relations, sindiran is in effect the usual means by which criticism is offered, accepted and negotiated. Without going into details it should be apparent that the appropriate handling of sindiran involves a subtlety and complexity which require a lengthy induction into social conventions for full appreciation, and that in special circumstances where the notion of sindiran itself is being celebrated as, for example, in Malay *pantun*, an almost professional skill is needed to operate successfully within this area of play.

Now Hamka as someone brought up firmly within the conventions of Minangkabau oral culture – of which he writes at length in Volume II – is fully conversant with sindiran, hence it is to be expected that when criticism is called for within the autobiography he should employ this convention, as he employs other traditional conventions, within the repertoire of his stylistic techniques. The chapter already alluded to in which he builds up his hero's expectations of high office falls within this notion of sindiran. There, however, there was a humorous edge to the satire. Here, by contrast, the reference to the pocketing of the gold badge is more damning and the criticism more pointed. The raison d'être of making the criticism oblique – in order not to offend against codes of interpersonal behaviour – is retained: Hamka the autobiographer does not wish to offend Hamka the hero, since direct criticism, even self-criticism, is aesthetically and socially intolerable, but on the other hand honesty demands some recognition of error.

As the description proceeds, the attention to the hero and his mental state becomes even more intense, but still the focus is from without, as the convention demands. It is the significant externals which are related: he bursts into tears, he is restless, his actions are disorganized, he cries again. Once again, limits are being reached in relation to what is acceptable within linguistic and cultural conventions. The description of a man crying, this implicit acknowledgement of his own weakness by the autobiographer, is coming close to the boundaries of what is aesthetically feasible. (And the penalty of any transgression would be the forfeit of the reader's respect not only for the man but also for the autobiography.)

Shortly after this, however, we see that what might have seemed a perilous loss of control by the writer, has in fact been a carefully measured and calculated piece of composition, since the actions of the hero are not only made fully intelligible, but the climax of the description draws us back to the mention of the crying and enables us to re-evaluate its function within the structure of the narration. Hamka is having a nervous breakdown – this is clearly what is meant by *kurang beres*.

Interestingly, it is the crucial need to leave the reader in no doubt that this is what occurred which drives the autobiographer to abandon momentarily the convention of reticence described above, and appeal directly to the reader through indicating what occurs to the hero, although it is the hero at a later date. With sindiran there is always some room for ambiguity – the hint might not be taken – but so important is it to the writer that here at least there should be no ambiguity, that the reading of the hero's behaviour be fully comprehensible, that he allows himself an interpolation, risking the consequences, with an explanatory sentence. 'Lama kemudian baru dia tahu, bahwa disa'at itu dia sudah mulai "kurang beres"' (It was only much later that he realized that it was at that moment he had begun to be 'mentally unstable').

The description of his subsequent actions, his loss of appetite, his incoherent sermon, all work to give substance to this statement. At one further point, again to stress the change which has come over the hero, the autobiographer again allows the convention to slip, not perhaps in this case leading to a demonstration of the special knowledge of the autobiographer, but, by contrast, this time with a pretension to the authorial omniscience of a novelist. 'Tidak diperhatikannya muka kawannya yang agak sudah tercenang melihat perubahannya' (He didn't observe the faces of his friends who wondered at this change in him). In that case, the alert reader asks, how did he, the autobiographer, know that the friends were wondering at his behaviour? Either he was told about it subsequently, in which case it is ostensibly autobiographical special pleading similar to the earlier example, or it is imaginative recreation – the omniscient novelist. Both possibilities raise doubts, although they are insignificant ones in terms of the overall response to the stream of the narrative.

A great deal, then, has been accomplished in this passage. In particular an explanation has been offered of the hero's behaviour, but it is an explanation which does not wholly exonerate him: as the explanation which Jim gives to Marlow is also not an exoneration. There is sufficient indication, of an oblique kind, that Hamka realizes he was at fault. As the narrative continues, this tension between the acknowledgement of guilt and the struggle to absolve the hero of that guilt is exploited further, but a critical demonstration of the operation of this tension would risk making an already lengthy article tedious and, with respect to analysing the autobiographer's technique, would anyway be redundant. Sufficient has been said, I hope, to indicate that for any study of Indonesian autobiography Hamka's *Kenang-Kenangan Hidup* repays careful reading.

In looking at this short episode which, together with the next sixty pages of the book, in terms of both the underlying intention of the autobiography and its centrality to the ordering of its construction, I take to be the most important for any interpretation of the work, I have tried to demonstrate the way in which a variety of critical approaches to literature deployed in a catholic manner can be brought to bear to make an Indonesian text yield up its meaning. Reception theory, biographical information, linguistic analysis, narratology, and *explication du texte* are not, as some would have us believe, mutually exclusive.

The point of convergence for all such approaches, as also for the much maligned 'New Criticism', is close attention to the text, the sine qua non of all responsible literary criticism, as I am sure the author of *Tergantung pada Kata* and *Sastra dan Ilmu Sastra* would agree.

Bibliography

Ajikik
1965   'Aku telah dewasa', in: *Tuhan tidak buang-mu* (*Kumpulan cherpen 1958-1965*), pp. 41-8. Malaka: Abbas Bandong.
Dilthey, W.
1976   *Selected writings*. Edited by H.P. Richman. Cambridge: Cambridge University Press.
Gosse, Edmund
1983   *Father and son*. Edited by P. Abbs. Harmondsworth: Penguin. [First edition 1907.]
Hamka
1963   *Tenggelamnja Kapal van der Wijck*. Ninth printing. Bukittinggi/Djakarta: Nusantara. [First edition 1938.]
1974   *Kenang-kenangan hidup*. Third edition. Jakarta: Bulan Bintang. [First edition 1951-52.]
Laye, Camara
1959   *The African child*. Translated from the French by James Kirkup. Glasgow: Fontana/Collins. [First French edition 1954.]
Mihardja, Achdiat K.
1949   *Atheis*. Djakarta: Balai Pustaka.
Moenir, Darma
1983   *Bako*. Jakarta: Balai Pustaka.
Ngugi wa Thiong'o
1975   *The river between*. London/Ibadan/Nairobi: Heinemann. [First edition 1965.]
Tamara, Nasir, Buntaran Sanusi and Vincent Djauhari
1983   *Hamka di mata hati umat*. Jakarta: Sinar Harapan.
Teeuw, A.
1980   *Tergantung pada kata*. Jakarta: Dunia Pustaka Jaya.
1984   *Sastra dan ilmu sastra; Pengantar teori sastra*. Jakarta: Pustaka Jaya.

Toer, Pramoedya Ananta
1952   'Sunat', in *Tjerita dari Blora*, pp. 77-86. Djakarta: Balai
             Pustaka.
Wimsatt, W.K.
1964   'The intentional fallacy', in: *The verbal icon; Studies in the
             meaning of poetry*, pp. 3-18. Lexington: University of Kentucky
             Press. [First published 1949.]
Zuhri, K.H. Saifuddin
1974   *Guruku; Orang-orang pesantren*. Bandung: Alma'arif.

P.J. WORSLEY

Mpu Tantular's kakawin Arjunawijaya and conceptions of kingship in fourteenth century Java

I

At some time between 1365, the year when *Mpu* Prapañca completed the writing of his *Nāgarakṛtāgama*, and 1367 when Rājasanagara, the ruler of Majapahit, issued the Bungur Inscription, Rajasawardhinī Princess of Pawwan-awwan and later of Kahuripan, who must have still been a girl in her early teens at the time, married Raṇamanggala of Paṇḍan-Salas. Both were close kinsmen of the king. Rājasawardhinī was the youngest daughter of the king's youngest sister Īśwarī, the Princess of Pajang, and her husband, Raṇamanggala, was the son of Raden Sotor, Rājasanagara's elder brother by another mother of lesser status. The couple lived until 1400, dying on the eve of the wars between the eastern and western branches of the family. Their daughter, Jayawardhinī *dyah* Jayeśwarī, who assumed the title of princess of Daha in 1429, married her cousin, Wijayaparākramawardhana dyah Kṛtawijaya, the Prince of Tumapĕl who was to rule Majapahit between 1447 and 1451. When she died in 1464 she had been the Queen Mother for thirteen years and she must have been regarded as something of a grand lady in the court of the time.[1]

It was in these circles close to the throne of Majapahit that Mpu Tantular, 'The Unwavering', lived and worked in the second half of the fourteenth century. Indeed it was with the support of Rājasawardhinī and Raṇamanggala that he wrote his two *kakawin*, the *Arjunawijaya* and the *Sutasoma*, at some time between 1367 and 1389, the year in which Rājasanagara died. It may have been that Mpu Tantular enjoyed the special favour of Rājasawardhinī and Raṇamanggala. Supomo has suggested that Mpu Tantular might have been dyah Parih, the beneficiary of the freehold confirmed and recorded for posterity in the Bungur Inscription mentioned above. In confirming the grant, Rājasanagara certainly makes particular mention of dyah Parih's relationship with Rājasa-

---

[1] See Supomo 1977:8-10; Noorduyn 1978:211-8 and the literature cited there.

wardhinī and Raṇamanggala, noting his steadfast loyalty (*kadṛḍhabhaktin*) and competence (*kawidagdhan*) in their service (Supomo 1977:8, 332-3). Mpu Tantular, writing in the *Arjunawijaya* about his choice of Raṇamanggala as the *manggala* of his poem, also seems to have considered the relationship between himself and this prince of the royal family as a special one. Certainly the relationship between the two appears to have endured, for the poet mentions the continued and sympathetic support (*anumata*) of Raṇamanggala again in his second kakawin, the *Sutasoma*, which he must have written some years later.[2]

Both Supomo and Zoetmulder argue that the *Arjunawijaya* was the first of the two kakawin to have been written. In the introduction to his edition of the *Arjunawijaya*, Supomo argues that it could not have been written before 1367 and may have been written as late as 1379; the possible existence of direct references in the poem to the Bungur Inscription of course suggests that the earlier of these two dates is the more likely. Supomo goes on to argue that the *Sutasoma* could not have been finished until 1384 or 1385, dates first suggested by Berg. Whether we accept these particular dates or not, Supomo and Zoetmulder have given us good reason to accept that the *Sutasoma* is the later of the two works. Supomo points, in particular, to its size and more complex structure and the poet's greater skill in the handling of language and prosody. And as I will suggest below, there may be other important thematic considerations which support such a view.[3]

Mpu Tantular's purpose in composing the *Arjunawijaya* appears to have been entirely conventional for writers of this genre. While he clearly intended the poem as a means of expressing his gratitude to his patron Raṇamanggala, like other *kawi*, he also speaks of his poem as an act of worship (*stuti* 1,2; 73,2) and reverence (*sĕmbah* 1,2) towards his tutelary deity (*iṣṭadewata*), whom he names as śrī Parwatarājadewa, *paramārtha*-Buddha (1,1), manifest (*sakala*) in the god Wiṣṇu (73,2). His reference to his poem as a *caṇḍi bhāsa* 'a temple of words' (1,2; 74,4), 'a temple composed of language', indicates that he intended it as a *yantra*, a receptacle in which his *iṣṭadewata* could be present so that he might meditate upon this godhead and, momentarily at least, experience the bliss of union with him. It is then with some poignancy that Tantular makes reference

---

[2]   The special quality of this relationship is expressed in the *Arjunawijaya* in terms of a physical closeness and accessibility permitted to the poet by Raṇamanggala, who is described in 1,3 as 'sira sang śṛddha n parĕkninghulun' (who condescends to allow me into his presence) and in 1,4 as 'tapwan madoh ring mangö' (who is never far from me, the poet).

[3]   For discussion of references to the Bungur Inscription see below. On the question of the date and authorship of the *Arjunawijaya* and the *Sutasoma* and mpu Tantular's relationship with Rājasawardhinī, Raṇamanggala and the king Rājasanagara, see Zoetmulder 1974:342-49 and Supomo 1977:1-16, 332-3 and the references cited there.

to this god in the very last lines of his poem. There, at the moment when his poetic efforts were finally at an end, he speaks of this godhead – whom he describes as 'the object of the poet's relishing' – as being 'immaterially present in the pages of the poem' ('sang sūksmĕng lĕpihan tanah' 74,5).[4] In the same passage in which he refers to his poem as a caṇḍi bhāsa he indicates too that he intended the poem – like many a temple – as the means of channelling the protective and purifying influence of his tutelary deity into the world, which was for him the Javanese realm, thus ensuring its prosperity and the long life and stability of the Javanese ruler, Rājasanagara, and his descendants.[5]

Zoetmulder, Hooykaas, Aichele, and other scholars too have drawn attention in their writings on ancient Javanese kakawin to the ornate language which is characteristic of this genre. Mpu Tantular himself also speaks of this aspect of his poetry, drawing his readers' attention to it by contrasting *parwa* and kakawin; he describes the process of composing his kakawin as *angracana parwacarita*, 'embellishing a simply told story (*parwacarita*)' (74,2).[6] Deploying his knowledge of prosody (*guru-laghu canda* 74,4), and of the subtleties of *aksara* (*inggitaning aksara* 74,4), of grammar and lexicography (*śabdika* 74,4), the poet has transformed the story (*kathā, carita*), which he found in the Old Javanese *Uttarakāṇḍa,* into a form which the *Wirāṭaparwa* describes as verbose (*wākya wistara*), filled with ambiguities (*wakrokti*), embellishments (*bhūṣaṇa buddhiracana*), illustrations (*dṛṣṭānta*) and 'the playful liberties which poets allow themselves (*kawilīlālālana*)'.[7]

The *Arjunawijaya*, as Supomo points out, may well be lacking in particular in embellishments of sound (*śabdālangkāra*). Nevertheless, there are in the poem, most notably in the passages following the entrance of Arjunasahasrabāhu into the story, elaborate embellishments of narrative content and passages rich in figures of speech (*arthālangkāra*) (Supomo 1977:16-46, in particular 36-46). The poem in this respect then conforms to a pattern of

---

[4] For a discussion of Śrī Parwatarājadewa see Supomo 1972:281-97 and Supomo 1977:69-82. For further discussion of the religious aspect of *kakawin* see Zoetmulder 1974:173-86.
[5] The word *siddha*, referring here to the poem as caṇḍi bhāsa (1,2), means as it does in Sanskrit 'successfully accomplished'. However, it also has the sense of 'endowed with supernatural qualities' (Zoetmulder 1982, II:1756). It is this sense which is intended here, where the poem is referred to as the site of the poet's iṣṭadewata and therefore of a material power which is the occasion of prosperity and well-being. That the poem was intended to engender these qualities in the ancient East Javanese realm we can conclude from the juxtaposition of mention of the poem as a locus of such power and the poet's expressed hope that the ruler of Java would prosper.
[6] The word parwa cannot refer here to the narrative of the *Mahābhārata* but to the style of language employed in the narration of such stories.
[7] See Zoetmulder 1974:87-8 for a discussion of this passage in the Old Javanese *Wirāṭaparwa* (Fokker 1938:3).

language use which draws attention to its formal characteristics and away from the apprehension of the simple narrative (*parwacarita*). Kakawin poetry is an illusory form (*māyākāra*), as the kakawin *Sumanasāntaka* expresses it (Zoetmulder 1974:479). The poem, like the phenomenal world, is *māyā*, at once a false, illusionary appearance and at the same time that in which is embodied an essence which alone is real. Poetic creativity, the analogue of divine creativity, brings a world of language into being which seduces the mind, obscures and renders distant and half-hidden that essence which is the object of the poet's relishing.

In the metaphor, contrived in this meeting in poetry of language and cosmic design, we discover that for the ancient Javanese connoisseur, poetry was not regarded finally as something separate and aesthetic. It participated in a category of experience the parameters of which were determined on the one hand by a longing for an end to all that is tangible, perceptible, sensually and aesthetically pleasing, and on the other by the strategies of a yogic discipline which made of that longing something which might be realized. What is experienced as *langö* by the connoisseur of poetry in the case of kakawin cannot then simply be the beguiling sensuous surface of the poem, its embellishing language. As a truly yogic experience, it must have involved the apprehension and relishing of that more essential object in the poem which we know to be the poet's tutelary deity and which put an end to delight in the wretchedness of phenomenal existence, the *saṃsāra*. Between the two, the immediate seductive lingual surface and the final blissful end to phenomenal existence, narrative (*kathā, parwacarita*) has been singled out by our poet as the object of his embellishing design.

Ghosh in his book *Epic Sources of Sanskrit Literature* argues that much of the classical *kāvya* literature of ancient India, a genre upon which ancient Javanese kakawin were modelled, was inspired by the two epics, the *Mahābhārata* and *Rāmāyaṇa*. Speaking of the relationship between epic narrative and its kāvya form, he makes it clear that what he describes as the 'ransacking' of the two epics for their narrative content involved a great deal more than either the innocent retelling of the episodes, legends, myths, fables, and didactic stories from these two works or the simple desire to change the prosaic into something aesthetically pleasing. The poet, says Ghosh, appears to have quite intentionally set out to produce new meanings in the telling of his tale (Ghosh 1963:193-4 in particular).

Robson in a recent article has drawn our attention once again to the subject of narrative and its meaning in ancient Javanese kakawin. He returns to Berg's allegorical reading of the *Arjunawiwāha*, which linked the narrative of

Arjuna's meditation, triumph over Niwātakawaca, coronation and marriage
with the biography of the eleventh century Javanese king Airlangga. To this
example Robson adds Aichele's suggestion of a similar relationship between the
Rāmāyaṇa and the biography of the ninth century ruler Rakai Pikatan, and
discusses the possible allegorical references of a number of other kakawin. This
aspect of kakawin writing, argues Robson, is referred to by the word
palambang, a word which he interprets as meaning 'allegory'. The narrative, he
says, refers 'on the one hand [to] the events as told in mythology, and on the
other [to] the events as known to the author from history or current
happenings. [...] The text has an obvious, literal, meaning, but also a hidden
one, clear only to those who know which identifications have to be made.' If we
follow Robson further and adopt the suggestion he makes following his
discussion of the *Nāgarakṛtāgama*, that 'allegory' may be too narrow an
interpretation of palambang, then it might be possible to recognize in this word
reference to narration as an interpretative mode in which the retelling of old
tales afforded the poet and his reader the opportunity to create new meanings,
but new meanings endowed with the authority of an ancient lore. Poetic
meditation meant not only the creation, by means of lingual ornamentation, of a
material yet illusory form in which a godhead was present in immaterial form.
Between lingual ornament and the immateriality of the godhead was also a play
of meanings. At times purely allegorical in its reference to historical events, on
occasion it bore upon considerations of a more generalized kind, to political,
religious, economic, and cosmological ideas and values which were relevant to
the times. However, the very narrative fabric of the poem was so designed that
it obscured these meanings. The once simple narrative was woven into a
complex pattern with other new and unexpected motifs and further
embroidered by embellishments of sound and figures of speech. Poetic
contemplation involved both the creation and unravelling of these designs.[8]

Now Mpu Tantular describes his poem as a palambang (73,2) and Supomo,
Tantular's editor and commentator, points out that the most significant embellishments to the *Uttarakāṇḍa's* tale of Rāwaṇa and Arjunasahasrabāhu, which
the poet had taken as his subject, are elaborations of narrative content, in
particular those which occur after the moment when Arjunasahasrabāhu
appears in the story. While Supomo is undoubtedly correct in explaining these
changes as arising from a poetic impulse to ensure that the work conformed to
a list of formal criteria prescriptive of the genre, we hope to demonstrate that a

---

[8]   Robson 1983:299-309. I. Kuntara Wiryamartana (1981 and 1986) has made important
observations concerning the interrelationship between narrative and different levels (*taraf*) of
meaning in kakawin.

number of these changes are of paramount importance for an understanding of the thematic interests of the poet, and the poem's commentary on issues of the day.

II

The *Arjunawijaya* is the story of a virtuous king, Arjunasahasrabāhu, whom we might designate the World Maintainer, and his virtueless enemy Rāwaṇa, the World Destroyer. In the margins of the story is yet another figure, the priestly World Renouncer. To be more exact, the poem is the narrative of their journeys through the world. In the case of the virtuous Arjunasahasrabāhu it is a story of a leisurely royal tour about his realm, while in the case of Rāwaṇa it is the tale of a military expedition intended to conquer the world. The journeys meet on the banks of the sacred Narmadā River, where the two kings join battle. The virtuous Arjunasahasrabāhu triumphs over the virtueless Rāwaṇa. The intervention of Rāwaṇa's grandfather, Pulastya, and the pleadings of Arjunasahasrabāhu's Queen Citrawatī, however, ensure Rāwaṇa's release, and following his recognition of Arjunasahasrabāhu's royal authority, he is free to return to his capital in Lĕngkā. Then, following the resurrection of all those who had died in the great battle between Arjunasahasrabāhu and Rāwaṇa, the triumphant Arjunasahasrabāhu returns with his queen and court to his capital in Mahispati.

The story opens with the *Daśāsyacarita* (73,1), a narrative sequence which, as Supomo points out, remains close to the account of events in the *Uttarakāṇḍa*. It is the tale of the world-conquering journey of Rāwaṇa, the virtuous king's enemy. Before proceeding to its account of Rāwaṇa's journey in the world, however, the poem contains an introduction in which the poet establishes the origins of Rāwaṇa's character and power in the world. These are accounted for in terms of kinship, physiognomy, and meditational practice. We learn that he, his two brothers Wibhīṣana and Kumbhakarṇa, and his sister Sūrpaṇakhā are the issue of a marriage between the powerful sage (*brahmarṣi*) Wiśrawa, whose descent the poem traces back through the sage Pulastya to the God Brahma, and Kaikaśī, who is of demonic descent (*rākṣasa*). Rāwaṇa's monstrous physique, which doubtless betrays these origins, is symptomatic of an inner obtuseness, violent passion and self-interest. The passage to the start of his world-conquering journey is a period of ten thousand years spent in the practice of a rigorous asceticism on Mount Gokarṇa in the company of his two brothers for which he is rewarded by the God Brahma with the gift of qualities that enhance his martial character. Already in the introduction then, as he seizes control of his stepbrother Waiśrawaṇa's kingdom of Lĕngkā, the character of Rāwaṇa's kingly rule is established and the narrative of each of the events which mark the progress of his quest to conquer the world in the poem is, as we shall see, thematically reiterative. Each serves only as a further exposition of the self-interested and violent character of Rāwaṇa's rule and the fear, chaos, and destruction in the world to which his unrivalled power gives rise.

The narrative of his journey begins with a description of the capital of Lĕngkā and the war between Rāwaṇa and his elder brother Waiśrawaṇa, who had been Lĕngkā's ruling king. Waiśrawaṇa's rule over Lĕngkā is said to have been an untroubled one, described in the introductory passage of the poem in the following terms:

> 'He (Waiśrawaṇa) was at ease, dallying (*līlālālana*) in the mountains and by the seashore (*ring pasir wukir*)' (1,7).

This description of political order, in its evocation of dalliance on mountain and seashore, anticipates, as we shall see, the poem's later account of the virtuous king's rule. Moreover, the mention of Waiśrawaṇa calls to mind another model of orderly kingly rule as it is explicated in the *aṣṭabrata* in the Old Javanese *Rāmāyaṇa*. There Waiśrawaṇa, the god of wealth, has a place in the explanation of the functions of the virtuous king, representing the generosity which the virtuous king should display towards his subjects. This is an association which, as we shall see, is made much of in the *Arjunawijaya*'s accounting of kingship (see below). Rāwaṇa's victory over his brother Waiśrawaṇa can be read then as a curtailment of the generous influence of the latter in the world and his seizure of the throne of Lĕngkā, as a sudden and violent usurpation of an untroubled political order. The extent of that political order is intimated by the theatre of war traversed by the two kingly brothers. Beginning in Waiśrawaṇa's palace, the two rival kings traverse the world of men, enter the heavens, shaking the Mahāmeru; they churn the oceans, descend into the nether world, and finally return to the palace, which is the site of Waiśrawaṇa's final defeat. The macrocosmic expanse traversed in this fraternal conflict is a reminder of a universality that was ascribed to the Javanese realm and of the absolutism of kingly power within it. The realm could not be divided nor could kingly power be shared.[9]

The motif of the war between two brothers over the throne is an ideal one to have begun a story of kingly rule such as that of Rāwaṇa, one which results in

---

[9]   For a discussion of the notion of the universality of royal authority in ancient Java, see for instance Weatherbee 1968: Chapter 3, especially 120-32.

political chaos. The poem's narrative of Rāwaṇa's seizure of the throne of Lĕngkā is a version of a mythological paradigm which appears to have been well known in Majapahit times. Briefly, it concerns the conflict between two brothers, one older and one younger, who fight over their respective rights to the throne, and the chaos which ensues from this fraternal conflict. Other versions of this mythological paradigm in ancient Javanese literature are to be found in accounts of the conflict between Airlangga's two sons, between whom their father's realm was divided. A number of accounts of this story exist. The *Calon Arang* is perhaps the best known. There are others too, one in Kṛtanagara's Simpang Inscription and, more importantly for our purposes, another is to be found in the *Nāgarakṛtāgama* by way of explanation of the sacredness of Kamal Paṇḍak, the place where the temple was situated in which the Rājapatnī was enshrined in 1362. Another version is found in the Garuḍa story in the Old Javanese *Ādiparwa*. Here is told the story of the conflict between the two brothers Supratīka and Wibhāwasu. This episode from the Garuḍa story is depicted on the southern wall of the temple base at Caṇḍi Kĕḍaton, a temple in eastern Java which dates from Majapahit times. In the case of these stories, much is made of the priestly intervention which puts an end to the deleterious effects of the conflict.[10] Of course the most elaborate and best known version of this paradigm is the epic narrative of the conflict between the Korawa and Pāṇḍawa known in ancient Java in the form of the prose parwa, a number of kakawin and bas-reliefs on ancient Javanese temples. An exemplary exposition of the resolution of such conflict between brothers at a time when the succession to the throne is in question, is to be found in the Old Javanese *Rāmāyaṇa*'s treatment of the relationship between Rāma and his brother Bharata when the former was exiled from Ayodhyā. This is a work with which mpu Tantular must have been acquainted, given the references which we find to it in the *Arjunawijaya* and its depiction at Caṇḍi Panataran.[11] Such a paradigm, which explains the origins of political chaos, would of course have been particularly apposite in a society such as that of ancient eastern Java, where the existence of multiple marriages and large kin-groups provided an ideal

---

[10] For the *Calon Arang* see Poerbatjaraka 1926, for the Simpang Inscription see Poerbatjaraka 1922:427-8; 432-5 and for the *Nāgarakṛtāgama*'s treatment of this story see Pigeaud 1960-63, I:52-3.

[11] The references take the form of a number of curses laid on Rāwaṇa by a number of protagonists in the story of his world-conquering journey (see below). There is also reference to Rāwaṇa's death at the hands of Rāma in the poet's remark at the end of the poem (73,2–74,1) (see below). It is not unlikely that mpu Tantular would have known the *Rāmāyaṇa* illustrations sculptured on the base of the main shrine at Panataran, a structure that dates from 1347. The temple at Palah was visited by Hayam Wuruk during his royal progresses of 1359 and 1361 (Krom 1931:423, Krom 1923, II:245-8, 256-68 and Pigeaud 1960-63, I:14, 46).

breeding ground for intrigue and conflict between kinsmen over the succession to the throne. As far as the Majapahit royal family is concerned, its dynastic genealogy, the *Pararaton*, provides us with ample evidence of such conflict in its account of events surrounding succession to the Singhasari-Majapahit throne. Indeed we have every reason to believe that already in Hayam Wuruk's reign, perhaps as early as 1377, the seeds of the conflict between the eastern and western branches of the ruling family had been well and truly sown.[12]

Following the defeat of Waiśrawaṇa, the narrative of Rāwaṇa's journey describes his progress through wooded mountains and comes to a close with his conquest of Ayodhyā. There is no evident reason for the ordering of the narrative in the logic of the narrative itself; there is no interior causal or chronological imperative that explains the order of events, only abrupt and seemingly arbitrary changes of time and place of action. The logic of the narrative's progression is to be discovered in the narrational ordering of the story. Here a thematic reiteration marked at every turn by the intervention of the storyteller is clearly evident. At each stage the inspiration for Rāwaṇa's journey is a desire to conquer the world, and the subsequent violence, fear, and chaos which his quest engenders are emphasized. At every turn the death of Rāwaṇa at the hand of Rāma in a future narrative time is announced in the form of curses.

Immediately following his victory over Waiśrawaṇa, Rāwaṇa proceeds to disturb Śiwa and Umā copulating on the peak of Mount Kailāśa, provoking the playful wrath of the god and inviting the curse of the monkey-headed guardian of the mountain, Nandi. He then visits the hermitage of the beautiful anchoress Wedawatī and provokes, with the defiling touch of his lips on her hair, her self-immolation in a sacrificial fire. Again he is cursed to die at the hands of Wedawatī's future husband Rāma. He disturbs the sacrificial ritual performed by King Māruta on Mount Uśinara, challenging him to an armed conflict which he cannot accept, at least not until the ritual has been terminated. Finally the narrative closes with his attack on the virtuous king of Ayodhyā, Anaraṇya, whose realm he conquers, once again provoking disorder where once order prevailed, and inviting yet another curse which prophesies his destruction at the hands of a future prince of Ayodhyā.

We have here in this first narrative sequence a vision of a virtueless king, the World Destroyer. We have watched Rāwaṇa rampaging about the poem's landscape, obtuse, arrogant, driven by an egotistical ambition to conquer the world. He displays no forbearance toward those whose virtuous actions

---

[12]   Brandes 1920. On the conflict between eastern and western kings see Noorduyn 1975. See also Soeroso 1984.

promote peace and order: gods, kings, and priests. His rule, all but universal at the moment when the narration of his journey is broken off, has given rise only to fear, chaos, and universal disorder and has sown the seeds of his own future destruction.

With an abrupt shift of narrative focus at this point, one clearly marked in the narration, the poem's account of the rule of the virtuous king Arjunasahasrabāhu begins. As was noted above, there is a clear parallel in the narrational context of the poem's accounting for both World Destroyer and World Maintainer. The second part of the poem also contains a story of a royal journey. This time, however, it is the story of a royal progress through a virtuous king's own realm and the thematic interest of the narrative is very different.

When talking above of the reign of Waiśrawaṇa over the kingdom of Lĕngkā, we saw that the poem sought to describe the quality of his reign in terms of a dalliance (līlālālana) on wooded mountain and seashore (pasir wukir). The story of Arjunasahasrabāhu's journey to the Narmadā River is nothing more than an elaborate exposition of this theme. The essential quality of this virtuous king's rule is sought in an exemplary royal progress which wends its leisurely way through the realm depicted as wooded mountain and seashore in the month of Kārtika, a season of the year associated in kakawin poetry with the arrival of the cooling rains and a renewal of life in the world of nature. It is the same season in which the poet wanders the same landscape seeking to capture, in the dalliance which his poetic meditation is, the quality of kalangwan with which the natural landscape is imbued. The king's rule is made the analogue of an ascetic poet's meditation.[13]

As was also the case in the narrative of Rāwaṇa's journey, the story of Arjunasahasrabāhu's progress begins in the palace. However, instead of a description of the wonderful design and fabric of the palace with the statue of the malevolent world-destroying Gaṇeśa situated emblematically in its midst which we read at the start of Rāwaṇa's story, the description of the palace of this ruler of the Hehayas at Mahispati is dominated by the motif of his queen. It seems that it is in the person of the virtuous king's royal spouse Citrawatī that his rule finds its emblem.

---

[13] It will be remembered that poetic writing was described as dalliance in the *Wirāṭaparwa* where the term *kawilīlālalana* 'the playful liberties which poets allow themselves' was used (see above). On the ascetic meditational aspect of poetic activity, see above and on the ascetic aspect of kingly rule, see below. It seems that the poem seeks to ascribe what is necessary, virtuous, and orderly to a category of experience which we might call meditational. While this category is essentially a priestly one, it embraces not only priestly meditational practice but also poetic meditation, love-making, heroic struggle on the field of battle (see below), and virtuous kingliness as well.

Before the description of the queen properly begins, however, the royal couple are described in the following terms:

> For those who beheld them, the royal couple were like Smara joining Ratih, the bee and the flower/
> (They were) like the beauty of the ocean and of the mountains increased a thousand-fold by the charm of the fourth month/

The similes here, intended to describe the inseparableness of the king and queen, associate their sexual intimacy – alluded to in the references to Smara and Ratih and the image of the bee and flower – with the beauty of the natural landscape of seashore and mountains in the month of Kārtika. The enduring intimacy of the royal couple – the king always responding to his partner's beauty – and their harmonious interaction with the natural landscape – indeed their integration with it – these are themes picked up in the description of the queen in the very beginning of the poem's treatment of Arjunasahasrabāhu and extended further in the narrative of their royal progress. Throughout the narrative of the royal progress, and later too in the account of Rāwaṇa's release, in the play of imagery and in the accounts of narrative incident in particular, the enduring sexual response of the king to his queen's enticing beauty suggests that the queen is not simply an emblem. She is, as the allusion to her as Śrī Lakṣmī in Canto 41,2 suggests, an essential element and one which binds the king to the natural fertility of the realm. Royal authority then resides not in the king alone but rather in the royal couple.[14]

It cannot be fortuitous then that the poet has chosen to place so much emphasis on the description of Citrawatī in the opening passages of the story of Arjunasahasrabāhu's royal progress. In doing so, he highlights an essential difference between Arjunasahasrabāhu's kingship and that of Rāwaṇa. The most singular absence in the account of Rāwaṇa's rule is a queen. This absence appears to be the result of deliberate narrational intervention on the part of the poet. In the work which appears to have been the source of his story, the *Uttarakāṇḍa*, we are informed of Rāwaṇa's marriage to Mandodarī but no mention at all is made of Citrawatī, Arjunasahasrabāhu's queen, about whom we hear so much in the kakawin. The poet, by depriving Rāwaṇa of his queen and so royally assigning Citrawatī to Arjunasahasrabāhu, has created for himself an opportunity to associate the virtuous king's rule with the motifs of sexual dalliance and the natural landscape of seashore and wooded mountain, an opportunity of which he avails himself already in the very first description of Arjunasahasrabāhu's palace.

---

[14] On Śrī Lakṣmī see Supomo 1977:321 and below.

The story of the royal progress properly speaking commences in Canto 22. The king, seated on a splendid cart and all the while caressing his queen, sets out for the Narmadā River as the first light rains of Kārtika fall. The many onlookers along their way, which first takes them by fields where people work and children tend cattle, marvel at the sight of the splendid calvacade of tributary kings (*bhūpati*) and officials with their armed retinues mounted on elephants and horses and the palace household of maids, servants, and nurses. They go on into the mountains resplendent with blossoming plants and trees and inhabited by all kinds of animals and birds which their progress scatters before it. It seems as if the whole of nature welcomes them. Delighted with all they see, the king and queen come upon an abandoned hermitage and a hamlet inhabited by cowherds and witness the drama of a poet and his mistress pursued by her brother. They halt a while to bathe their horses in a limpid mountain stream and, setting off again, pass by ricefields and hamlets interspersed with hermitages and cloisters. Finally they arrive at a great temple complex (*dharma*).

The passage in the poem in which the visit of the royal couple to the Śaiwa-Buddhist temple complex is described is notable for the directness of its style of language, which is quite in keeping with the didactic character of the narrative at this point. The king's request for an explanation of the Buddhist shrine (*Boddhadharmākuśala*) is greeted by a long response in which the priest first expounds the essential oneness of Śiwa and Buddha. He explains then the distinction between *dharma haji*, temples built and maintained for the use of noble families, and *dharma lĕpas*, temples built for the communities of Rṣi, Śaiwas and Buddhists, and allocated gifts of land (*bhūdāna*) for their upkeep. The priest dwells at some length upon the question of the establishment and maintenance of such temples, arguing that these form an important aspect of the duty (*dharma*) of a king. Prompted not by his own self-interest but by a concern for the welfare of his subjects, the king should give liberally to his kinsmen and the warriors who protect him. But more particularly, the king's generosity should be directed towards the creation and maintenance of dharma lĕpas. In fulfilling his obligations in this respect, he must carefully distinguish between the property of the three different clerical orders, Buddhists, Śaiwas, and Rṣi, and protect them against interference by others. The merit of such generosity, the priest assures the king, is no less than that which comes to one who dies a valiant death in battle. Failure to perform his duty in this respect, however, can only have disastrous consequences, not only for the king himself, but for everybody else as well. Arjunasahasrabāhu takes the advice of the priest to heart and assures him that he recognizes his special duty towards the religious establishments in his realm. In the narrative which follows this event, the poet takes up the theme of the king's generosity in descriptions of a royal audience given to village people who arrive laden with gifts of food, the sumptuous feast provided by the king for his retinue, and his distribution of gifts to the Śaiwa and Buddhist abbots (*sthāpaka*) and clothing to a variety of lower officials including the heads of villages and *sīma*. As their progress continues, we read of visits by the king and queen to a variety of religious institutions on which he liberally bestows gifts, the case of one dilapidated Śaiwadharma lĕpas being mentioned in particular.

The story of the royal progress reaches its climax in the account of the couple's sojourn at the seaside and on the banks of the great Narmadā River. Here the theme of royal dalliance reaches its most elaborate exposition in the story. The narrative is replete with references to the entrancement of the court at the beauty of surrounding nature, references to naked or semi-naked women bathing, to the sexual dalliance of king and queen and their love-making, which in one passage the poet transforms into a yogic discipline (*smaratantrayoga*). This is not the only place in the narrative of the royal progress where dalliance is associated with the motif of ascetic meditation and the ensuing experience of blissful enlightenment. It appears also in Canto 33, for example, where the royal couple are described as being in such a state of reverie, induced by their contemplation of the charming view of the seashore, that they are on the point of being transported to the abode of the gods. In the description in this same passage of mist rising and a storm dissipating to reveal an island in the midst of the sea, is there not also to be read some reference to the blissful liberating experience of ascetic meditative practice or poetic contemplation?

Perhaps the most perfect image of the virtuous king as producer of wealth is to be found in the description of Arjunasahasrabāhu in the form of a colossal monster lying across the Narmadā River blocking it, all the while caressing the Queen Citrawatī. The couple are guarded by the army under the command of their general Suwandha while all about them their retinue are pictured delightedly gathering up the great profusion of fish, gold, silver, pearls, and precious stones which lie in the dry river-bed. Here we have a passage which captures well the mood of sexual dalliance and playful delight characteristic of Arjunasahasrabāhu's reign. The poet continues to make of kingship a pleasurable game. However, he identifies a strangeness which inhabits his depiction of king and queen. The transformation of Arjunasahasrabāhu into the form of a colossal monster is noted as being out of place in the presence of the queen ('dūra kita, masku wĕnang umulatê sĕḍĕng wibhū', 38,9). The transformation of Arjunasahasrabāhu into this form is an outward mani-

festation of a great and violent physical strength which we shall later see is
appropriate on the field of battle. The contiguity of this monstrous physical
form of the king and the queen surrounded by the court at play is poignant, for
it draws attention to the restraining influence – even the control – which the
presence of the queen exercises over the power of the king. The poet explains
the king's damming of the river as a response to the queen's pouting resistance
to his advances until he concedes to her desire that he dam the river. The poet
describes his gentle fondling of her as a response to her flirtatious rubbing of
her own body as she bathes. Having done her bidding and conceded to her
charms he finds himself unable to copulate with her for fear of the devastation
which would follow the removal of his body from the river. He can but meekly
lie across the river and caress her. She has roused him to action but redirected
his energy away from herself to another activity, which provides the
opportunity for his retinue to accumulate vast wealth in the form of gold and
silver, pearls, and other precious stones which lie in the bed of the river.

On this poignant note, the narrative of the virtuous king and queen comes to
an end and another abrupt narrational gesture carries us from one narrative
subject to another. We leave the World Maintainer and his queen to their
delightful games and return again to a world in which Rāwaṇa's vain glory and
his quest to conquer the world are the principal preoccupations. Disturbed from
his meditation of a Śiwa *lingga* by the flooding Narmadā River, he contemplates
yet again taking up arms against another virtuous king.

Until this point in the poem, the difference between World Destroyer and
World Maintainer has been quite apparent. The one, motivated by a self-
interested desire to conquer the world, has created only fear and disorder; the
other, able only to imagine a world in which kings are concerned for the well-
being of others, has inspired only delight and created harmony and order. In
the narrative sequence that now follows, where the battle between
Arjunasahasrabāhu and Rāwaṇa is narrated, both protagonists display the same
violent martial qualities. Arjunasahasrabāhu, following his transformation into
the form of a colossal giant, exhibits in his very physical being the same
monstrous characteristics which have always been Rāwaṇa's. In this aspect, he
finds an appropriate space to inhabit; on the field of battle some equivalence
between the characters of Rāwaṇa and Arjunasahasrabāhu is established in the
narrative. Both behave as heroic warriors should behave. Both are impervious
to the hail of frightful weapons hurled at them by their opponent. Both are
resourceful and brave even in moments of impending defeat when lesser spirits
might have failed. The way the narrative orders the battle according to the
status of the various protagonists is also suggestive of an equivalence between

the two. First the lesser drama of the minor protagonists is recounted, a preface to the more consummate conflict between the two principal protagonists which follows. The episode in which Suwandha, Arjunasahasrabāhu's general, challenges Rāwaṇa's advancing army illustrates the point well. At first Rāwaṇa accepts Suwandha as a worthy opponent, mistaking him for his king, Arjunasahasrabāhu. When he discovers who Suwandha is, however, Rāwaṇa retreats from the battlefield, quite unprepared to join battle with someone so unworthy to be his opponent. He scoffs at Suwandha, 'To kill a rice bird or a water swallow would take more time and be more difficult' (43,9). He leaves his army to deal with Suwandha, returning only when it seems that they will be defeated by Suwandha, whom he kills.

Finally, of course, Rāwaṇa is defeated by Arjunasahasrabāhu and so the narrative establishes in the end the inefficacy of Rāwaṇa's rule in the world. The World Maintainer's violence is master. Despite this defeat at arms, however, the poem separates the ethical quality of the rule of World Maintainer and World Destroyer not just in terms of their capacity as warriors on the field of battle. The one is not simply braver or more heroic than the other, the one is not just stronger or more violent than the other in the end. The difference is to be discovered in the greater loneliness of the World Destroyer in the hour of his defeat (compare 69 with 70,2). The existence of this great loneliness is accounted for in terms of the difference in values which motivate the two protagonists. In the cautionary words addressed to Rāwaṇa by Arjunasahasrabāhu at the request of Rāwaṇa's priestly grandfather in the final passages of the poem, the difference is described as one between obtuse arrogance (*mūrkhâwamāna*) (70,1) and a selfless concern for the good of others (*parārtha*) (70,4). Arjunasahasrabāhu upbraids Rāwaṇa for his selfishness and urges him to behave virtuously (*sādhu*) (71,1) and to act in future in the interest of the welfare of the world (*jagaddhita*) (71,1). If we recall the discussion of the story of the damming of the Narmadā River above, it would seem that the poem explains the more clement disposition of the World Maintainer by the presence of a queen who has the capacity at once to excite and to restrain the energy of the king, thus ensuring his benevolent concern for the welfare of others. In the absence of the queen, on the field of battle, Arjunasahasrabāhu manifests in his physical form and in his actions the same violence and aggression as does Rāwaṇa. Indeed it will be recalled that the queen kills herself while the battle is in its final stages, believing her husband to have been slain. Her death and then her revival, on Arjunasahasrabāhu's return, draws our attention in a quite dramatic fashion to the inseparability of king and queen away from the field of battle. It is the queen, it seems, who separates civilization from barbarity. The failure of Rāwaṇa's kingship resides in the absence of a queen. His loneliness gives to his rule its one-sided endless aggression, which can only destroy a prosperous and harmonious world order.

In the same narrative context where Arjunasahasrabāhu and Rāwaṇa's priestly grandfather Pulastya converse, another distinction is made which is important for our reading of the poem. However, on this occasion it is a distinction which the priestly Pulastya makes in his accounting for Arjunasahasrabāhu's triumph. He invokes the image of the realm as a natural landscape of wooded mountains, but in doing so he refers not to dalliance but to another kind of activity in that landscape. He makes a distinction between king and ascetic priest: the king in the enchanting beauty of his mountain-like kingdom displays the same steadfastness of mind as does the ascetic in his retreat. However, unlike the priest whose continued refusal to attend to the beguiling nymphs drives them from his presence, the king must at all times be alert to the presence of the dangers which threaten him and be active in the eradication of evil in the world about him. The priest in his own way seeks the same end as the king (71,6): the king kills evil-doers and the priest's ritual and meditative practices ensure the incarnation of Wiṣṇu's power (*prabhāwa*) in the world so that there might be just such a king in the world. Pulastya proposes then an alliance of priestly and kingly power in the interests of the welfare of the world. He even addresses Arjunasahasrabāhu as if he were just such a kingly incarnation of Wiṣṇu.[15] At this point, the poem takes an ironic turn, for Arjunasahasrabāhu politely but firmly sets aside Pulastya's accounting for his triumph and the nature of his kingly power. He disabuses Pulastya of the assumption that he is an incarnation of Wiṣṇu. Throughout the story of Rāwaṇa's journey, the references in the curses laid on him which are made to the narrative future prophesy his end at the hands of Wiṣṇu in the incarnation of Rāma born in the second world age, the Tretayuga. Arjunasahasrabāhu now makes reference to his own death in the same narrative future at the hands of another incarnation of Wiṣṇu, Paraśurāma, who will also be born in the Tretayuga and who will be responsible for the extermination of all *kṣatriya*. An alliance of lasting value between priestly and kingly power appears then not to be inevitable.

We know that the narrative return of World Maintainer and World Destroyer to their respective capitals brings no hope of lasting peace and that the world will continue to be divided between them. The poem, however, foretells a future in which not only will world-destroying kings cause chaos and

---

[15] Note the use of *-ta* ('your') in 71,5c in the middle of a verse in which general reference is being made to the incarnation of Wiṣṇu's power in the world.

disorder, but even the clement order created by a triumphant and virtuous king who is motivated by the interests of others will prove in the end to be more apparent than real. The future promise of order seemingly lies only in the hands of a warrior priest who will purge the world of all kṣatriya princes.[16] And here perhaps we recognize the priestly hand of the World Renouncer who wrote the poem. Speaking from the margins of his poem and in anticipation of the end to royal authority which the final ironic twist of his pen so clearly announces, this priestly presence has also put words of advice into the mouth of the priest of the Śaiwa-Buddha temple complex about the dire consequences for a king who does not properly maintain the material interests of an institutionalized priesthood, and which introduces into Pulastya's remark on the relationship between king and priest a further reminder of the king's duty to protect the priestly hermits in the wooded mountains (*Arjunawijaya*, Canto 71,2 and above). Or is there another future that mpu Tantular imagines? There is perhaps reason to believe that as he wrote his *Arjunawijaya* Tantular looked forward to a future Buddhist world order. In the poem's final two cantos he explains the poem as a song of praise to the god Wiṣṇu, Maintainer of the Universe (*Arjunawijaya* Cantos 73,2–74,1). In this same passage where he makes such clear reference to those incarnations of Wiṣṇu who will be responsible for the destruction of Rāwaṇa and Arjunasahasrabāhu, mpu Tantular also invokes Wiṣṇu as a material manifestation (*sakala*) of Buddha. In this equation of Buddha and world-maintaining incarnations of Wiṣṇu do we perhaps glimpse Tantular's intention to compose the *Sutasoma,* in the narrative of which the ravages of a World Destroyer give way to a singular royal Buddhist world order? If this is the case, then a tale from the *Uttarakāṇḍa* that once prefaced the future narrative world of the *Rāmāyaṇa* has been transformed by mpu Tantular into the prelude of a Buddhist epic about kings and queens and political order (Soewito Santoso 1975 and Zoetmulder 1974:329-41).

III

We have discovered mpu Tantular's kakawin *Arjunawijaya* in a space not between the *Uttarakāṇḍa* and the kakawin *Rāmāyaṇa*, where we might have expected it to be, but between the *Uttarakāṇḍa* and another kakawin, the *Sutasoma*. This discovery has been possible because of a reading of the poem which has initially sought its accounting in terms of narrational motifs which

---

[16] *Arjunawijaya*, Canto 72,1 and Cantos 73,2-74,1. On Paruśurāma see Dowson 1961:230-1.

situate the meanings of the poem in the context of a narrative world. It is in the language of narrative that the poem has discovered the grounds of an intelligibility which permits it to join in a trafficking of meanings with other narrations. It is in the language of narrative then that the poem's vision of kingship has taken material form and it is here that our reading of the poem has thus far sought to find it.

Legitimate royal authority, in the moralizing view of the poem, is universal and therefore absolute. It is the natural attribute of a royal couple, for it comes into being in the intimate embrace of a king and a queen. There can be but one centre of such authority in the world. Although it is clear that in the view of the poem the universality of Arjunasahasrabāhu's royal authority is only temporarily achieved in Rāwaṇa's submission to his authority, there is in the poem itself and in its immediate narrative context sufficient reference to its consummate establishment in the narrative future of a *Rāmāyaṇa* or a *Sutasoma* for us to accept that royal authority in the view of the poem is indeed singular and therefore absolute. However, in order to prevail, such authority must be virtuous. Royal authority is self-righteous and the poem only imagines opposition to such virtuousness being virtueless, violent, and barbaric. Virtuous itself, it propagates and protects only what is virtuous. An analogue of godliness, kingly being has a beneficent and a terrific aspect. In its terrific aspect, it turns upon all that is evil and opposed to it. Alert to the presence of evil and separated from the community of the queen's embrace, the king gives shape to violent energy which he deploys to purge the world of all that is morally corrupt and inimical to his sovereignty. Towards the good and the loyal the king turns the beneficent aspect of his authority. Inspired by an abiding desire to promote and maintain the welfare of the world, the king, in the gentle embrace of the queen, displays a splendid generosity towards kinsmen, priestly institutions, and commoners alike. In the poem such generosity is exhibited in exchanges of food and donations of gifts to village officials and grants of tax-exempt lands and other gifts to royal kinsmen and various religious orders for their material sustenance. Wealth is something which is accumulated. The wealth-producing activity of the king and queen is described as a delightful game which uncovers gold and silver, pearls, and other precious stones. Labour as a source of wealth is mentioned only in passing and as an activity of others who inhabit another world only momentarily visible from the court.

Only a priestly righteousness might lay claim to equivalence with such royal virtue. We hear the voice of priestly authority in the narrative of the poem itself. Its statements are pronounced by the priest of a Śaiwa-Buddha temple complex and we listen to its words in what *bhagawān* Pulastya has to say to Arjunasahasrabāhu at the end of the story. However, we also recognize it in the voice of the teller of our tale; it is the voice with which mpu Tantular would speak from beyond the narrative of the poem. And when we listen to what it has to say, we discover that this other source of virtuous authority is filled with paradox. The efficacy of its power derives from a condition of continual obliviousness to the world all about and yet it is not only dependent upon the world for its material sustenance, but seeks also to exercise its authority in the world. Apart from the world, it collaborates with the world, willing through the conduct of its rituals the continued presence of a virtuous royal authority, one which incarnates the world-maintaining influence of a divine Buddha Wiṣṇu. Indeed, it even threatens to intervene in the world to purge it once and for all of any royal authority which does not conform to this model.

The sources of the poem's intelligibility of course do not only exist in the narrative itself, for the poem is not a world apart. The same narrational motifs which situate the poem in the context of a narrative world establish its place in other worlds beyond the narrative itself. The poem refers directly to practices and institutions which were quite commonplace in the times in which it was written and listened to. These practices and institutions were ones which formed the active centre of royal authority in the ancient Javanese social order (Geertz 1977:151). Reference to such practices and institutions in the context of the moralizing view of the poem situate it ideologically and open the way for our historical imagination to understand how it was that the poem participated in the activities of that royal centre and partook of its authority.

In the case of the *Arjunawijaya* the major motifs out of which its narrative world has been constructed – the association of political authority with the tender intimacy of king and queen; the progress of the royal couple through the realm with its associated audiences to villagers and their officials, the feasting, the sightings of hermitages and ruined sanctuaries, the visits to temple complexes, and the concern for their proper maintenance; the conflict between kinsmen for the throne and the violent disruption of military campaigning – all these things would have been quite familiar to mpu Tantular and his contemporaries.

Donald Weatherbee has drawn attention to the special place which the relationship of king and queen occupied in thought about kingship in ancient Java. The queen embodied the king's royal authority (*rājalakṣmī*) and the king's marriage to the queen ensured him legitimate possession of the authority he required to rule. The royal couple were the analogue of a divine couple. The king's sexual contact with his queen activated his royal energy in the same way as the goddess, the god's *śakti*, activated the god's divine creative power through sexual contact with him. The emphasis we note here on the possession of a woman as the source of vital royal authority no doubt provided an important ideological focus in the politics of marriage in the courts of ancient Java. It explains the practice of *hañang*, the forcible abduction of women as booty in war, and no doubt was also considered quite compatible with the practice in Majapahit times of legitimating succession to the throne by tracing descent through the female line.

If the evidence of the *Nāgarakṛtāgama* can be taken as a reliable guide, then it seems that royal progresses were a regular occurrence in the Majapahit of the second half of the fourteenth century. The *Nāgarakṛtāgama* lists seven such progresses: in 1353 to an area near to where Surabaya is presently situated, another in 1354 to Lasĕm on the north coast of Java, and a further one in 1357 to Loḍaya on the south coast; in 1361 the king travelled to Palah near Blitar and in 1363 to Simping, both on the southern reaches of the Brantas River. The most detailed description is reserved for the progress of 1359, when Rājasanagara, with an enormous entourage which included royal kinsmen, the chief minister Gajah Mada, the king's many wives, bodyguards and servants, about 400 ox-drawn carts, elephants, horses, and large numbers of people on foot carrying regalia and other burdens, set out along narrow, badly made roads to visit some 210 localities which were scattered over some 30,000 to 45,000 square kilometres. Stops were made at forest hermitages and mountain sanctuaries, ancestral shrines and state temples all along the way. The king held public audiences, and received gifts which he redistributed; he attended ceremonies and rituals in a variety of Buddhist, Śaiwa, and Śaiwa-Buddhist domains where he on occasion engaged in learned discussion, for example, on the true character of priestliness (33,2). A visit was made to the seashore, where the king stopped for his pleasure. Hunts were organized and performances of masked dances and sporting competitions were arranged. Clearly it is in such a royal progress that we discover the likeness of the royal tour described by mpu Tantular in the *Arjunawijaya*.[17]

When discussing the narrative motif of the brothers' war above, we have already commented on its possible reference to the kind of political intrigue which prevailed between royal kinsmen in ancient eastern Java and which on occasion appears to have broken out in assassinations and open warfare. One finds also quite easily in a work such as the *Pararaton* references to military campaigning involving the movement of armies over the Javanese landscape

---

[17]   See Pigeaud 1960-63, I:14-47, IV:40-213 and Geertz 1977:157-60, who gives a brilliantly evocative description of the character of royal progresses in Majapahit times.

(see note 12). Before drawing this segment of the discussion to a close, however, I want to address the issue of the royal duty to provide for the material maintenance of priestly institutions. It is an issue upon which the author of the poem has placed some emphasis. And doing so provides us not only with another instance of the kind of direct reference to familiar practices and institutions which we have seen are so characteristic of the poem, it will also allow us to examine the possibility of the poem referring to particular historical personalities and events.

In its narration of the visit of Arjunasahasrabāhu and Citrawatī to the Śaiwa-Buddhist temple complex, the poem distinguishes between *dharma sīma* (*dharma haji*) and *dharma lĕpas*. Here the poem refers to the practice of creating *sīma* or tax-exempt territories, which were intended amongst other things to provide for the building and maintenance of temples and monasteries. The *dharma sīma* or *dharma haji*, as the poem makes clear, were for the benefit of noble families, while dharma lĕpas were tax-exempt lands placed at the disposal of three priestly orders, the Ṛṣi, the Śaiwas and Buddhists. Such tax exemptions were created by the ruler but appear on occasion to have also been created by other powerful royal persons. The right to tax exemption was not transferable by the recipients and was granted in perpetuity and could therefore not be revoked by the grantor or any successive ruler. This was not the only way in which religious establishments were maintained, but the practice appears to have formed an important basis for providing for the material needs of such institutions throughout the period between the eighth and the fifteenth centuries.

The manner in which the poem treats this subject – the strongly didactic character of the priest's comment with its precise reference to details and the accompanying warnings of the dire consequences of mismanagement – gives reason to believe that some tension existed between religious establishment and court in the matter of this practice. A number of inscriptions have survived which record the outcome of legal proceedings concerning rights to such tax exemptions and, as we will see, there are also examples of the reissuing of charters granting such rights. Spectacular is the case of the Sarwadharma Charter, issued in 1269 on the authority of the ruler of Singhasari Kṛtanagara at the very beginning of his reign. The issuing of this charter appears to have been initiated by the heads of various religious establishments who complained of the heavy burden of taxes and other contributions required from them and carried through with the assistance of their allies in the royal court. The charter records Kṛtanagara's decision that the separation of religious lands from secular lands (*thāni bala*) which had been instituted by his father Wiṣṇuwardhana be put into effect through a variety of measures, including the exemption of religious domains from payment of taxes and the performance of duties for the court and other secular authorities and the placement of the religious domains directly under the authority of their respective *dharmādhyakṣa*.[18] Following the death of Gajah Mada in 1364, a reorganization of the administration appears to have taken place which may have resulted from pressure similar to that exercised early in the reign of Kṛtanagara. Certainly the *Nāgarakṛtāgama* devotes considerable space to the subject of the administration of grants of tax exemption, mentioning a register of tax-free lands, listing the court officials charged with their administration, and recording the names of some 218-odd institutions divided into various categories. Here again it is clear that the registration and administration of these tax-free lands involved the careful distinction of a variety of categories of institutions including the three categories mentioned in the *Arjunawijaya*, Ṛṣi, Śaiwa and Buddhist. The *Nāgarakṛtāgama* also mentions the initiative of Rājasanagara, following the death of Gajah Mada, to complete a number of important dharma and to issue charters, presumably recognizing claims to tax-free privileges on the part of a number of such institutions. The Bungur Inscription, which has already been mentioned, appears to have been just one of a number of decisions taken by Rājasanagara to recognize such claims in the years following the death of Gajah Mada.[19]

This last inscription records a decision by Hayam Wuruk made in 1367 to restore tax-free privileges to lands at Bungur under the name of Śri Bodhimimba. The beneficiary was a certain dyah Parih, whose loyal and intelligent service to Rājasawardhinī and Raṇamanggala the inscription notes. It seems not unlikely that the recognition of the tax-free status of these lands may have been due to the intervention of this couple. In recording Hayam Wuruk's decision, the inscription cites an earlier decision made in the month of Kārtika in the Śaka year 782 (A.D. 860) by the Javanese king Lokapāla, described in the inscription on a couple of occasions as an incarnation of Wiṣṇu on earth. His decision to create tax-free lands (*dharmasīma lĕpas*) was for the benefit of the *mpungku* of Bodhimimba and his descendants and involved lands in North Bungur and Asana. The mpungku of Bodhimimba was the teacher (*guru pangajyan*) of the king; he was of kṣatriya family and by persuasion a Buddhist. The inscription likens him in character to Wairocana. The grant was intended

---

[18] Pigeaud 1960-63, I:99-103, IV:381-90. On the subject of such grants generally see Christie 1985:13-6 and 1983.

[19] See above. On the *Nāgarakṛtāgama*'s reference to grants of tax exemption, administrative reforms following the death of Gajah Mada and the organization of the religious orders see Pigeaud 1960-63, IV:214-66.

for the building of a temple in which a statue of the Buddha was to be placed and in whose honour a *puja* was to be celebrated each year in the month of Kārtika. Following consecration of the temple the tax-free lands were to be known by the name of Kañcana, and its priest (*sthāpaka*) was to be a Buddhist. It seems that the tax-free lands were also intended to support another temple of which the priest was a *brāhmaṇa* and who Kern suggests was a Śaiwa. Furthermore, the mpungku of Bodhimimba undertook to devote himself continually to the conduct of pūjā, meditation, and prayers that the king might live long, defeat his enemies and rule over a united and peaceful realm (Kern 1917).

Supomo has seen in the description of the Śaiwa-Buddhist temple sanctuary described in the *Arjunawijaya* a possible reference to an important temple mentioned in the *Nāgarakṛtāgama*, the dharma of Kagĕnĕngan, the temple in which the founder of the Majapahit dynasty, bhatāra Girināthaputra, was enshrined. Supomo goes on to conclude that the *Arjunawijaya's* reference to this complex suggests that Prapañca's appeal for the restoration of this decayed dharma in the *Nāgarakṛtāgama* had been successful. While one should take this possibility seriously, there is another, and in some ways more obvious, possibility to pursue in the case of *Arjunawijaya's* reference to the Śaiwa-Buddhist sanctuary. On the basis of those details which have been extracted from the Bungur Charter above, is it not possible to see in the poem's account of a visit by a reigning monarch in the month of Kārtika to a Śaiwa-Buddhist sanctuary an allusion to a similar complex at Bungur whose ancient rights as a tax exempt domain had been restored through the intervention of Rājasawardhinī and Raṇamanggala in the month Asuji 1367, just one month before the annual pūjā was due to take place in the month of Kārtika? An immediate reference of this kind is quite apposite in a part of the poem which addresses itself in such an obviously didactic manner to the question of royal responsibilities in the matter of providing for the material maintenance of religious establishments. The positive response of Arjunasahasrabāhu captures well the apparently enthusiastic support of Rājasawardhinī and Raṇamanggala, and ultimately of Rājasanagara too, for dyah Parih in the case of his claims to tax exemption. One does not have to accept that dyah Parih and mpu Tantular are identical, a suggestion which Supomo has put forward, to agree with this proposal. It is clear that dyah Parih and mpu Tantular were contemporaries and both had close connections with the court of Rājasawardhinī and Raṇamanggala. It is not at all improbable that mpu Tantular would have been aware of the import of the Bungur Inscription and of the role of his patron Raṇamanggala in the restoration of dyah Parih's rights (Supomo 1977:332-3).

This may not be the only such reference to Raṇamanggala in the poem. In

canto 53 we find Suwandha's speech to the commanders of Arjunasahasrabāhu's
army in which he urges them to stand fast in the face of the enemy. In a passage
in which the activity of warriors in battle is transformed into an ascetic ritual
leading to release from saṁsāra, the first stanza contains an apparent allusion to
the name of Raṇamanggala, 'One who brings good fortune in battle'.
Suwandha's words are directed in particular to those whom he addresses as
'rulers who bring good fortune' ('para ratu pinakādimanggala'), and his
subject: their goal on the field of battle ('pinakeṣṭining apĕningan ing
raṇānggaṇa') (53,1b,d). It is as if Suwandha's words were addressed to Raṇamanggala, and other of his royal contemporaries, in much the same didactic
fashion as the comment of the priest of the Śaiwa-Buddha temple complex was.
The description of Raṇamanggala in the very first canto of the poem as 'the
embodiment of the fourth month' ('sang sākṣāt paśarīraning masa kapat') also
opens the way for the discovery of an allusion to the quality of his rule, as one
of the *prabhu* of the Majapahit realm, in the description of the leisurely
progress of Arjunasahasrabāhu and his queen through the natural landscape of
their realm during the fourth month (Weatherbee 1968:148-75).

Perhaps even the way in which mpu Tantular speaks of his purpose in
composing his poem contains allusions to the Bungur Inscription. The
inscription records, as we have already noted, the intention to construct a
temple in which a statue of the Buddha would be placed and in honour of
which, in every month of Kārtika, a pūjā would be celebrated. It notes also the
intention of mpungku Bodhimimba, through the conduct of rituals appropriate
to his office as a Buddhist priest, to ensure the long life of a king who is likened
to Wiṣṇu, and to facilitate his victory over his enemies and the continuance of
his peaceful rule over a united kingdom. Mpu Tantular's poem too was intended
to be a temple of words (*caṇḍi bhāsa*), a locus for the priestly poet's praise of
his tutelary god, who we have learnt was none other than the lord Buddha,
manifest in the world as the god Wiṣṇu, a kingly presence whose influence
ensured the maintenance of the same kind of world order as that which mpu
Tantular hoped his temple of words would promote when he associated his
poem with the long life and welfare of his own ruler, Rājasanagara. Perhaps
there is too, in the person of the priestly mpungku Bodhimimba, a reference to
the mould in which mpu Tantular saw himself formed in his relationship to
Rājasawardhinī and Raṇamanggala and to royal authority more generally.
Mpungku Bodhimimba's function as royal tutor finds its analogue in the
moralizing intent of mpu Tantular's poem to teach kings how to rule.

But if the poem has the occasional character which this kind of reference
suggests it had, what are we to make of the poem's grander allusions to conflict

between rival kings and to tension between a virtuous ruler and the clerical orders in his realm, and even to the spectre of a warrior priest who might one day bring down a virtuous king's rule? In such questioning of the roots of royal authority are we to recognize a pessimism about political order in Majapahit in the second half of the fourteenth century? Following the disappearance of the strong hand of Gajah Mada in 1364, did there appear inevitable and enduring rivalries between Rājasanagara and powerful royal kinsmen? Is there perhaps particular reference to the influential position which was occupied by Wijayarājasa, the Prince of Wĕngkĕr, in the Majapahit court of the time and in which the wars of 1400-1406 between royal kinsmen appear to have originated? Is there then in mpu Tantular's advocacy of a future Buddhist order some attempt to discover a new foundation of royal authority? Was it a response to the same circumstances which had led others to seek novel ways of thinking about kingship in the tales of Pañji and other stories which appear for the first time as illustrations on temples and shrines in the second half of fourteenth century and in the fifteenth century? Was he even perhaps attempting to counter a quite alien explanation of things, promoted by an Islamic community which was establishing itself at the heart of the Javanese realm at the same time?[22]

---

[22] Noorduyn 1975 on Wĕngkĕr and the conflict between Eastern and Western kings. On the presence of a Muslim community in Majapahit in the second half of the fourteenth century Robson 1981:271-2 and Damais 1954:34a. Pañji stories for example appear on the *pendopo* terrace at Candi Panataran (1375) and on shrines on Mount Penanggungan (15th century). The *Sri Tañjung* is illustrated at Candi Jabung (mid 14th century), Candi Surawana (1400) and also on the *pendopo* terrace at Candi Panataran. The *Calon Arang* is on Candi Gambar Wetan (1410-1438) and the *Sudamala* Candi Tigawangi (1388). See Bernet Kempers 1959, Suleiman 1978 and 1981, Terwen-de Loos 1971.

Bibliography

Berg, C.C.
1972   'In memoriam Walther Aichele', *Bijdragen tot de Taal-, Land- en Volkenkunde* 128:209-13.
Bernet Kempers, A.J.
1959   *Ancient Indonesian art*. Amsterdam: Van der Peet.

Brandes, J.L.A.
1920   *Pararaton (Ken Arok) of het boek der koningen van Tumapĕl en van Majapahit.* Tweede druk, bewerkt door N.J. Krom. 's-Gravenhage: Nijhoff; Batavia: Albrecht. [Verhandelingen van het Bataviaasch Genootschap van Kunsten en Wetenschappen 62; First edition 1896.]

Christie, Jan Wisseman
1983   'Rāja and Rāma: The classical state in early Java', in: Lorraine Gesick (ed.), *Centres, symbols, and hierarchies: Essays on the classical states of Southeast Asia,* pp. 9-44. New Haven: Yale University Southeast Asia Studies. [Monograph Series 26.]
1985   *Theatre states and Oriental despotisms: Early Southeast Asia in the eyes of the West.* Hull: Centre for South-East Asian Studies, University of Hull. [Occasional Paper 10.]

Damais, L.-C.
1954   'Etudes Javanaises; 1. Les tombes musulmanes datées de Trålåyå', *Bulletin de l'Ecole Française d'Extrême-Orient* 48:353-417.

Dowson, J.
1961   *A classical dictionary of Hindu mythology and religion, geography, history and literature.* London: Routledge and Kegan Paul.

Fokker, A.A.
1938   *Wirātaparwa opnieuw uitgegeven, vertaald en toegelicht.* 's-Gravenhage: Smits. [Ph.D. thesis, University of Leiden.]

Geertz, C.
1977   'Centres, kings and charisma: Reflections on the symbolics of power', in: J. Ben-David and T.N. Clark (eds), *Culture and its creators,* pp. 150-71. Chicago: Chicago University Press.

Ghosh, J.
1963   *Epic sources of Sanskrit literature.* Calcutta.

Kern, H.
1917   'Over eene Oudjavaansche oorkonde (gevonden te Gĕḍangan, Surabaya) van Çāka 782 (of 872)', in: *Verspreide geschriften.* Zevende deel, pp. 17-53. 's-Gravenhage: Nijhoff. [First published 1881.]

Krom, N.J.
1923   *Inleiding tot de Hindoe-Javaansche kunst.* Tweede herziene druk. 's-Gravenhage: Nijhoff. 2 vols.
1931   *Hindoe-Javaansche geschiedenis.* 's-Gravenhage: Nijhoff.

Kuntara Wiryamartana, I.
1981   Struktur dan estetik; Tinjauan Kakawin Arjunawiwaha sebagai
            karya seni. Paper presented to Penataran Tenaga Ahli
            Kesusastraan Jawa dan Nusantara, Yogyakarta.
1986   'Beberapa pokok tentang penelitian kakawin', *Basis*, Majalah
            Kebudayaan Umum 35:13-7.
Noorduyn, J.
1975   'The eastern kings in Majapahit', *Bijdragen tot de Taal-, Land-
            en Volkenkunde* 131:479-87.
1978   'Majapahit in the fifteenth century', *Bijdragen tot de Taal-, Land-
            en Volkenkunde* 134:207-74.
Pigeaud, Th.
1960-63   *Java in the fourteenth century; A study in cultural history; The
            Nāgara-kĕrtāgama by Rakawi Prapañca of Majapahit, 1365 A.D.*
            The Hague: Nijhoff. 5 vols.
Poerbatjaraka, R. Ng.
1922   'De inscriptie van het Mahāksobhya-beeld te Simpang
            (Soerabaya)', *Bijdragen tot de Taal-, Land- en Volkenkunde*
            78:426-62.
1926   'De Calon-Arang', *Bijdragen tot de Taal-, Land- en Volkenkunde*
            82:110-80.
Robson, S.O.
1981   'Java at the crossroads; Aspects of Javanese cultural history in the
            14th and 15th centuries', *Bijdragen tot de Taal-, Land- en
            Volkenkunde* 137:259-92.
1983   'Kakawin reconsidered: toward a theory of Old Javanese poetics',
            Bijdragen tot de Taal-, Land- en Volkenkunde 139:291-319.
Soeroso, M.P.
1984   'Kedaton Wetan dan Kedaton Kulon pada Masa Majapahit',
            Amerta 9:1-6.
Soewito Santosa
1975   *Sutasoma; A study in Javanese Wajrayana.* New Delhi:
            International Academy of Indian Culture.
Suleiman, Satyawati
1978   *The pendopo terrace of Panataran.* Jakarta: Proyek Pelita
            Pembinaan Kepurbakalaan dan Peninggalan Nasional.
1981   *Batur pendopo Panataran.* Jakarta: Proyek Penelitian Purbakala.

Supomo, S.
1972   '"Lord of the Mountains" in the fourteenth century kakawin',
            Bijdragen tot de Taal-, Land- en Volkenkunde 128:281-97.
1977   *Arjunawijaya; A kakawin of mpu Tantular*. The Hague: Nijhoff.
            2 vols. [KITLV, Bibliotheca Indonesica 14.]
Terwen-de Loos, J.
1971   'De Pandji-reliëfs van Oudheid LXV op de Gunung Běkěl
            Pěnanggungan', *Bijdragen tot de Taal-, Land- en Volkenkunde*
            127:321-30.
Weatherbee, D.E.
1968   *Aspects of ancient Javanese politics*. [Ph.D. thesis, Johns Hopkins
            University, Baltimore.]
Zoetmulder, P.J.
1974   *Kalangwan; A survey of Old Javanese literature*. The Hague:
            Nijhoff. [KITLV, Translation Series 16.]
1982   *Old Javanese-English dictionary*. 's-Gravenhage: Nijhoff. 2 vols.

E.U. KRATZ

Criticism and scholarship
The study and teaching of Indonesian literature in a non-Indonesian context

When the organizers of this symposium suggested the theme of 'Variation and Transformation' I presume they had in mind primarily the study of past and current manifestations of Indonesian literatures. Yet, in further considering the intention of the organizers of trying to provide a picture of current trends in the study of Indonesian literatures, I could not help but think of this theme of 'Variation and Transformation' in the context of the teaching of Indonesian literatures. There is of course nothing special about this thought and it is one which had to emerge, given the significance of this symposium, which is to mark the retirement of Professor Teeuw. Looking for variation and trans-formation in the field of Malay and Indonesian literatures one would do quite well by simply consulting the published work of Prof. Teeuw which, over a period of 42 years now, has been a witness to this theme, synchronically and diachronically, thematically and historically, displaying a wide topical range and methodological variety.

One of the most significant aspects of the study and teaching of Indonesian literature today is a changing attitude to the subject. I am not so much thinking of the high profile that literary theories have developed of late, if Indonesian and other publications of the last few years are anything to go by,[1] but of the fact that we are moving out of the era of the pure eyewitness record into a different phase. That is, besides being critical students, recorders, and analysts of current events, which has been the major occupation of students of Indonesian literature so far, observers of that literature have now to look back as well and deal with happenings which only yesterday were still contemporary, i.e. the creation and birth of a new literature, as historical events. The fact that

---

[1]   It would go beyond the context of this paper if I were to list all the relevant literature on this as well as on any other issue raised here. Therefore a brief selection will have to be sufficient. Concerning the prominence literary theory has gained in Indonesian literary studies there are, amongst others: Damono 1978, Darma 1983 and 1984, Hardjana 1981, Nadjib 1984, Sumardjo 1984, Teeuw 1984, Yudiono KS 1986.

many of the original participants in this happening and many of its consenting critics and original mentors are still actively engaged in this literature, as well as the fact that much of what was topical in the 1930's and 1940's, such as the Polemik Kebudayaan or the issue of popular literature, are still topical today, should not distract us from the other fact that these events and developments have gained a considerable historical dimension since, which requires a different approach from that applied in day-by-day criticism, analysis, and description.[2] It is here that newcomers to the field are at a disadvantage for, without intending to take away anything at all from the work done so far, both bibliographically and analytically – work which students of Indonesian literature are familiar with and for which they are grateful – there still exists a dearth of proper documentation and published studies. Some of the questions which emerge in consequence of this different and in some respects more detached approach and which are pertinent to our study and teaching, I would like to touch upon in this paper. I intend to address myself in particular to the questions of a linguistic and literary definition of this literature, its origins and links with other literatures, its literary assessment and historical appraisal, and its social and political context.

When teaching a course on Indonesian literature and its history one needs to face the important questions of how to define this contemporary literature which is written in Indonesian, what it consists of and where it begins. To begin with, the first step to make when looking at the literatures of today's Indonesia is probably to differentiate between those forms of literature that only live in the memory of people and at best are merely reproduced or 'reproductive', as are some of the more traditional forms, such as the *syair*, and those that are creative and productive, and generate new texts. Having distinguished between 'dead' and 'living' literatures on a very superficial basis, as there has been hardly any research into the demarcation line between the two, we need to make a further differentiation of those living ones which we are primarily concerned with in the teaching of this course. Here concepts such as national, regional, and provincial literature will have to be introduced. There may be some argument as to whether there is a distinction to be made between Indonesian regional and provincial literatures; yet, if we take regional to be an

---

[2]   If I have understood Prof. Teeuw correctly, given the genesis of his invaluable study which has grown together with the literature it discusses from *Voltooid Voorspel* (Teeuw 1950) and *Pokok dan Tokoh* (Teeuw 1952) into the present *Modern Indonesian Literature* (Teeuw 1967), it is this necessary difference in approach which made him decide against a change in format for the second, enlarged, edition (Teeuw 1979) and to opt for a discussion of more contemporary manifestations of Indonesian literature. Needless to say, however, the new second volume reflects in its description and analysis of recent texts its author's historical knowledge and insight.

exclusively linguistic criterion, given that national and regional literature share common themes, and provincial a thematic and qualitative one, the two are clearly distinct from each other and the difference between them and a national literature which can be defined both linguistically and thematically, becomes evident. Linguistically, national literature would be that which aims to address itself to everybody speaking and reading Indonesian regardless of whether it is his or her first or second language and, perhaps even more importantly, it is the literature which, through the language it uses, is able to reach all speakers of Indonesian. In other words, if the linguistic idiosyncrasies of an author can still be understood and appreciated by readers who do not share the author's mother language, or, at the least, if these idiosyncrasies do not form an obstacle to such understanding, then this literature may be called national.

This linguistic definition of a national literature can equally be applied when trying to distinguish thematically between national literature on the one hand, and provincial literatures on the other.[3] By defining national literature linguistically and thematically as the one with quantitatively the widest reservoir of readers, regional and provincial literature have been defined already in a negative way as being of appeal only to restricted audiences. Expressed more positively, it has to be recognized that thematically regional literature, although linguistically aimed especially at the speakers of only one regional language, does not deal exclusively with problems and issues particular to that language community only, but it will deal with these and other, wider (national and universal) problems in a way to which this linguistic group can relate particularly well. Provincial literature, in contrast, would be the literature which, using national or regional languages, concerns itself exclusively with the local problems and parochial issues of one particular social or cultural group within a given community. Provincial literature does not desire to reach a wider audience, but produces texts for the consumption and appreciation of that specific, narrow group.

The relationship between regional and provincial and national literature has hardly been studied so far, and it would be an extremely interesting and worthwhile exercise to try and find a satisfactory explanation for the fact that some writers who, it would seem, are successful authors in their regional tongues seem keen to venture into the national arena. To say that the rewards appear

---

[3]   Taken one step further and going beyond the confines of a given national language, universal literature would then be the literature which is able to appeal to a readership larger than that of the text's original language, and a literature which can be appreciated by other readers within their own specific, intellectual and social context regardless of the text's particular origins and frame of reference.

higher nationally might be too simple an answer, as it is not yet certain that the recognition of a 'national' writer is more rewarding than that of a writer who is appreciated and esteemed in his own regional community and society.

Turning now to the national literature as such, this literature needs urgent further definition in addition to the one provided above, that is, as the literature aiming linguistically and thematically at all readers of Indonesian, since it still means different things to different people. In the Indonesian case, especially a text's theme, its way of publication, and its particular social, cultural, historical, and even geographical context are used to allot it its place on a scale between what is considered 'good' and what 'bad' literature. Frequently too the term *susastra* is brought up in this context, implying some kind of belles lettres: the 'real, good, true, and serious' literature which, by some undefined consensus of opinion, has been produced in a 'recognized' way by 'recognized' authors in 'recognized' journals and by 'recognized' publishers. Terms such as *sastra majalah*, or *sastra koran, sastra hiburan, sastra pop*, and *bacaan liar* are widely used to discredit the 'unrecognized' literary expressions thus described and produced. Yet, if we look more closely into the history of publishing in Indonesia and if we follow the publishing history of the works even of 'recognized' authors, we find that particularly the division between sastra majalah and sastra koran, namely the texts published outside the generally 'recognized' literary and cultural journals – the 'bad' literature – and those published inside – the 'good' literature of susastra – is an artificial one. To give some examples: In his *Ichtisar Sedjarah Sastra Indonesia* Ajip Rosidi (Rosidi 1969) lists a total of 35 'recognized' outlets, not all of which were purely literary journals, from *Jong Sumatra* to *Horison*. For a bibliographical study on literary texts in journals which I have conducted recently[4] I have consulted 113 different periodicals and I still carry a list of names of periodicals which I would like to have seen but which so far I have been unable to obtain. In this study I found that of the twenty-one authors who have more than 100 titles to their credit (according to my data), and who, by and large, belong to the 'recognized' authors, six authors published in more than twenty periodicals, nine used less than twenty but more than ten journals, and six less than ten periodicals.

Those who published in less than ten periodicals were: A.M.D.G. Myala, Or Mandank, Armijn Pané, Amir Hamzah, and M.R. Dajoh. Of these authors, whose names are largely linked with the pre-war years, only M.R. Dajoh published the major part of his work after Independence but still during the

---

4   The study has since been published (Kratz 1989).

Revolution, when periodicals were as few in number as they had been during the colonial period.

The following published in between ten and twenty periodicals: Sitor Situmorang, Sapardi Djoko Damono, Subagio Sastrowardojo, Abdul Hadi W.M., Taufiq Ismail, Toto Sudarto Bachtiar, Mansur Samin, Harijadi S. Hartowardojo, and Suradal A.M.

And these are the writers who used more than twenty periodicals: Ajip Rosidi, Rendra, Rijono Pratikto, Trisno Sumardjo, Muhammad Ali, and Motinggo Boesje.

Clearly not all of the journals used by the authors mentioned can be found in Ajip Rosidi's list. Among them are a number of journals which are rarely mentioned by serious critics. One of them, *Aneka*, lists among its contributors, to mention just some of the better-known names, Muhammad Ali, Yusach Ananda, S.M. Ardan, Motinggo Boesje, Sjuman Djaya, Sirullah Kaelani, Ramadhan K.H., Titie Said, Sori Siregar, Sitor Situmorang, Utuy Sontani, Djamil Suherman, Purnawan Tjondronegoro, and Pramoedya Ananta Toer. *Brawidjaja* and its successor *Widjaja* are journals from Surabaya which many may never have heard of, yet among their contributors were Sapardi Djoko Damono, Muhammad Fudoli, and Gerson Poyk, in addition to some of the other authors I have just mentioned.

A closer study of the general periodical literature reveals that what many Indonesian critics consider entertainment, *sastra picisan, hiburan*, and *pop*, cannot be approached properly with an a-priori air of condescension and belittlement. None of the writings have been studied sufficiently yet to allow any kind of general judgement, let alone a negative one. The *picisan* authors of the 1930's, for example, saw themselves as religious writers and as the only truly Indonesian authors (Kratz 1986:64). The three published volumes of Pramoedya Ananta Toer's tetralogy (Toer 1980a, 1980b, 1985a) which are hailed as high points of contemporary literature, show as much affinity to the bacaan liar [5] as they are examples of current literary expression.

When looking at studies in Indonesian it becomes obvious that when speaking and writing about Indonesian literature, it is generally implied that what one is referring to are those texts which are regarded as belonging to 'serious, recognized' literature, to susastra. The occasional protest by a few Indonesian authors such as Nasjah Djamin (Djamin 1984) against this bias in approach has received little attention so far. It would be a highly useful topic of research to establish the criteria for this Indonesian understanding of what is serious

---

[5]   This affinity becomes particularly obvious in a comparison with the fiction written by R.M. Tirto Adhi Soerjo which has been edited by Pramoedya Ananta Toer himself (Toer 1985b).

literature and to identify the conceptual basis for Indonesian literary appreciation. Simply to blame 'the West', however, would be too easy an answer.

For the purposes of our course it would probably be better to define Indonesian literature as every creative text written in Indonesian which displays individuality in authorship and strives for originality in expression. The thematic nature of the text and social background of its author are and remain as irrelevant in this definition as the text's place and mode of publication. Terms such as 'good' and 'bad' would merely serve to indicate how close a text has come to the aim of originality of thought and expression (taking individual authorship for granted). Measuring Indonesian literature by the yardstick of individuality and originality, then, good and bad texts can be found spread over a wide spectrum of media and genres.

But now to the naming of this literature. Usually one is offered the terms 'modern' (Indonesian) literature (Sastra Indonesia Modern) or 'new' (Indonesian) literature for its description. The last term of course begs the question as to whether the 'new' refers to Indonesia or to the literature. Unfortunately, the Indonesian forms 'sastra Indonesia baru' and 'sastra baru Indonesia' seem to be used indiscriminately, thus making an answer difficult. What then is this modern and new Indonesian literature and where does it come from?

The terms new and modern might indicate that there is, or rather was, another literature: a traditional and old or perhaps even old-fashioned literature. It would not be unreasonable to assume that this old and traditional Indonesian literature preceded this modern new literature of today. But, as Prof. Teeuw has said in the first chapter of his *Modern Indonesian Literature,* there is no such thing as an old and traditional Indonesian literature. Indonesian literature was only born with Indonesian nationalism, and the concept of an Indonesian literature is as young as the political concept of Indonesia. Of course, prior to the Indonesian literature of today there existed other literatures, but those were the literatures of the various ethnic groups of the Archipelago written in their respective languages, and none of these regional literatures can be seen to have preceded Indonesian literature directly. Most of these traditional regional literatures came to an end in the course of the 19th and 20th centuries. Regional languages are no longer used to create written literature except for a few languages, such as Sundanese and Javanese (Ras 1979, Rosidi 1966), which still flourish in their respective environments. Today there exists a considerable body of modern texts in those two languages, Sundanese and Javanese, thus justifying the use of the adjective 'modern' with reference to the contemporary literatures of the Sundanese and Javanese. With reference to Indonesian, however, the case seems different for the reasons which I have just tried to indicate.

It has been suggested that this 'modern' Indonesian literature is a continuation of that in Malay, be it called Classical or Traditional.[6] It has further been suggested that Indonesian literature was preceded directly by various types of literature of the late 19th and early 20th centuries written in Malay which had developed as the indigenous press began to grow from the 1850's onwards. Here it still has to be clarified which, of the various types of contemporary Indonesian literature I have referred to above, these earlier texts are supposed to precede. While serious research has begun on some aspects of this earlier literature (Salmon 1981, Sykorsky 1980, Watson 1971) and, to a limited extent, on what the authorities of the day called bacaan liar (Chambert-Loir 1974, Tickell 1981), most of these pre-1920's texts still remain unstudied. Yet, these limitations in our knowledge have not prevented the formulation of far-reaching theories and the publication of broad generalizations on the narrow basis of whatever research has been done concerning in particular the roots of Indonesian susastra and its development. As so often happens, these theories are based in part on non-literary, ideological arguments on account of the shortage of literary studies based on an intensive investigation of all the available literary evidence. Without pretending to have been engaged in any kind of study myself, I would like to take this opportunity to add my own theory and hypothesis and negate any direct link between those early literatures and the belles-lettres as generally understood today. If one is looking for a continued development of these early literatures, it might prove more fruitful to look into the connection between them and the so-called trivial literature of the 1930's, the well-known sastra picisan, and, more recently, the sastra hiburan of the 1950's and 1960's, and the sastra pop of the 1970's and early 1980's.

Where then does susastra, the recognized belles-lettres of the 20th century, written in Indonesian, come from? There are two links always dutifully referred to in textbooks and surveys, Abdullah and the Dutch generation of the 1880's, the famous Tachtigers. Let us discuss Abdullah first. Indeed, his work is important and worth studying for several reasons which concern his subject matter, form, language, and style, but so far nobody has really demonstrated

---

[6] Use of the term *classical* is misleading and has to be rejected because of its European connotation of representing 'the best of its kind' as defined under the heading 'Classicism ' in the Encyclopaedia Britannica, Micropaedia, vol.II: 973 (Chicago 1974). It still has to be proven that what we possess of traditional Malay literature today is the best, since the fact that we happen to have a certain number of manuscripts from certain regions of the Archipelago, written and copied over a certain period of time in the past, is insufficient reason to justify the use of the term *classical* for their description.

that Abdullah created a literary tradition and all we can conclude at the moment and present to students is the exceptional nature of Abdullah's personality and work. But Abdullah was not the only one who responded to the challenges of the 19th century. Amin Sweeney (Sweeney 1980) has shown that there were others who in a far more natural and evolutionary way have attempted to change the nature of traditional literature, and it would be interesting to see how one might possibly be able to link modern developments to these changes. Raja Ali Haji could be mentioned here as well, as an example for the tremendous movements that took place in traditional literature during that time and the different responses. Yet in both cases, Abdullah and Raja Ali Haji, it would seem that despite the innnovative changes made to the nature of traditional literature, it and its normative poetics were not the appropriate means with which to respond creatively to the challenges of the day.

To establish a link is made even more difficult since in the works of Abdullah (and of Raja Ali Haji) we are dealing with non-fictional texts, whereas in the case of contemporary Indonesian literature we are generally discussing texts of a fictional nature.

There still remains what might be called Abdullah's journalistic work. Here indeed it might be possible to find a link between texts such as the famous *Syair Kampung Gelam Terbakar* (Skinner 1973) and features in the newly emerging press, of which the contemporary *kisah nyata* type of real-life story seems a late successor. But then this use of the syair is not particular to Abdullah. The syair always seems to have offered itself more easily than the *hikayat* to the narrative description of current events and of personal emotions (albeit in a very indirect form). As we realize that Abdullah was not the only one to have produced literature of the kind, we may even go one step further and postulate that the 'transitional' literature proposed by Skinner (Skinner 1978) still exists today side by side with Indonesian belles-lettres and other types of Indonesian contemporary literature.

This still leaves us with the the European link of Indonesian susastra. Studies of Indonesian literature always refer to the link with the Dutch generation of the 1880's, the Tachtigers, which, it is explained by both sympathetic and hostile critics of the development of Indonesian literature alike, is a result of colonial education and indoctrination. But does the colonial context really suffice to explain the emergence and future growth of this new and different literature? If, for example, Balai Poestaka literature was forced upon an unwilling, unresponsive, and unconditioned public, why is it then that these artificial texts, as their critics call them, are still being reprinted today? Not all of the Balai Poestaka publications which are still popular are set books at school.

Perhaps our study of Indonesian literature might be taken further if one were to compare in more detail the historical circumstance of the rise of both literatures, that of the Tachtigers and that of the young Indonesians.[7] In purely literary terms, both might be studied and compared as a response to the shackles of some by then unproductive, normative, and sterile poetics which no longer allowed for any creative expression. In wider cultural and social terms perhaps they could be studied and seen in connection with the emergence of the individual (and the middle classes), which, as we know from detailed studies of other, European, literatures of the late 19th and early 20th centuries is part of that general upheaval and movement which has come to be known under the banner of modernism (Bradbury and McFarlane 1981, especially pp. 104-9). The term Modernism covers the tremendous social, economic, cultural, intellectual, and political changes which were felt worldwide over a period of time at the turn of the century and which, it would seem, have provoked similar responses in different places at different times, and which no doubt have been intensified in their interrelationship and force by the considerable technical advances made in international communications which allowed for a much faster exchange and turnover of ideas.[8]

Returning to early Indonesian literature and its direct link with the Tachtigers, one of the questions that might be considered is for example whether the Indonesians would have accepted any other poetic form but the sonnet? Might it not be worthwhile to pursue further the thought expressed first by Armijn Pané well over 50 years ago in 1933 (Pané 1963) of the formal and structural compatibility of sonnet and *pantun*, rather than emphasizing the fact that the sonnet was the favourite poetic form of the Tachtigers? That the old norms and forms had outlived their purpose even though they were still well known in the 1920's was probably shown most entertainingly by Roestam Effendi in his very successful, witty parody of the traditional form, his poem 'Bukan beta bijak berperi' (Effendi 1953:28), which is a formally highly accomplished witness to traditional poetics but which in every sentence and line rejects the philosophy of the old poetics. This does not mean that with the arrival of new and foreign forms, the indigenous, Indonesian spirit was abandoned as well. On the contrary, this spirit was still alive, as was shown most successfully before the war by Amir Hamzah. What needs to be discussed

---

[7]   Noticeable too is the fact that in discussions of the early beginnings of Indonesian literature no reference is made to developments on the Malay Peninsula, although this comparative approach is bound to produce valuable insights.

[8]   To give another example of the undeniable importance of communications we only have to refer to the movement in 19th century Indonesian Islam which, it has been argued, was greatly helped and fostered by the improved shipping facilities following the opening of the Suez Canal.

in teaching, however, is the irony that while in Amir Hamzah's case this Malay
spirit was held against him, probably because of his aristocratic background,
even though his poetry is undeniably modern and can be shown and proven to
be so,[9] in the 1950's in the case of Sitor Situmorang and in the 1970's in that of
Sutardji Calzoum Bachri, it was exactly this evocation of the traditional spirit
of Malay poetry which has enhanced their reputation. It might be worth
remembering too in this connection that Chairil Anwar himself is said to have
considered his most successful poem to be 'Cerita buat Dien Tamaela' (Anwar
1966:33), a poem which is highly evocative in its recollection of the spirit of
traditional poetry. A further study would be to investigate which of these early
texts and, in particular, which of the early poetry is of more than historical
interest today. Many of the Indonesian poets of that period we still consider as
outstanding today, such as Sanusi Pané and Amir Hamzah, made little or no use
at all of the sonnet form, and it might be found in the course of such an
investigation that many though not all of the poems we still enjoy are precisely
the ones which do not use the sonnet form.

Connected with the question of the origins of Indonesian literature as part of
the history of Indonesian literature is also the much-discussed problem of
generations (Siregar 1980). Given the young age of Indonesian literature it is
understandable if even slight changes in form and direction assumed at times
considerable proportions in the eyes and minds of participants and eyewitnesses. Yet, with the benefit of time, generations and periods of Indonesian
literature will need re-inspection, and it would seem that when teaching the
history of Indonesian literature the divisions employed by Indonesian critics
need careful discussion. Should it not be argued that until today we find side by
side a range of genres and themes, and that contemporary Indonesian literature
accommodates everything from the 'Transitional' to the Angkatan 80? Is not
one of the problems of generations as presented in Indonesia that it does not
leave room for all those writers and texts whose work never fitted into any of
these neat and exclusive divisions? Seen in retrospect, do not some of the
distinctions seem rather exaggerated? Studying directly what was said to justify
their existence at the time, it appears that affinities clearly existing between
these so-called generations have been lost and forgotten as distinguishing
features and trends were highlighted. The concept of generations is tidy when
teaching, but since there does not seem to be an end to this rather biological
proliferation, a distinction will eventually have to be made between generations,
periods, and movements; and most probably greater emphasis will have to be

[9]   Compare for example his poem 'Di tepi pantai' (Kratz 1980:43) with his later 'Teluk
Jayakatera' (Hamzah 1977:25-6).

given to the concept of movements and periods than has been the case so far. Considering movements, they would have to be distinguished even further between those that are self-proclaimed and those that emerge through the display of common features. This of course can best be done if a highly selective, exclusive, and microscopic, generational approach to Indonesian literature is augmented by a more inclusive, macroscopic view for which there is now sufficient material available, historically and quantitatively.

This new analysis might help to identify moments of real importance in the development of Indonesian literature other than non-literary events. Again, attention might focus on the language and the change of use of Indonesian from formal to colloquial, and from impersonal 'standard' to colourful, personal idiom. Might not some of the attention then be focused on the fact that many though not all of those who proclaim new trends and generations have been expressing their own vested interest as artists rather than as critics and literary scholars? Is it not another remarkable feature of Indonesian literary criticism that much of it has been and is being written by the very same persons who are doing most of the creative writing as well? Many of this group of excellent people are very conscious of the fact that they are involved in a historical process; and very self consciously they are determined to play their part.

Needless to say, theirs is the work we study, write, and lecture about, but can we allow ourselves to refer to their material in the first place other than as objects of study? An answer to this question depends entirely on one's own position at that particular moment in time, either as recorders who present findings and analyses (to our own non-Indonesian audience) regardless of personal opinion, or as personally involved critics. Normally the two can only be separated with great difficulty when dealing with a living literature, which makes a detached approach rather hard, as can be seen from the following example which I find extremely interesting and relevant as an academic observer as well as a personal witness. I mention this example here, because it shows well the dilemma of the non-Indonesian student of Indonesian literature who tries to stay in contact and dialogue with his object of study. In December 1985 Ariel Heryanto published *Perdebatan sastra kontekstual* (Heryanto 1985), an anthology of programmatic articles, statements, polemics, and discussions on the concept of 'sastra kontekstual', which was first launched by Arief Budiman as a test balloon in late 1984 and which was then further inflated by Ariel Heryanto. No doubt, Arief Budiman and Ariel Heryanto have addressed themselves to very important issues of Indonesian literary, cultural, intellectual, social, and political history and are dealing with an issue which recently has also found the attention of some of our Australian colleagues (Foulcher 1986).

The book, which runs to 501 pages, is extremely impressive as an exercise in industrious documentation, far superior in comprehensiveness to Achdiat Karta Mihardja's *Polemik Kebudajaan* (Mihardja 1948) and the recent *Pengadilan Puisi* by Pamusuk Eneste (Eneste 1986a). The collection consists of eight parts, which are entitled

> Bagian 1 Lahirnya serangkaian perdebatan (Birth of a series of debates);
> Bagian 2 Umpan pertama (First bait);
> Bagian 3 Umpan kedua (Second bait);
> Bagian 4 Laporan media massa (Mass media reports);
> Bagian 5 Beberapa tanggapan (Some reactions);
> Bagian 6 Tanggapan atas tanggapan (Reactions to reactions);
> Bagian 7 Beberapa tulisan terdahulu (Some initial writings);
> Bagian 8 Beberapa tulisan pendorong (Some stimuli).

The book has short biographies of the contributors, and an annotated bibliography of additional reading up to July 1985.

A key problem in our study of Indonesian literature which is not discussed at all but which is amply and implicitly exemplified by the contents of the book is that of our material basis.[10] There is almost no reference to an individual literary text. A further problem thrown up but not discussed openly by the

---

[10]   At source level there is the unique collection and documentation of Dr H.B. Jassin in Jakarta. There is also the excellent private collection of D.S. Moeljanto and there are others still. There are also the various public libraries in Jakarta, Leiden and Ithaca to name but the best known ones. Although there is very little by way of bibliographical access to these untold treasures, their disregard cannot be excused as the following example will show. The latest edition of the poems of Chairil Anwar claims to contain all his original poems together with variant readings in one volume (Eneste 1986b). Apart from the fact that the editor of this collection too does not seem to have made use of Chairil Anwar's autographs for his edition, the volume still contains translations and adaptations. Poems which almost 20 years ago had been identified by J.E. Tatengkeng as translations and adaptations are still included here as originals. What is even more annoying, Tatengkeng's article is listed in the book's copious bibliography (Tatengkeng 1967). This is just one obvious example of the need for a proper documentary basis for research and teaching, as well as for the isolation in which much of the research on Indonesian literature takes place. In the light of the great importance of Chairil Anwar and his work, and because of the excellent work done on some of his poems, his oeuvre is a splendid illustration of our achievement and dilemma. It shows that on the one hand that there are substantial, yet selective and disconnected studies, and that there are not yet enough comprehensive, substantial ones based on these monographs. On the other hand we have the broader and more general studies which lack the backup of the substantial specialists' studies. Unfortunately it seems that many people inside and outside Indonesia rely on the easily accessible, that is what has been printed in books. It is one of several merits of Prof. Teeuw's *Modern Indonesian Literature* that it contains a very detailed and careful bibliography of primary and secondary sources referred to and discussed in his study, but at the same time this merit seems to turn into a disadvantage if Indonesian literature is only what can be found in 'Teeuw', an unfortunate but common assumption which the author of the study most certainly does not encourage, as he has made very clear in the Epilogue to the second edition.

book is the question how far study and teaching of Indonesian literature are subject to current political conditions, yet the accusation is made that susastra is produced by and for an affluent middle class, generally referred to as the universal humanists. This of course brings with it the other accusation that criticism has a middle-class orientation too. Elsewhere this critical assessment has been extended recently to embrace the suggestion that there is a conspiracy of silence by the Universalist International to negate the contribution of the Left to Indonesian literature and, generally, to deny its existence (Hill 1984). As an observer one might say that if this were so and LEKRA, because this is what we are talking about, had been neglected, it had suffered a fate neither better nor worse than that of many other groups, movements, and individuals such as 'religious' writers, 'trivial' ones, those living outside Jakarta, let alone outside other big cities and towns. However, in my view, the theory of a conspiracy of silence has to be rejected out of hand. If a reason had to be sought for this alleged neglect, again one might look at the youthfulness of Indonesian literature and its particular (contextual) way of expressing itself. It is a fact plain to see that Indonesian writers and critics concern themselves seriously but in their own way with the problems they have to face today. Therefore it seems unfair to ask them to write in the explicit manner their critics want them to, while on the other hand to disregard and discard what is on offer, namely texts which in their own implicit ways deal critically with the human problems of the day (which as everyone knows are the immediate result of and bound by their given historical context).

No doubt the issue of *sastra kontekstual* will be with us for a long time to come, not least due to the existence of this publication, which will continue to engage and stimulate writers and critics. However, when reading the book one is inclined to conclude that the programmatic articles, and in their wake many of the texts generated by them, are discussing a literature which exists largely in the minds of the two main authors, Ariel Heryanto and Arief Budiman, a caricature of a literature which bears no resemblance to the realities of Indonesian literary and cultural life.[11] What is more, every Western textbook cliche of a bourgeois, alienated, and socially irrelevant literature has been repeated, in order to defend, rather patronizingly and in a Western way, the literature of the Indonesian people, which is understood to mean texts published in journals and magazines, which concern themselves explicitly with the social issues of the day, against un-Indonesian influences and Western theories. From

---

[11] Another example of this approach was offered recently by the journal *Horison* in an interview with the writer Bokor Hutasuhut (Mahmud 1986:44), when the interviewer elaborated on his understanding of the *Manifes Kebudayaan*.

a literary point of view the approach is disappointing, since the issues raised – those of high and low, good and bad, serious and light, of book and magazine literature, of education, edification, and entertainment – have been seen as being of only relative merit and importance for some time now, and have given way to other approaches already. Due to the reliance on outdated and uninformed Western stereotypes of literature and rigid notions of society, and failing to produce a coherent definition of their own, sastra kontekstual does not help us in any way to understand and interpret Indonesian literature further. It fails to relate in any way to any specific form of Indonesian literature, be it bourgeois or of the people, be it susastra or sastra majalah.

Having said all this, it still remains that the book touches upon fundamental questions of Indonesian literature which have not yet received the scholarly attention they deserve and require, but which are difficult to deal with by using a non-literary approach. In the Indonesian context, 'seni untuk seni' and 'seni untuk rakyat', cliches which have been passed on polemically for a long time, are as empty as the concept of sastra kontekstual when inspected more closely. When discussing these concepts with students one would have to point out the extra-literary approach implied in these concepts and their non-literary roots. Even though it is true that people may have defended the concept of seni untuk seni, it never was postulated in the way claimed first by LEKRA, and it still needs to be proven that those who supported this slogan and rejected the other slogan of seni untuk rakyat were, to chose a neutral phrase, antisocial and non-committal in their literary work. Without even resorting to the equally well-worn cliche that we all are conditioned socially, the point has to be made that one of the striking features of Indonesian literature is that even the 'highbrow', 'recognized' literature of the middle classes, which is attacked by the protagonists of sastra kontekstual, is probably more relevant in its social comment and more eloquent in its social commitment than much of the (frequently escapist) texts found in the literature of the people as defined in sastra kontekstual (Tickell 1986).

A few years ago I said in a talk in Jakarta, without any objections from the Indonesian audience, that quite deliberately I did not distinguish between research done by Indonesian and research done by other scholars and critics, since I assumed that both shared a theoretical and aesthetic basis; a basis which was also shared by the creative writers themselves. This is challenged by the initiators of sastra kontekstual, who argue for unrelated, separate, socially conditioned, contextual bases not only between East and West but also within the classes of one society. While I accept that our own criticism as non-Indonesians is equally conditioned by our given contextual circumstances, and while I also believe that the interests, priorities, and methods of Indonesian and other scholars and critics may differ at times, given for example possible differences in task as involved participants or as observant intermediators for a non-Indonesian public, I still believe my original assumption to be true. I am still convinced that there is an interaction between Indonesians and non-Indonesians, not because of some economic, political, and social pressure but because of the existence of a basic level of understanding and of shared emotions among thinking beings. How else could we appreciate and relate to literary and non-literary texts written in different ages in different places, using different languages, and in entirely different historical and socio-economic contexts? True, our interpretation may quite differ from the intentions of the author, as even the appreciation of the author's contemporaries might be different from his own, yet this appreciation, albeit for different reasons and in different contexts, would not be possible if there were not something universal in a text which goes beyond the temporal and spatial limits of any given, incidental context.

I have come to the end of my remarks. Let me stress once again that, if I have not referred to the work of Professor Teeuw directly and in every instance, this does not imply any form of disregard. On the contrary, I simply assume that everybody here is familiar with it. Suffice it to say that each and every person, be he or she a native or non-native speaker of Indonesian who concerns him or herself with Malay and Indonesian literatures, owes a tremendous debt to Professor Teeuw. It is impossible not to be confronted with his work at some stage of one's own particular study and teaching and it is unwise not to take note and concern oneself with what he has written on a particular topic. If I have looked at Indonesian literary studies from the point of view of the teacher and his requirements, it is with gratitude and in the recognition that much of what has been achieved in this field has been achieved by Professor Teeuw, and that much of what we will be able to do in the future is based on the foundations laid by him. After all, despite his professed love affair with Old Javanese literature, Professor Teeuw is the one non-Indonesian scholar who has been most persistent in his concern for and interest in the study of Indonesian literature.

Bibliography

Anwar, Chairil
1966   *Deru Tjampur Debu.* Djakarta: Jajasan Pembangunan.

Bradbury, M. and McFarlane J.
1981   *Modernism*. Harmondsworth: Penguin.
Chambert-Loir, H.
1974   'Mas Marco Kartodikromo (c.1890-1932) ou l'education
            politique', in: P.-B. Lafont and D. Lombard (eds), *Littératures
            contemporaines de l'Asie du Sud-Est*, pp. 203-14. Paris:
            l'Asiathèque.
Damono, Sapardi Djoko
1978   *Sosiologi Sastra; Sebuah pengantar ringkas*. Jakarta: Pusat
            Pembinaan dan Pengembangan Bahasa Departemen Pendidikan
            dan Kebudayaan.
Darma, Budi
1983   *Solilokui; Kumpulan esei sastra*. Jakarta: Gramedia.
1984   *Sejumlah esei sastra*. Jakarta: Karya Unipress.
Djamin, Nasjah
1984   'Si Tambi dan Si Buyung Ketek', in: Pamusuk Eneste (ed.),
            Proses Kreatif; Mengapa dan bagaimana saya mengarang. Vol.
            II, pp. 21-50. Jakarta: Gramedia.
Effendi, Roestam
1953   *Pertjikan permenungan*. Djakarta: Fasco.
Eneste, Pamusuk
1986a   *Pengadilan puisi*. Jakarta: Gunung Agung.
1986b   (ed.) *Chairil Anwar, Aku ini binatang jalang; Koleksi sajak
            1942-1949*. Jakarta: Gramedia.
Foulcher, K.
1986   'Sastra kontekstual: Perkembangan Mutakhir dalam politik sastra
            Indonesia', *Horison* 21-9/10:311-3, 315, 332-9.
Hamzah, Amir
1977   *Buah rindu*. Cetakan kelima. Jakarta: Dian Rakyat.
Hardjana, Andre
1981   *Kritik sastra; Sebuah pengantar*. Jakarta: Gramedia.
Heryanto, Ariel (ed.)
1985   *Perdebatan sastra kontekstual*. Jakarta: Rajawali.
Hill, D.
1984   *Who's left? Indonesian literature in the early 1980's*. Clayton:
            Monash University, Department of Indonesian and Malay.
Kratz, E.U.
1980   '"New" poems by Amir Hamzah', *Indonesia Circle* 21:40-4.

1986   'Islamic attitudes towards modern Indonesian literature', in: C.D. Grijns, S.O. Robson (eds), *Cultural contact and textual interpretation*, pp. 60-93. Dordrecht/Cinnaminson: Foris. [KITLV, Verhandelingen 115.]

1988   *A bibiliography of Indonesian literature in journals; Drama, prose, poetry*. Yogyakarta/London: Gadjah Mada University Press/School of Oriental and African Studies.

Mahmud, Damiri

1986   'Wawancara dengan Bokor Hutasuhut; Sastrawan harus diberi kesempatan meninjau pembangunan', *Horison* 20-2:41-4.

Mihardja, Achdiat K. (ed.)

1948   *Polemik kebudajaan*. Djakarta: Balai Pustaka.

Nadjib, Emha Ainun

1984   *Sastra yang membebaskan; Sikap terhadap struktur dan anutan seni modern Indonesia*. Yogyakarta: Pusat Latihan, Penelitian dan Pengembangan Masyarakat.

Pané, Armijn

1963   Sonnet dan pantun, in: H.B. Jassin (ed), *Pudjangga Baru; Prosa dan puisi*, pp. 259-66. Djakarta: Gunung Agung.

Ras, J.J. (ed.)

1979   *Javanese literature since Independence; An anthology*. The Hague: Nijhoff. [KITLV, Verhandelingen 88.]

Rosidi, Ajip

1966   *Kesusasteraan Sunda déwasa ini; Sebuah tindjauan*. Bandung: Tjupumanik.

1969   *Ichtisar sedjarah sastra Indonesia*. Bandung: Binatjipta.

Salmon, C.

1981   *Literature in Malay by the Chinese of Indonesia; A provisional annotated bibliography*. Paris: Maison des Sciences de l'Homme.

Siregar, Bakri

1980   'Telah lahir suatu angkatan: sebuah tinjauan sastra', *Prisma* 9-2:32-48.

Skinner, C.

1973   (ed.) 'Shaer Kampung gelam terbakar oleh Abdullah b. Abdul-Kadir', *Journal of the Malaysian Branch of the Royal Asiatic Society* 45-1:21-56.

1978   'Transitional Malay literature, Part I: Ahmad Rijaluddin and Munshi Abdullah', *Bijdragen tot de Taal-, Land en Volkenkunde* 134:466-87.

Sumardjo, Jakob
1984   *Memahami kesusasteraan; Untuk sekolah lanjutan dan umum.*
              Bandung: Alumni.
Sweeney, Amin
1980   *Reputations live on; An early Malay autobiography.* Berkeley:
              University of California Press.
Sykorsky, W.V.
1980   'Some additional remarks on the antecedents of modern
              Indonesian literature', *Bijdragen tot de Taal-, Land en
              Volkenkunde* 136:498-516.
Tatengkeng, J.E.
1967   'Tudjuh belas tahun sesudah wafatnja Chairil Anwar', *Horison* 2-
              4:100-4, 122.
Teeuw, A.
1950   *Voltooid voorspel; Indonesische literatuur tussen twee
              wereldoorlogen.* Djakarta: Pembangunan/Opbouw.
1952   *Pokok dan tokoh dalam kesusasteraan Indonesia baru;* Dengan
              sebuah sumbangan dari Dr. R. Roolvink. 2 vols. Djakarta:
              Pembangunan.
1967   *Modern Indonesian literature.* The Hague: Nijhoff. [KITLV,
              Translation Series 10.]
1979   *Modern Indonesian literature.* Second edition. The Hague:
              Nijhoff. 2 vols. [KITLV, Translation Series 10.]
1984   *Sastra dan ilmu sastra; Pengantar teori sastra.* Jakarta: Pustaka
              Jaya.
Tickell, P.
1981   (ed.) *Three early short stories by Mas Marco Kartodikromo.*
              Clayton: Monash University, Department of Indonesian and
              Malay.
1986   'Subversion or escapism? The fantastic in recent Indonesian
              fiction', *Review of Indonesian and Malaysian Affairs* 20-1:50-67.
Toer, Pramoedya Ananta
1980a   *Bumi manusia; Sebuah roman karya pulau Buru.* Jakarta: Hasta
              Mitra.
1980b   *Anak semua bangsa; Sebuah roman karya pulau Buru.* Jakarta:
              Hasta Mitra.
1985a   *Jejak langkah.* Jakarta: Hasta Mitra.
1985b   *Sang pemula dan karya non-fiksi (jurnalistik), fiksi
              (cerpen/novel) R. M. Tirto Adhi Soerjo.* Jakarta: Hasta Mitra.

Watson, C.W.
1971   'Some preliminary remarks on the antecedents of modern
            Indonesian literature', *Bijdragen tot de Taal-, Land en
            Volkenkunde* 127:417-33.
Yudiono KS
1986   *Telaah kritik sastra Indonesia*. Bandung: Angkasa.

A. TEEUW

The text

It doesn't say what it says – or does it?

My subject for this farewell lecture is simple: 'The Text'; that would seem appropriate for the occasion, as the text always stands at the beginning and at the end of all reading and study of literature. My text for this lecture you may find in the poem *Awater* by Martinus Nijhoff, line 36: 'Lees maar, er staat niet wat er staat' – but as reading is rewriting (the reader writes the text, I shall return to that), with a small addition 'Lees maar, er staat niet wat er staat – of toch soms?' (Just read, it doesn't say what it says – or does it?)

In our culture we are used to reading printed texts, ready-made, as a book or journal; we accept them as they are, at best we may be irritated by misprints or bad typography or messy bindings; but the main thing, the printed words on the page, are a fixed datum. As for the whole process of the author's mental concoctions ultimately leading to the text in front of us: a fat lot we care! which means that we don't care a bit: for 'it doesn't say what it says'.

However, there are people who do care about printed texts. Students of texts, textual critics, have shown in many cases, ranging from Shakespeare to Fitzgerald, that printed texts are often no good, whether on account of accidental misprints or through more or less drastic interventions by one or other actor in the long chain between writer and reader.

An example which I like to quote can be found on the first page of what is usually called the first modern Indonesian novel: *Sitti Noerbaja atau Kasih ta' Sampai*, by Marah Roesli (1922). The female protagonist is waiting for her father's gig which will take her home from school. In the extensive description of her appearance and outfit it is told that she has a red ribbon in her hair while wearing yellow stockings and shoes. Simple and clear. But in post-war editions of the novel the ribbon has become black, whereas the stockings and shoes have turned dark brown. Who was responsible for this intervention will probably never be cleared up; most probably a fashion-conscious typesetter provided the girl with an outfit which he considered more suitable for his time!

However, today my topic is not primarily printed literature, which in

Indonesia is a relatively recent phenomenon; nor shall I deal with orally transmitted texts, which of old have been the normal form of 'literature' in the country, and which are still very much alive in various forms.

Between the oral text culture and the technology of the printed book there is the period of manuscript culture, which in Indonesia probably started with the coming of the Indian civilization in our early Middle Ages, and which in fact has still not come to an end. In that culture texts were transmitted by hand: on prepared palm-leaves, on bark, on copper or stone (in that case we call them inscriptions), and later on various kinds of paper.

Anyone who copies makes mistakes; I think you all know that from experience. So when a text was disseminated through repeated copying, for instance because it was successful or authoritative, or was found useful by those in power, and when it subsequently was considered fit to be saved through the ages, then chances are that in later copies more and more deviations from the original were to be found, and that these later copies would show more and more differences among themselves. In Leiden alone there are many thousands of Indonesian manuscripts, often there are several manuscripts of the same text, and all of these are always more or less different from one another.

In Europe ever since classical times there have been keen and critical readers who did not accept these differences, certainly not in the case of authoritative texts by the master, by the great author, or of the divine Word itself. They wanted to know what had really been written. These lovers of the true word, philologists, set themselves the task of restoring texts to their original form and purifying them of all copying errors which had crept in in the course of time.

In Indonesia too there have always been readers of manuscripts who did not copy a text as they had it before them without further ado, but who dealt with it critically and who endeavoured to correct real or putative errors. This can be proved by critical study of the preserved manuscripts. But philology as a scholarly discipline in Indonesia only started to develop after the technology of printing had been introduced, when people who wanted to publish handwritten texts discovered that usually more than one manuscript existed of a certain text, and that in order to publish an authoritative version, for school, for scholarly study, or for a larger audience, they had to make a choice.

In this way during the last two centuries a large number of Indonesian texts have been edited and published, on the basis of preserved manuscripts. Scholars in the Netherlands, in particular Leiden, have played an important role in Indonesian philology, and they still do. I just want to mention the Bibliotheca Indonesica, a series of scholarly editions of Indonesian texts with English translations, which was set up by Dr Robson and me in 1968. Volume 26 has now appeared. Dr Robson, who already for years now has been the editor of the series, still groans daily under this burden!

Editing texts on the basis of manuscripts is not an easy task. It has become a job, a discipline, with its own methods and techniques, its own principles and assumptions, and by now with quite a respectable tradition. Especially during the nineteenth century in the West a philological method was developed which pretended to be objective and strictly scientific; under certain conditions corrupted texts in manuscripts could be restored, so it was said, to the form in which the original author had created them. This is called the stemmatic method; stemma means pedigree, and the method is based on a technique for restoring the pedigree, the genealogical relation between manuscripts of a given text. On the basis of such a stemma it should be possible to decide which readings in manuscripts stem from the original text and which ones have come about through subsequent corruption.

Due to various circumstances Indonesian philology followed the development of Western philology only slowly, and from a distance: the philological study of classical and medieval European texts was rather a far cry for students of Indonesian literature; even professionals for a long time were not aware of the fact that for the study of languages and literatures too some form of theory was essential. Moreover many editors of texts were complete or part amateurs, who had more common sense and practical knowledge of the languages and literatures concerned than insight into theoretical problems of philology; and, one should add, luckily so! For even without much theoretical knowledge one can produce quite acceptable text editions, provided one has enough common sense and factual knowledge. The reverse, theory without a sound factual basis, leads to regular calamities.

The pretensions and the refinement of the stemmatic method did not really penetrate Indonesian philology; my teacher Professor Gonda in the thirties applied it for the first time and with great acumen in a number of Old Javanese text editions; and my former student and present colleague Ras in his impressive dissertation of 1968 showed that even in an extremely confusing situation of a large number of heterogeneous and partly rather corrupt manuscripts of a Malay text the application of the stemmatic method can produce fine results; with proper self-confidence Ras at the end of his job testifies: 'despite their corruptness [of the manuscripts] we are able to reconstruct the text almost precisely in the form in which it must have been when the last writer [of a number of successive versions] laid down his pen'.

Yet neither Gonda's example nor Ras's success have led to a regular and systematic application of this apparently so objective and scientific method. This holds good for Javanese philology; but also in the rather numerous Malay text editions published during the last few decades all over the world the stemmatic method at best receives lip service without ever being in fact applied. Even in cases where the editor sets up a stemma of the manuscripts, he does not actually use it for the text edition, because he considers the method inapplicable. In other cases either tacitly or explicitly another method is preferred; often an edition is based on a single manuscript, with at best incidental corrections of 'errors' on the basis of variants in other manuscripts.

I shall mention a few examples; and on this rather special occasion I would like to start with recent dissertations by three academic teachers in Malay philology in the Faculty of Letters at the Universitas Indonesia in Jakarta. All three belong to a group of tender but most charming female students whom I as a budding 'extraordinary lecturer' was privileged to initiate into the secrets of philology at the brand-new Universitas Indonesia in 1950. The fact that a number of them thirty years after this first initiation still managed to crown their academic training with a Ph.D. degree testifies more to the tenacity and perseverance of these Indonesian women than to the quality of my teaching at the time! And the fact that some of these former pupils from long ago, friends of today, were able and willing to be present at this farewell lecture makes my wife and me feel happy and grateful!

Thus three dissertations, defended in three continents, with three different supervisors: first of all Dr Mulyadi, with a Malay text edition begun in Leiden, continued and completed in London in 1980 with Dr Russell Jones as supervisor, and finally published again in Leiden in 1983 – who was talking about a Leiden and a London school? Dr Mulyadi discusses all thirty manuscripts of her text known to exist, but without presenting a stemma or engaging in any discussion on methodological or theoretical problems she sums up her approach and her choice: 'my choice fell on the neat earliest manuscript'; and this manuscript turns out to be so neat that she manages to edit her text of 160 compact pages with a critical apparatus of one page, altogether 40 brief notes. Dr Achadiati Ikram, after a careful study of all 22 manuscripts of the Malay Rama story, which proved to contain four different versions of the story, convinced me as her promotor in Jakarta in 1978 that in this case too the best choice would indeed be to base the edition on a single, relatively old manuscript; but she needed 40 pages for the inclusion of the most important variants of her 320-page text. Number three, Dr Panuti Sudjiman, acquired her Ph.D. degree in 1979 with my colleague Anthony Johns at the Australian National University in Canberra. In the introduction to her text edition she managed to establish the textual history in great detail on the basis of a careful study of the manuscripts, and to construct a stemma which represented this textual history quite neatly. Nevertheless her edition too, for sound reasons, was in the main based on a single manuscript, corrected with the help of relevant variant readings from other manuscripts.

Elsewhere we see the same tendency: Russell Jones, till recently teaching in London, but himself also not quite free from Leiden taints, in his 1969 dissertation saw no possibility 'to reconstruct a good composite text' from his five manuscripts, and so he built his edition 'around a base manuscript'. And in the 1985 edition of the thesis, which contains a preface dated 1981, he thinks that in retrospect he made the right choice 'on theoretical grounds'. Similarly Henri Chambert-Loir in his edition of the *Hikayat Dewa Mandu* (1980), after an exemplary study of the 16 manuscripts, resulting in a classic stemma, concluded that application of the stemmatic method was impracticable, and that the variants were far too numerous and too arbitrary to construct a basic text, an archetype, as philologists would call it.

Two Leiden promovendi came closest to applying the stemmatic method: Liaw Yock Fang and Lode Brakel. The former, supervised by R. Roolvink in 1976, on the basis of a careful study of a great number of manuscripts, constructed an impressive stemma which, however, creates fundamental problems because it shows what in philological jargon is called horizontal contamination: a blending of two sub-branches in the pedigree of the manuscripts; therefore Liaw Yock Fang, more often than is strictly admissible according to the rigid rules of the method, was forced to resort to common sense or good taste, two qualities which he fortunately has amply at his disposal. The late Lode Brakel wrestled with a complicated family of 30 manuscripts, the oldest and historically most interesting of which were incomplete. He managed to present a careful grouping of the manuscripts according to their historical relationship, even though he avoided calling this a stemma. In his edition he tried to reconcile as much as possible two points of view: doing justice, as far as possible, to the oldest manuscripts, while at the same time endeavouring to produce a critical version of the complete text.

These viewpoints in practice turned out to be contradictory, and from the other side of the English Channel Brakel was severely taken to task: for fundamental reasons Russell Jones and Ulrich Kratz passed judgement on Brakel's approach which could not but result in a new hybrid text, a new manuscript of the *Hikayat Muhammad Hanafiyyah*, but one 'made in Leiden', which in this form had never been available to any Malay reader.

Willem van der Molen, in his Leiden dissertation of 1983, has shown that in view of the experiences gained so far in Javanese philology 'application of the stemmatic method in many cases will not be possible'; he pointed out that also in Middle Dutch philology – and one may extend this to the whole of European medieval studies – the classical method of philology has fallen into discredit. The situation in Malay philology, both practically and theoretically, is no different. Let me try to summarize what the problems involved are. A number of factors, partly interdependent, may be pointed out.

1. In many cases it seems uncertain whether 'in the beginning' there always was a specific author of a particular text, as we on the basis of experience in our book culture too readily assume. Many texts are anonymous, and not accidentally so.

2. Presumably in quite a few cases an oral tradition preceded the written text; oral texts in Indonesia by definition have a variable form. In such cases pluriformity rather than monogenesis may be underlying the written tradition.

3. The criterion of correctness in selecting a proper reading, apparently so self-evident, in many cases is inapplicable; choices between a correct or a corrupt reading often seem arbitrary. This affects the stemmatic method at its very roots.

4. Like elsewhere, in Indonesia too copyists in many cases were not automata. Often they were creative, language-conscious rewriters, sometimes even philologists *avant la lettre*, who when copying older texts used to compare manuscripts, thereby cutting the grass from under the feet of their later Western colleagues.

5. The idea that the original text was the best, the most perfect and the most coherent one and that later changes were corruptions is not correct as a general statement. Here too the experiences of Indonesian textual critics agree with those of European medievalists: the textual history often shows a development from a crude and clumsy to a linguistically and literarily more perfect form. This has of course something to do with the transition from oral to written texts.

6. Finally scholars have come to see, again just like European medievalists, that even in cases where the stemmatic method by itself can be applied successfully, the obvious gain of having recovered an original text is not without its drawbacks as well. In modern literary studies, which show more interest in readers and users of texts than in authors, the particularities of each individual manuscript, whether dialectal, stylistic, orthographic, or as a reflection of a special readers' or reception situation, are often considered more relevant than an archetype which is composed on the basis of a great variety of manuscript material.

In this manner, students of Indonesian philology, both through their own experiences and in view of insights gained elsewhere, in more advanced domains of philological study, have become doubtful about textual criticism and the ideal way of editing the kind of texts which they are usually dealing with. But also from outside their own field the traditional study of texts is being undermined. Lee Patterson, in a fine article entitled 'The Logic of Textual Criticism and the Way of Genius' (1985), recently pointed out the inner contradiction in which textual criticism, at least of literary texts, is entangled. It is impossible for a textual critic to establish correct or corrupt readings on the basis of a sound knowledge of language, style, idiom, literary conventions and the like, while at the same time in learned words and theories parroting Nijhoff's 'it doesn't say what it says' and maintaining the uniqueness and unpredictability of the text. It is impossible to be at the same time reader as a literary critic and reader as a textual critic, in other words to extol ambiguity as the most essential characteristic of literary texts, while simultaneously positing unequivocal norms of correctness and corruption for the selection of variant readings. This inevitably leads to insoluble conflicts.

Fredson Bowers presents beautiful examples of literary critics being infatuated with a poetical abstruseness which is exposed by textual critics as a simple error. Just one case: in Herman Melville's story *White-Jacket* the first person protagonist ends up in the ocean where he is floating semi-conscious under water. Suddenly he is touched by 'some inert, soiled fish of the sea' which returns him to life. A literary critic is ecstatic about this soiled fish: 'Hardly anyone but Melville could have created the shudder' which is caused by this shocking stylistic figure: the purity of the sea so surprisingly coupled with the dirtiness of the soiled fish. Bowers casually observes: 'The only difficulty with this critical *frisson* about Melville's imagination [...] is the cruel fact that an unimaginative typesetter inadvertently created it, not Melville.' For 'soiled' in this passage is a printing error for 'coiled'. Bowers concludes: 'it is indeed somewhat indicative of the over-subtlety of our times [1959, the heyday of New Criticism] to find the complexities of a misprint so eloquently preferred to the relative simplicity of the author's own phrase'.

It would be wrong to think that this problem only turns up with the more sophisticated forms of modern Western literature. Nijhoff's 'er staat niet wat er staat' also holds good for all kinds of Indonesian texts. Recently Ras again drew attention to the essential function of *pasemon*, the hidden meaning behind the literal texts of so-called historical works. Similarly the many mystical texts in Malay and Javanese time and again testify to the validity of Riffaterre's formulation of the same truth: 'A poem says one thing and means another'. Even simple folksongs like the Malay *pantun* or the Javanese *paparikan* abound with ambiguities. Or, to mention an example on a quite different level: Professor Berg's theory about Javanese historical texts as optatives, as an imagined, alternative reality created by the poet in order to replace the historical facts, imposes upon the reader creative obligations which are in continuous conflict with the text-critical interpretation of the real meaning of the words of the text. I shall return to this later on.

Thus for literary theory the apparently simple datum of the text as such has become more and more problematical. After the nineteenth century, which both in literature itself and in literary theory put full emphasis on the author as a person (the Dutch poet Willem Kloos echoed the English romantic poets in his well-known saying 'Ik ben een God in 't diepst van mijn gedachten', I am a God in my innermost thoughts), the twentieth century shifted the accent to the text as an objective fact: the impersonal 'it says'; the line preceding our motto in *Awater* runs:

> De schrijfmachine mijmert gekkepraat
> (The typewriter muses crazy talk)

Biographical interest in the author or affective involvement of the reader were considered irrelevant or even 'heresies'. The words should speak for themselves. New Criticism, close reading, a 'wereld in woorden' (world in words, the title of a book on the art of the novel by my Leiden colleague Dresden), autonomy of the text were the slogans of the day.

That time too has passed; the reader was discovered as the most important link; Paul Valéry already announced this new development in his pronouncement: 'mes vers ont le sens qu'on leur prête'. Ingarden was the first who as a theoretician drew attention to what he called *Leerstellen*, the empty spaces which have to be filled in in every text by the reader, even though with Ingarden the text itself kept absolute precedence. Mukarovsky and his student Vodička go one step further: the reader does more than just filling in empty space: he concretizes, re-creates the dead artefact of the mere text through his creative reading into an aesthetic object. For Jausz too the reader is essential; he argues that alongside the usual *Produktionsaesthetik* and *Darstellungsaesthetik*, which approach the work from the viewpoint of the author and the text itself, it is literary history which stands in need of a *Rezeptionsaesthetik*: the literary work is not a timeless monument; it derives its significance in literary history from the reception by, from the continuous confrontation with the horizon of expectations of ever-changing readers. In the work of Jausz and Vodička the dialectic tension between reader and work is fundamental.

With two French literary scholars who are particularly influential in the United States, Roland Barthes and Jacques Derrida, the scales have been turned completely in favour of the reader. The provocative adage by Derrida speaks for itself: 'The reader writes the text'. At the base of this idea lies the conception that the text has no original, real, objective, determinable, formulatable meaning. Any effort to explain the text is circum-scription, re-scription, trans-scription, which actually make the original 'script' disappear. In that sense every reader writes the text which he reads. Reading is never reconstructing the true meaning of a text, but a deconstruction, a debunking of what it seems to say, a replacement of the wording of the text by another construct of words which in its turn is basically open to deconstruction by the next reader. I shall return to this below.

In the field of Indonesian literary studies Berg, whom I have already mentioned, could be called the first deconstructivist *avant la lettre*; he exploits his freedom as a reader to an extreme in his occupation with Old Javanese texts. In many places in his publications he deconstructs, manipulates, debunks these texts and rewrites them, transcribing their words with his own Old Javanese words, thus forming a link in that process of endless transformation which is called literature. He is the reader to whom Nijhoff seems to refer when he says:

> De dichter hoort in ieder woord
> Geboorten van literatuur.
> (The poet hears in every word
> births of literature.)

Berg perplexes his colleagues, the present speaker included, by his form of textual criticism; we tend not to believe him with his emendations, we hardly dare to take him seriously; we are at our wits' end with his recent publications, as he, although nowhere giving evidence that he keeps up with the developments of literary theory, draws the most extreme consequences from Derrida's adage 'the reader writes the text'.

It should be added that at the same time he is not as ultramodern as would seem at first sight; in a way he is even quite old-fashioned, as he completely links up with our medieval manuscript culture, which preceded the book culture. In the former the man who was then called grammarian: investigator and commentator of literature, was at the same time the scholarly rewriter. For in contrast to the simple clerk-copyist, the grammarian had as his duty to rewrite the texts which he read, enriching and retesting, explaining and illuminating them. This he did not do creatively in our sense of the word, from a modern concept of originality – whatever that may be – but between the lines, interlinearly adding from other texts; to quote Gerald Burns from a fascinating paper on 'the originality of texts in a manuscript culture': 'the grammarian's originality is inter- rather than extralinear', he is: 'preeminently the schooled

writer, whose desire is to transcend the letters that limit and define him [...].'
Writing is always hermeneutic, interpreting: 'To write is to intervene in what
has already been written. [...] All writing is essentially amplification of
discourse.'

This takes us back to modern theory of literature; it seems to me the
quotation from Burns might as well have come from a work by Foucault; from
the Middle Ages to Foucault *il n'y a qu'un pas*; the text as an original,
independently signifying whole does not exist. That idea by now has also
penetrated Indonesian literary studies: Henk Maier begins his dissertation in
1985 with a well-known quotation from Barthes: 'A text is a tissue of
quotations drawn from innumerable centres of culture', also called an
intertextual bricolage, a mosaic of relations with and quotations from other
texts. Only the reader can create that tissue or 'texture' of the text. From his
own wide reading he creates a meaningful whole which in this form only exists
for him; for every reader has his own field of reading, and there is no end to
the weaving by readers. In that sense every reader indeed writes his own text.

This is doubtless a shocking idea for the traditional student of Indonesian
literature with his naive (whether one would like to take this word with a
negative or a positive connotation) approach to the text: not only does it not say
what it says, it says only what I read; and what I read is always determined
intertextually, it does not just depend on the words of the text in front of me,
but on the whole literary context surrounding these words, insofar as they are
available to me as a specific reader. Small wonder that in such an approach it
becomes senseless to search for the original text and the proper meaning. All
words are meaningful to the reader who knows how to give them meaning, and
text-critical choices between variant readings are essentially uninteresting,
irrelevant, futile. Reading, including text-critical reading, is by definition a
subjective matter.

As if this blow were not bad enough for those who simply want to know
what it says, recently a young scholar in Sydney defended a thesis (and, I hasten
to add, a capable and captivating dissertation) which takes us one step further
away from the idea that one could and should publish critical editions of texts.
The title looks promising enough: *The Desiring Prince; A Study of the Kidung
Malat As Text*. To students of Javano-Balinese literature *Malat* is well known as
a poem, probably written in Bali in a variant of Old Javanese, handed down in a
large number of manuscripts, but so far not tackled by modern textual critics,
due not only to its large size, but also to the diversity of the textual tradition
which is practically prohibitive for a scholarly edition. When I received
Vickers's manuscript for review, I opened it with great expectations: would he

at last have dared to undertake this edition and could he even have managed to complete it?

Alas, the reader interested in textual criticism is soon brought back to reality; on one of the first pages the book states: 'a critical edition following philological principles may not necessarily be the best starting point for a study of the *Malat*'. There is indeed a chaotic textual tradition, largely in fragmentary manuscripts; moreover there is the classical Balinese dance *Gambuh*, with libretto and music, which is also *Malat*; there are paintings, including ones at some royal courts, which are also *Malat*. What actually is *Malat*? Certainly not one of these abstract reconstructions by dull Western (read Leiden) philologists. Here too we soon meet Barthes as the saving angel, who relieves Vickers of the editorial job in the traditional sense; the text, so the Master says, is an 'activity of production; the Text [with a capital letter! beware! we are talking about abstractions!] only exists in the movement of discourse'. In short, the text is a process; no further definition is given, but the following circumscription comes closest to it: 'it is the communication of different producers and audiences around a common set of interests that are conveyed as text'. Whereas with Maier the text is still an intertextually Malay, intra-literary phenomenon, with Vickers it becomes an intra- and even inter-cultural (Javanese and Balinese) texture of lingual and other expressive means and elements, through which Balinese communicate, but which we shall never be able to grasp in its real or full or proper meaning by picking out loose threads, as for instance is done by philologists in text editions.

Yet, in spite of this bias against badly understood philology I consider Vickers's study important, as he makes an effort to interpret various aspects of Balinese culture (or rather a Balinese subculture) such as language, literature, dance, music, theatre, and painting in one coherent interrelationship. But the text in the conventional sense of the word we have lost in the process; it not even does not say what it says, it no longer says anything in Old Javanese; Vickers's text is trans-scribed, written across the Old Javanese text which he read in the way a good reader should read: the reader writes the text. Anyone who might want to read the *Malat* as a Balinese poem has to start all over again from the manuscripts and write his own text. Fortunately Hedi Hinzler in her Leiden dissertation of 1981 had a different idea about text; she too studied a Balinese story, in this case as a shadow theatre performance, and she too did this in a broad cultural context of dance, music, theatre, and social structure. But to her a text remained a text: words which can be re-read and read over by others in her book.

In all this I have not yet mentioned the most basic problem which had been discovered, or rather rediscovered, by modern students of literature such as Barthes and especially Derrida, even though it was implicit in the paraphrase quoted by Maier: it is argued that it is even fundamentally impossible to explain, to expound texts, linguistic utterances of any kind. It is impossible in the present context to discuss this problem in any detail; let me just try to give a simple, one might say oversimplified, example to show what is behind this reasoning. We start from a line of poetry, such as the famous beginning of Gorter's poem *Mei*, known to every Dutchman: 'Een nieuwe lente en een nieuw geluid'; let us now try to look up the words of this line in a Dutch dictionary, in order to find out what the line means. We leave the complicated issue of the article out, and start with 'nieuw'; in my old school dictionary, which will do for this purpose, 'nieuw' is explained as 'het tegengestelde van oud' (the opposite of old); would this imply that once I know what 'oud' means I also know what 'nieuw' means? Wrong; for according to the same source 'oud' is 'het tegengestelde van jong' (the opposite of young). And what is 'young'? The first meaning which is given is 'onbejaard' (unaged). I do not seem to be making much progress. Let's try again with 'lente'. My source says: 'jaargetijde 21 maart tot 21 juni: voorjaar' (season from 21 March till 21 June: spring); but 'voorjaar' is explained again by 'lente'; and 'jaargetijde' is 'een der tijdperken, waarin het jaar verdeeld wordt: lente enz' (one of the periods into which the year is divided: spring etc.). We turn around in word-circles; and of course those numbers are of no use either in a dictionary.

Now my colleague Van Sterkenburg, with all the formidable gadgets in his Instituut voor Nederlandse Lexicologie, makes dictionaries which are much better than my old school 'Koenen'. But basically I never get out of these circles when I want to explain a linguistic utterance. I am always being referred to other words, which in their turn are explained by yet other words, either synonyms or opposites or complements of the words which we are looking up. And this is how language is: ever since De Saussure we know that the meanings of words – and of other linguistic elements as well – are oppositional, that they always mean non-other words; chair is not-bench, not-stool, not-seat, not-stall, and so forth; to explain words by definition is to replace them by other words which in their turn have to be explained. It is essentially the same problem we had with those unexplainable texts; texts too can only be rewritten, transcribed in the double etymological sense of the word: we can rescribe them by scribing across them. Every word, every text disappears under its own explanation.

Well, if all this is true, if textual criticism is so futile, editing so dubious, analysing so ambivalent, interpreting so fundamentally impossible, what next? Patterson says: if one does not accept the basic assumptions of textual criticism,

'Then the only alternative is not to edit at all'. Should one go one step further and say: if one does not accept the basic assumption of textual criticism and literary criticism, then the only alternative is: no more textual criticism, no more text editions, no more textual analyses, no more translations, no more interpretations? Then there is only one conclusion: the rest is silence.

This would be a nice ending for a farewell lecture, a crowning experience at the end of a professorial career. 'Das Lied ist aus'. A pity, of course, for the successor; but a windfall for you, ladies and gentlemen: a few minutes before five o'clock you can be off for the handshakes and the well-deserved drink.

Alas, I must disappoint you; you shall not have these few minutes off; in all my lectures as a teacher – perhaps some 7,000 – I rarely gave my students minutes off; there is still time left, to quote Nijhoff once more:

> voorwaar,
> Dit is geen einde nog, maar
> Een voorgoed begonnen begin.
> (truly, this is not the end yet, but
> a forever begun beginning)

Therefore, in the remaining minutes I will offer a few suggestions as to how we, textual critics and literary critics, can proceed together on the road of Indonesian literary studies.

1. Against the deadlock that every linguistic utterance is unique and basically can never be explained by any other linguistic utterance because of the very fact that the meaning of linguistic elements is oppositional: new means not-old, not-young, and spring means not-summer, not-year, the no less basic defence should be adduced which I originally learned from Reichling's dissertation 'Het Woord': language is not only a system of oppositional signs but also an instrument for action: linguistic signs are means to deal with things. Every speaker of Dutch knows which things he can 'act' upon through words like *nieuw* and *lente*, and how he, by applying grammatical rules, through a clause like 'Een nieuwe lente' and other words can interact sensibly with a speech partner, e.g. about the Keukenhof or the first plover's egg: it says what it says, and if a philosopher wants to make this a problem, 'tant pis pour le philosophe'.

2. Vickers is quite right in arguing that a text such as *Malat* gets its full meaning only within the whole of Balinese culture or one of its subcultures. But this does not mean that the understanding of a text outside such a particular context is impossible or senseless. *Malat* is also readable, and even enjoyable, as a text in the conventional sense, and therefore it should be edited and published, of course according to the method which is most suitable in view of the study of the manuscripts concerned. Vickers's appeal to Jausz is one-sided, if only for

the fact that Jausz, with all his emphasis on the interaction between text and reader, never disavows the text as a linguistic document, as is shown by all his fine studies which are based on written and edited medieval and other texts. That is why we cannot make progress without edited and published texts, and why editing is vital, in whatever form.

3. Maier too, in his understandable inclination to react against the one-sidedness of his predecessors, in turn does not escape being one-sided himself. For a text is not only an intertextual tissue, a mosaic of quotations. Words do not only mean in opposition to each other, in an endless vicious circle. Through their referring function words also create a world of their own, an alternative to reality, but knowable and recognizable thanks to the 'action knowledge' with respect to reality which we have acquired through this self-same language. That is why a reader is not just seesawing between what it says and what it does not say (poetry), and between what it says and what is said elsewhere (inter-textuality), but also between what it says and what it refers to (reality). Intertextual analysis cannot do without textual analysis, as Maier fortunately understood quite well, as his book shows; but textual understanding in its turn cannot do without the referential function of language.

4. In brief, what it does not say or what is said elsewhere we can only get to know by reading and understanding what it says and what it refers to. That is why we need texts. For a manuscript culture that inexorably means: editing, transforming them to the book culture of our times. The question is: how? Linking up with the quotation given earlier that the alternative would be 'not to edit at all', Patterson says: 'To be sure, not editing has many different degrees'.

5. How then should we go about the editing of Indonesian texts? It is obvious that there is not just one single method which is sacrosanct. The textual critic in each particular case will have to pose a number of questions, for instance with respect to the nature of the available manuscript material and the situation of its transmission, the number of manuscripts, their distribution in space and time, their physical qualities, their degree of variation, the characterization of the copyists and their masters, the local copying traditions and conventions, and so on.

Still more important is the nature of the text itself. Attention should be paid to the following questions.

1. The origin of the text: there is a rich range of possibilities, from texts which have their roots in the anonymous oral tradition to typical authors' texts. In the latter case, in spite of all the freedom allowed to the present-day reader, it is nevertheless completely legitimate, and even essential, to make an effort to restore the text as it was written by the author in a critical edition, as close to

the original as possible in view of the quality of the manuscripts and the expertise of the editor. This does not preclude the possibility that it might be interesting to study what happened to the text at the hands of later copyists or critical readers. A good example is the mystical poetry by Hamzah Fansuri, the sixteenth century poet from Acheh, an edition of which was recently completed by Drewes after Brakel started the work. We have to be grateful to the authors that we have these texts at our disposal in a form which corresponds as precisely as possible to what the original poet wrote. This indeed is an absolute condition for a better knowledge of Indonesian Islam and its history.

2. We can also distinguish the texts according to the way they were transmitted: there are typical audience texts, sometimes even libretti, in which the copyists acted as readers, reciters, re-tellers, or performers. In such cases little can be gained by a stemmatic method, and we had better leave the manuscripts to speak in their own right. But there are also texts for individual reading, study books; in such cases the copyists may have acted as critical readers, but may not have been out to re-create the text in a suitable form for a new audience; for them in such cases the authority of the teacher-writer may have prevailed over their own critical sense.

3. The texts can also be distinguished according to their function: Vickers was not the first to point out that Balinese copyists showed much more respect for the very prestigious, sacral Old Javanese *kakawin*, works of literary art also according to our norms, than for *kidung* like *Malat*. Therefore, whoever undertakes editing a kakawin in a form which comes as close as possible to the text written in Java in the Middle Ages – I can speak from some experience – is not at the outset facing a hopeless task. Worsley's reservations with respect to the edition by Robson and me of the kakawin *Kuñjarakarṇa Dharmakathana* would therefore seem to me somewhat begging the question, a *petitio principii*, even though it is true that also after our publication and Van der Molen's edition of the prose version of the same story from Java a lot more remains to be done with respect to the later Balinese transformations of the text, where the copyists showed fewer scruples about preserving the original.

4. One should also pay attention to the aim of the edition one has in mind: whether it is strictly for scholarly purposes, for education, for a general public, and take into account this practical function of the edition in dealing with the manuscript material. In an interesting little volume Jerome J. McGann recently dealt with various aspects of textual criticism, especially for modern English literature, from this point of view; and it would seem to me that future editors of Indonesian texts can profit from his ideas.

5. Finally – nothing new certainly, but most important of all: the lesson

which has to be drawn from developments both in textual criticism and in literary criticism, both in Indonesia and elsewhere, is that the two need each other as badly as ever. They are two sides of one coin. It is an illusion that one might be able to practise textual criticism without literary analysis and interpretation; and it is as wrong to think that one can study literature without the capacity to deal text-critically with the material one studies. For one cannot really know what it does not say or what is said elsewhere, if one does not know what it says or what it refers to, or even – I hesitate, for this is a dangerous heresy – what has been meant.

So if one does not manage or want to be a textual critic and a literary critic at the same time, in view of ever-growing specialism or by bent or preference, one should at least have a knowledge of the other one's branch, of the other side of the coin. The fact that, unless I am much mistaken, shortly in our department four of my former promovendi, together representing the whole scale from fanatical textual criticism to rabid literary criticism, from solid philology in the sense of *Altertumswissenschaft* to functional textual study, will meet each other daily, physically and one hopes also in a scholarly way, is a gratifying thought for a parting professor who in his own work always tried to keep an eye on both sides of this, as well as of all other coins!

Ladies and gentlemen! I would like to end with Nijhoff once more, but then in the spirit of the now concluded symposium with a variation, or if you like, a transformation:

> De tekstverwerker mijmert gekkepraat.
> Lees maar. Er staat ook wat er staat.
> (The text-editor/word-processor muses crazy talk.
> Just read. It also says what it says.)

Bibliography

Berg, C.C.
1938   'Javaansche geschiedschrijving', in: F.W. Stapel (ed.), *Geschiede-
                nis van Nederlandsch Indië*, II, pp. 5-148. Amsterdam: Joost van
                den Vondel.
1955a   'Twee nieuwe publicaties betreffende de geschiedenis en de
                geschiedschrijving van Mataram', *Indonesië* 8:97-128.
1955b   'Geschiedenis en geschiedschrijving van Mataram', *Indonesië*
                8:231-69.
1955c   'De zin der tweede Babad-Tanah-Jawi', *Indonesië* 8:361-400.

1969, 1980   *Maya's hemelvaart in het Javaanse Buddhisme.* Amsterdam: Noord-Hollandsche Uitgevers Maatschappij. 3 vols. [Verhandelingen Koninklijke Akademie van Wetenschappen, Afd. Letterkunde, Nieuwe Reeks 74-1/2, 102.]

Bowers, Fredson
1959   *Textual and literary criticism.* Cambridge: Cambridge University Press.

Brakel, L.F.
1975   T*he Hikayat Muhammad Hanafiyyah; A medieval Muslim-Malay romance.* The Hague: Nijhoff. [Bibliotheca Indonesica 12; Ph.D. thesis, University of Leiden, 1975.]

Burns, Gerald L.
1980   'The originality of texts in a manuscript culture', *Comparative Literature* 32-2:113-29.

Chambert-Loir, Henri
1980   *Hikayat Dewa Mandu; épopée Malaise; I. Texte et présentation.* Paris: Ecole Française d'Extrême-Orient.

Drewes, G.W.J. and L.F. Brakel
1986   *The Poems of Hamzah Fansuri.* Edited with an introduction, a translation and commentaries, accompanied by the Javanese translations of two of his prose works. Dordrecht/Cinnaminson: Foris. [Bibliotheca Indonesia 26.]

Gonda, J.
1932   *Het Oud-Javaansche Brahmāṇḍa-Purāṇa.* Prozatekst en kakawin uitgegeven en van aanteekeningen voorzien. Bandoeng: Nix. [Bibliotheca Javanica 5.]

Hinzler, H.I.R.
1981   *Bima Swarga in Balinese wayang.* The Hague: Nijhoff. [KITLV, Verhandelingen 90; Ph.D. thesis, University of Leiden, 1981.]

Ikram, Achadiati
1980   *Hikayat Sri Rama; Suntingan naskah disertai telaah amanat dan struktur.* Jakarta: Penerbit Universitas Indonesia. [Ph.D. thesis, Universitas Indonesia, Jakarta, 1978.]

Jones, Russell
1980   'Problems of editing Malay texts; Discussed with reference to the Hikayat Muhammad Hanafiyyah', *Archipel* 20:121-7.

1985   *Hikayat Sultan Ibrahim Ibn Adham; An edition of an anonymous
               Malay text with translation and notes.* Lanham/New
               York/London: University Press of America. [Center for South
               and Southeast Asia Studies, University of California, Berkeley,
               California, Monograph Series 27.]

Kratz, E.U.
1980   'The editing of Malay manuscripts and textual criticism',
               Bijdragen tot de Taal-, Land- en Volkenkunde 137:229-43. [See
               also his review of Brakel 1975, in *Bulletin School of Oriental
               and African Studies* 41(1978):200-2.]

Liaw Yock Fang
1976   *Undang-undang Melaka; The laws of Melaka.* The Hague:
               Nijhoff. [Bibliotheca Indonesica 13; Ph.D. thesis, University of
               Leiden, 1976.]

Maier, H.M.J.
1985   *Fragments of reading; The Malay Hikayat Merong Mahawangsa.*
               Alblasserdam: Kanters. [Ph.D. thesis, University of Leiden,
               1985.]

McGann, Jerome J.
1983   *A critique of modern textual criticism.* Chicago/London:
               University of Chicago Press.

Molen, W. van der
1983   *Javaanse tekstkritiek; Een overzicht en een nieuwe benadering
               geïllustreerd aan de Kunjarakarṇa.* Dordrecht/Cinnaminson:
               Foris. [KITLV, Verhandelingen 102; Ph.D. thesis, University of
               Leiden, 1983.]

Mulyadi, S.W.R.
1983   *Hikayat Indraputra; A Malay romance.* Dordrecht/Cinnaminson:
               Foris. [KITLV, Bibliotheca Indonesica 23; Ph.D. thesis,
               University of London, 1980.]

Nijhoff, Martinus
1954   *Verzameld werk I; Gebundelde, verspreide en nagelaten
               gedichten.* 's-Gravenhage: Daamen; Amsterdam: Van Oorschot.

Patterson, Lee
1985   'The logic of textual criticism and the way of genius', in: Jerome
               J. McGann (ed.), *Textual criticism and literary interpretation*,
               pp. 55-91. Chicago/London: University of Chicago Press.

Ras, J.J.

1968 *Hikajat Bandjar*; *A Study in Malay historiography*. The Hague: Nijhoff. [KITLV, Bibliotheca Indonesica 1; Ph.D. thesis, University of Leiden, 1968.]

1986 'The Babad Tanah Jawi and its reliability; Questions of content, structure and function', in: C.D. Grijns and S.O. Robson (eds), *Cultural contact and textual interpretation*; *Papers from the Fourth European Colloquium on Malay and Indonesian Studies, held in Leiden in 1983*, pp. 246-73. Dordrecht/Cinnaminson: Foris. [KITLV, Verhandelingen 115.]

Reichling, Anton

1935 *Het woord*; *Een studie omtrent de grondslag van taal en taalgebruik*. Nijmegen: Berkhout. [Ph.D. thesis, Katholieke Universiteit Nijmegen, 1935.]

Riffaterre, Michael

1978 *Semiotics of Poetry*. Bloomington/London: Indiana University Press.

Roesli, Mh.

1925 *Sitti Noerbaja atau kasih ta' sampai*. Tweede druk. Weltevreden: Balai Poestaka. [Seventh impression: Mh. Rusli, *Sitti Nurbaja*; *Kasih tak sampai*, 1954. Djakarta: Perpustakaan Perguruan Kementerian P.P. dan K.]

Sudjiman, Panuti H.M.

1983 *Adat Raja-Raja Melayu*. Jakarta: Penerbit Universitas Indonesia. [Ph.D. thesis, Australian National University, Canberra, 1979.]

Teeuw, A. and S.O. Robson

1981 *Kuñjarakarṇa Dharmakathana*; *Liberation through the law of the Buddha*; *An Old Javanese poem by Mpu Ḍusun*, edited and translated; With a contribution on the reliefs of Caṇḍi Jago by A.J. Bernet Kempers. The Hague: Nijhoff. [KITLV, Bibliotheca Indonesica 21.]

Vickers, Adrian Hassall

1986 *The desiring prince*; *A study of the Kidung Malat as text*. 2 vols. [Ph.D. thesis, University of Sydney.]

Worsley, Peter

1985 'An Old Javanese poem; Methodological questions of textual analysis and translation', *Asian Studies Association of Australia Review* 9-2:104-8. [Review of Teeuw and Robson 1981.]

Index

Finding a satisfactory way to alphabetize Indonesian personal names is difficult. For the sake of easy reference, the system followed in the index below is to alphabetize on the basis of the last part of the name.

Printed in the United States
by Baker & Taylor Publisher Services